MULE

My Dangerous Life as a Drug Smuggler
Turned DEA Informant

C. A. HEIFNER
WITH ADAM ROCKE

LYONS PRESS
Guilford, Connecticut
An imprint of Globe Pequot Press

Lyons Press is an imprint of Globe Pequot Press.

Text design: Sheryl Kober
Project editor: Kristen Mellitt
Layout artist: Justin Marciano

Library of Congress Cataloging-in-Publication Data

Heifner, Chris A.
  Mule : my dangerous life as a drug smuggler turned DEA informant / C.A. Heifner with Adam Rocke.
    p. cm.
  ISBN 978-0-7627-8028-0
  1. Heifner, Chris A. 2. Drug couriers—Texas—Biography. 3. Drug dealers—Texas—Biography. 4. Drug enforcement agents—Texas—Biography. I. Rocke, Adam. II. Title.
  HV5805.H395H456 2012
  363.45092—dc23
  [B]

                                                                              2012015233

Printed in the United States of America

10 9 8 7 6 5 4 3 2 1

"*Pain or damage don't end the world. Or despair or fucking beatings. The world ends when you're dead. Until then, you got more punishment in store. Stand it like a man . . . and give some back.*"

—AL SWEARENGEN

This is not a drug story. This is a life story.

Contents

Each chapter of this book is named for a song.
Visit HeifnerOnline.com for a soundtrack playlist.

Linkin Park - In the End
Lily Allen - The Fear
Elvis Presley - Devil in Disguise
Glenn Frey - Smuggler's Blues
The Game featuring 50 Cent - Hate It or Love It
Notorious B.I.G. - Mo' Money, Mo' Problems
The Eagles - Hotel California
Tupac Shakur - Changes
Jay-Z - H to the Izzo
Linkin Park - Somewhere I Belong
Switchfoot - Meant to Live
Puddle of Mudd - Blurry
Moby - Extreme Ways
311 - Beautiful Disaster
Prince - Let's Go Crazy
N.W.A. - Fuck tha Police
Tracy Lawrence - Time Marches On
David Allen Coe - Take This Job and Shove It
N.W.A. - If It Ain't Ruff
Evanescence - Bring Me to Life
Pitbull - Dammit, Man
Steely Dan - Reeling in the Years
Alabama - My Home's in Alabama
Rage Against the Machine - Killing in the Name
Tina Turner - We Don't Need Another Hero
Frank Sinatra - My Way
Styx - Renegade

1

In the End

"Good morning, Professor Heifner!" said a former student, her smile warm enough to melt frozen butter. She added a saucy wink before we passed each other in the hall, reaffirming my decision to pursue a career in education. All the gold in Fort Knox can't buy you an ounce of true respect, yet I had amassed tons of it. Granted, the life of an adjunct faculty lecturer at El Paso Community College isn't one of decadent excess, but I loved it anyway. I had worked hard, and damned if I wasn't going to enjoy it.

It was the first day of spring 2010 classes, and the vice president of instruction had summoned me to his office. Dr. Dennis Brown had created a wide variety of special projects, and I was hoping that my efforts over the prior two years would result in some much-deserved recognition. The respect of the students meant a lot, but the respect of my peers and supervisors meant more.

My first meeting with The Man. His meek and rather goofy appearance surprised me. Wearing a peach shirt with a pink tie, he reminded me of a fashion–faux pas Mr. Rogers from the old kids' show.

With him sat a trashy bottle blonde from Human Resources, whose name—like her personality—was bland and forgettable. She had done her impossibly colored hair in a teased out perm that hadn't been in style since the '80s, and her makeup—sky-blue eye shadow, Pepto-pink lipstick creeping onto her teeth made her vampire pale complexion equal parts disturbing and frightening.

After customary introductions we took our seats at the conference table in Brown's large, drab office. An awkward silence ensued—hardly the immediate adulation my ego had been expecting. This low-key, risk-averse, no-pulse demeanor of most academics was nothing new, but the total absence of chatter meant that something was definitely wrong. My worst fears slid across the table.

"Mr. Heifner, are you aware that an article about you appeared in the January 17 issue of *El Paso Inc.*?" he asked, his voice monotone, almost sterile.

The born salesman in me quickly entered damage control mode and smiled wide—even though I wanted to crawl into a snow cave and hibernate. They say any publicity is good publicity, but I was less than pleased with the article. The reporter misstated facts, sensationalized tidbits, and turned a blind eye toward many of the positive aspects of my speeches. But that article, along with a recent piece in the *New York Times*, was helping me make significant headway in my speaking endeavors.

"Absolutely, sir," I said proudly. "This year I plan on speaking to 25,000 high school students as a free public service, and I'm trying to raise awareness of my efforts via any means possible, not to mention finding sponsors to help pay for travel expenses."

Dr. Brown and Blondie clearly were expecting a different response along the lines of an apology rather than pleased acceptance. Another pregnant pause followed.

"Mr. Heifner, we want to go over some aspects of your job application," Brown said, withdrawing a second document from the folder in front of him.

A knot bigger than a Texas ranch formed in my stomach. I no longer wanted to hibernate; I wanted to hole up for an entire ice age. What was about to happen became painfully obvious. This dynamic duo wouldn't have parsed every detail of my hiring packet unless they intended to shit-can me. I bet this was how the *Titanic*'s captain felt when frigid water began flowing over the transom. My ship was sinking—fast.

"Mr. Heifner, on your application you affirmed that you have *never* been convicted of a felony," he said, screwing up his face in disgust as if he had just stepped in fresh dog shit.

"Correct, I haven't. Otherwise, I would have disclosed it."

Reputation aside, Brown instantly revealed himself to be a ball-less, favorites-playing bureaucrat who had somehow ascended into management. He hid behind the rules and undoubtedly had never been forced to make a bold executive decision in his life.

"It also asks if you've ever been involved in a deferred adjudication," Blondie added.

Ultravanilla drones like this who keep their heads low, don't make waves, and live for midday cigarette and coffee breaks make me sick. No, they were worse than drones; they were sheep. The highlight of their week was probably a trip to the local $4.99 buffet after church. That kind of lifestyle stood against every motivational speech I had ever given or would ever give. It made me want to swallow a shotgun.

"Yes, it does," I agreed calmly, "and given my rather unusual situation, I called the HR hotline and asked for the proper way to answer that question. I followed their instructions to the letter. I was told that as long as I don't have a felony conviction, the question is a misnomer, and I should simply answer 'no.' Of course, I see my mistake now, but I have nothing to hide. If I did, I certainly wouldn't admit my past indiscretions in my speeches."

Why did it matter? Politicking hard and fast, I tried to spin the situation in my favor by mentioning the gobs of positive feedback from my speaking engagements. Any politician worth his soapbox would have praised my impromptu, impassioned speech. But despite my best efforts the garrote around the larynx of my career was pulling tighter and tighter. Brown and Blondie didn't give a crap about the inconsistencies on my job application or that I was one of the most popular instructors on campus. They didn't like the idea of a former drug trafficker and subsequent DEA informant getting any press, regardless of the knowledge I was imparting.

I poured my heart and soul into that meeting. I was honest, straightforward, and as upbeat and positive as humanly possible. I knew why I was there, and I knew what was at stake—both then and for years to come. Future aspirations aside, I truly loved my job and the opportunity it presented to touch the lives of so many people who might have headed down the same rocky, pitfall-laden path I had taken. But their minds were made up long before our meeting; they just wanted to cover their asses before firing me. Welcome to reality. It sucked—but I wasn't going down without a fight.

"Surely, you're both aware of my excellent teaching record and my stellar rapport with the students."

"Mr. Heifner, this meeting isn't about your ability as an instructor." Brown's emotionless voice went even flatter. "You are hereby suspended until further notice."

"But today is the first day of classes, and I have a class tonight."

"I'm well aware of that, Mr. Heifner. I'll inform you of my final decision this afternoon."

People make mistakes, and the good ones atone for them—or try to. *I* was trying and succeeding—or so I thought. I always wanted to do something noble with my life—something special—to become respected, to give back. So then why the fuck did I keep finding myself in unwinnable fights against impossible odds for ludicrous reasons?

My name is Chris Heifner, and this is my story.

2

The Fear

At an age when I shouldn't have been thinking beyond Little League and Pop Warner or which superhero was cooler, Batman or Superman, I had already conjured a plan to travel the world, experience incredible adventures, find fame and fortune, meet and marry the perfect woman, and raise awesome kids. I believed it was my destiny.

"All or nothing" is what I told everyone my life would be, courtesy of a God-given trifecta of looks, brains, and charm. I'm no Brad Pitt, but I'm no Steve Buscemi, either. I don't play in Albert Einstein's trivia league, but I'm definitely smarter than the average bear. As for charm, when Eskimos need ice, they come to me.

As I grew older and pondering my future became more and more frequent, I surmised that all I had to do was stay the course, continue making progress, and sooner or later my big break—an event that would transform my life into fairy-tale worthiness—would occur. But sitting in my Business Law class, taking notes, stressed out of my gourd because I was worried about whether I had enough gas to get home, much less enough money in my wallet to eat not just today but for the rest of the month, my vision of that perfect life felt like a delusion of grandeur.

It was 1997, six years after I had graduated from a small-town high school in Alabama, and I was struggling to hold it all together. Short on options, I desperately wished something—*anything*—would save me from my plight. Graduation lay more than a year away, and it felt like an eternity. I had followed the sage advice of those who I believed had life by the short hairs, yet I was still struggling mightily, feeling as if I were pushing a boulder up a flight of stairs.

Growing up a military brat gave me the privilege of traveling the world. By the time I was fourteen, I'd been to more incredible places and seen more fantastic sites than Indiana Jones. My parents worked hard, behaved by the book, and lived meager lives, raising me to appreciate and follow those same principles. From age sixteen I worked whenever I wasn't in school so I could afford some of the basic teenage wants my parents couldn't provide. That meant sacrifices—no high school sports or senior prom—but the long-term goal of a perfect life easily merited temporary pain.

In college I intended to put my master plan into effect and make my mark on the world. My fraternity elected me president, numerous student organizations welcomed me into their groups, and a series of internships gave me a taste of life after school. Like so many kids in the crucible of higher education, I still found time to unleash my dedicated party animal. I dated often, searched intently for my soul mate, traveled anywhere when funds and time allowed, and always kept my eyes peeled for opportunities to make a little money. I was burning the candle at both ends in a classic case of FOMO—fear of missing out. I wanted to experience it all because you never know when it's going to end. But the trouble with living for the moment because you fear you'll miss out is that your brain always focuses on what to do *next*. So I really didn't enjoy myself as much as I should have.

Eventually, the hectic pace caught up to me. Among the menial jobs, hours of schoolwork, and rowdy social life, I grew so tired that I wanted to sleep . . . for a month. I often went to a friend's house to hang out and accidentally passed out for the whole afternoon.

Then, one hot, humid summer night, my car broke down on a dark country road, leaving me sweaty, sticky, and stranded. Waiting hours for a friend to come get me offered me as a living feast to the mosquitoes—just one of rural Alabama's many summer pleasantries—and allowed my mind to register that I was miserable—not just about that moment but about my entire life. *Nothing* had worked out as planned.

So I decided to implement change, the most drastic measure being a transfer to the University of Texas at El Paso (UTEP). Unfortunately, that meant living with my grandmother—a less than ideal scenario for trysts with the opposite sex—but finishing my undergrad education, now seven years in the making, definitely justified some social obscurity.

About to turn twenty-five, I longed for financial stability, health insurance, a reliable car, and a sense of accomplishment. The monotonous cycle of working, studying, and socializing, with nothing to show for it, was wearing me out. I wanted to achieve something grander than simply keeping my head above water. I actually looked forward to the tedium of the corporate world, especially the opportunity to climb the ladder. I *wanted* a cubicle, business cards, my own coffee mug, a reserved parking spot, a 401(k), and a daily routine that didn't include worry and exhaustion. That kind of uniformity is easily tolerable while plotting a course to world domination, right?

"One more year, one more year, one more year," I repeated, accidentally speaking aloud.

"Hey, chief, what the hell are you mumbling about?" asked the guy seated beside me in Business Law. His name was Jeff Andes, but everyone called him Jake. I didn't know him. I had chatted with him a couple of times before—typical male small talk about sports, gambling, women—but I knew his type. He had that big-man-on-campus swagger, supreme confidence oozing from every pore. You couldn't help but like him and want to hang out with him. Reasonably smooth and confident in my own abilities, I had a hard time faking that I didn't have a care in world. But Jake really didn't, and I desperately wanted to know his secret.

Whenever he pulled into the parking lot, it was in a different ride. A new Trans Am one day, a flashy motorcycle the next, a sweet suspension-lifted Ford pickup after that. I didn't begrudge his slick clothes and expensive gold watch—okay, I was a *little* jealous—because I knew my time would come . . . but damn if I didn't wonder how he had figured it all out so soon.

"Huh?" I said, confused.

Jake laughed. "Yeah, this class does that to me, too. You should join our group. We're meeting in the library around noon."

"Sure, no prob," I replied casually.

Dropping papers and bumping into people, I rushed to the library while inhaling a bag of potato chips for lunch, bought with a handful of change found in my car. The palatial library inspired me to strive for greatness, but walking in there I felt like Atlas with the weight of the world on my back.

"Hey, chief, over here!" Jake yelled across the deathly quiet library atrium.

I chuckled, but I wasn't in a fun-and-games mood; I was in a get-shit-done-and-end-the-day mood. Business Law group work, laundry, and homework were on my list, and maybe I'd also have time to rub one out and grab a quick nap before night classes. Problem is, people in El Paso live on a different time line. They're late for everything. Naturally, the amigos in Jake's posse (now mine by default) didn't break tradition. But because this was a valuable opportunity to gain some insight, I bit the bullet and stayed.

Hailing from a small town in Kansas, Jake had spent long hours working on his father's farm, giving him a thick, muscular build that helped him become a champion wrestler in high school. Joining the army before his graduation cap hit the ground perfectly rounded out the dossier of the prototypical all-American country boy.

When Jake asked about my background, I got halfway through my depressing tale before he motioned for me to stop. "Damn, boy, you need a fuckin' drink. Your whining is gonna make me run into traffic."

"I could use a drink," I said.

His green eyes lit up. "Wait, I got a better idea. Let's go get a lap dance."

"Huh. Never had one."

He looked at me as if a dick were growing out of my forehead. "*What?* Shut the fuck up. You're kidding, right?"

"Wish I was."

"That's it, then. Screw these guys and the group work. You and I are outta here."

The laundry list of my responsibilities rolled through my head like a dung beetle pushing a ball of fresh elephant shit. Of course I wanted to say "fuck it" and have some fun, but I couldn't survive an eighth year as an undergrad. On the other hand, I hadn't had any *real* fun in a while. Then again, I was also flat broke—a severe problem for strip-club gratification.

Clocking my inner turmoil, Jake clapped me on the shoulder. "Look, I know you're a broke nigga, so don't worry. I got this. Just hang out. A beer won't kill ya."

Next thing I knew, we were in his Trans Am zipping in and out of traffic like Tony Stewart. Jake alternated between smoking a bowl, talking about his family, and cranking the wheel to avoid hitting anyone. He offered me a hit, but drugs—even pot—weren't my bag, and I was happy to let him do all the talking because I didn't want to think about my own life and I was big-time curious about where he got his money. The GI Bill took care of his tuition, but that didn't explain the cars, clothes, and flash-cash.

Jake rambled on about his two brothers and his large, extended family in Kansas, all living prosperous and happy lives. Admittedly, it made me jealous. My mom, sister, and I were anything but prosperous. My mom had divorced my stepdad, who raised and adopted me, and I had only just learned who and where my real father was, but what kind of relationship we'd have, if any, was still up in the air.

Seeking out my biological father was supposed to reveal my roots and a place where I belonged. Turns out I was an eyelash in the eye of his perfect life and far from welcome. So I listened to Jake's stories about his uncles, cousins, brothers, and father with a sense of forlorn disconnect, wondering if I would ever have an extended family like that of my own. Jake hadn't revealed the source of his financial well-being, so I chalked it up to the lottery—either state run or ancestral.

We pulled up to the club, and Jake walked in like he owned the place. He withdrew a fat, rubber band–bound gangster roll of bills to pay the cover. Shocked at its thickness, I was also unsure how to act, so I tried to follow his lead.

The club was dark as a cave at midnight, and while my eyes were adjusting, I must have bumped into every table and chair. Deafening countrified rock blared from the speakers, and the whole place smelled like cheap booze and sweaty sex. But hey, free beer is free beer.

When we sat down, I closed my eyes to help them adjust. When I opened them, gorgeous half-naked women had surrounded us.

"Whatcha drinkin', chief?" Jake yelled over the music.

"Any beer as long as it's cold," I shouted back.

He gestured to the waitress, and before I could blink a bottle of Bud Light, ice dripping down the side, appeared in my hand. To say we were getting the royal treatment would have been a gross understatement. The girls were caressing my hair, rubbing my chest, and treating me like a rock star. I slammed the beer. Before the empty bottle hit the table, a fresh one was waiting for me.

"You've really never been here before?" Jake asked.

"I told you, I've never been to a strip club before."

"I thought you were shittin' me."

I shook my head.

He motioned to the two girls on my lap. "Do you like them, or do you want different ones?"

My brain couldn't even process the question. Two busty Latinas with silky, coffee-colored skin were loving all over me. The other girls walking around were also slammin'.

Uncertain how to answer, I just nodded—while mentally kicking myself for not having the balls—or the funds—to visit a strip joint sooner. Truth is, I was also a little shocked. The media always portray strippers as nasty or trashy, but these girls were gorgeous and well spoken, with white teeth, perfect smiles, and beautiful hair. Any of them could have passed for the girl next door—if the girl next door was smokin' hot and walked around in a thong bikini.

"Do you know these girls?" I asked.

"You could say that," he said with a grin.

"Man, this sure beats the shit outta UTEP."

"*Now you're talking!*" Jake roared and thumped me on the shoulder. Then he whispered something to one of the girls. She smiled and nodded.

That's when I noticed that the guys at other tables weren't receiving the same king's treatment.

Just as the waitress slammed a third beer on the table, the girls on my lap stood up and led me to a bench on the far side of the wall. The fresh brew didn't last the walk, but one of the girls snatched another before we arrived. One girl held the beer and made me chug while the other stroked my back. I had no idea what was about happen, but I sure as hell wasn't complaining.

A new song started, and on cue both girls took off their tops and started doing a rhythmic dance on top of me. Words can't do their moves justice, so let's just say that their performance was magnificent and leave it at that. For three or four songs, they took turns straddling me, rubbing their perfect breasts in my face, and caressing my hair and chest. It was pure bliss.

But being out of my element made me go supernerd, trying to make small talk, asking their names, where they were from, how they liked dancing. They giggled and shushed me while rubbing my hands all over their bodies.

"Are you sure this is okay? I'm not breaking any rules?"

"Yes, sweetie, it's okay!" the strippers laughed before shutting me up with a three-way French kiss.

By the end of the marathon double lap dance, my head was spinning. When the show was over, the girls put me back together, tucking my shirt back in, letting their fingers do the walking and taking me by surprise. Normally, I prefer to get to know someone before swinging the bat, let alone trying for second base. But this was far from normal.

The girls walked me back to the table, fed me more beer, and took turns kissing my neck. I tried to play it cool and chat them up, but they only talked with each other as they downed the shots that Jake continued to order. They liked that I was a virgin to this experience, and it shocked me to hear them arguing about who would take me home.

Seven beers later, with a few more trips to the lap dance area, I was feeling a little dirty, a lot drunk, and very happy. That's when Jake came back to the table and shooed away the girls.

"It's time for the boys to talk," he said, handing each girl a crisp twenty-dollar bill.

"Are you sure?" I blurted, hesitant to let them out of my sight.

Bankrolling the action, Jake ignored the question. "So, whatcha think?" he said.

"What do I think? I think this is fuckin' awesome! But how could I ever take one of those girls home to Mama? Do you think they have diseases?"

"You're a funny guy, Chris. These girls are for partying, not for rings on their fingers." He looked me dead in the eyes. "You ready for a *real* party?"

What the fuck? I thought this was a real party. I looked at my watch; three hours had passed. So much for laundry, homework, and night class. Before I could object, we were out the door and about to climb into the car when Jake ordered me into the back seat.

Pontiac Trans Ams, especially Jake's 1997 WS6 model, have a backseat barely big enough to hold a gallon of milk. Just as I began to protest, two of the club's strippers ran over, and it dawned on me what he meant by a real party. Instead of her "work uniform," one of my lap dance beauties was wearing tight khaki shorts and a yellow tank top barely containing her large, perfect tits—and she was carrying a small duffel bag.

"I won," she said, arching her eyebrows, referring to the dispute with the other stripper about taking me home. "By the way, I recognize you from UTEP. We took a class together."

A lap dance was one thing, but fucking a stripper was a different barrel of fish. Despite a devil-may-care attitude, I have tried to be cautious my whole life. I would rather skip sex altogether with someone

I don't know than wear a condom. It's not PC, I know, but I *hate* them. Yes, I understand their benefits, but they give me penile claustrophobia. Which makes me dedicatedly monogamous. At that moment I was unattached. Then again, being superselective about whom I dated, I was single a lot.

Half of my brain continued our backseat chitchat while the other weighed the pros and cons of pursuing this impromptu "relationship." No freakin' way was Jimmy going to party without a hat. Another dilemma on top of my angst over blowing off work and class for reckless sexual abandon.

Rejecting my nerdy attempts at conversation, my "date" used all her womanly charms—charisma, eloquence, beauty—to seduce me, and she was making it hard to resist. Just the thought of nixing the tryst made me feel like a church-addicted Puritan, and she wasn't taking no for an answer, her continued kisses quickly converting me.

We pulled up to a house in central El Paso near the zoo, a shady part of town, and Jake's date hopped out and went into the house.

"Whatcha doin' back there?" Jake said.

"Studying."

"I'll bet you are." Then, when my date stopped nuzzling me, Jake looked at her and asked, "How come you never liked me like that?"

"'Cause you're married and not half as cute as Chris."

Wait, Jake is married?

Before I could dwell on what that meant, Jake's date came flying back out of the house like a bullet from a gun and jumped in the car, screaming, "*Go! Go! Go!*" as if our lives depended on it. Which apparently they did.

As Jake fumbled with the ignition, two *cholos* in red bandanas and tattered wifebeaters barreled out of the house behind her. As I was mumbling a silent prayer, Jake's TA fired up, and we blasted out of there.

"Did you get it?" Jake asked a few streets later.

"Sure did, baby," she said, holding up a small plastic baggie filled with white powder . . . just as a police cruiser swung out of a side street and jumped on our ass, lights flashing.

Jake's gal instantly flung the baggie onto my lap. I froze as if it were a hand grenade with the pin pulled. My date snatched it and stuffed it in her bra.

"What are you doing?" I asked.

"Don't worry, I'll put it where the sun don't shine if we have to get out of the car. For now it's safe."

Sweat broke out across my forehead, and my hands started squeezing reflexively.

"Relax," she said, kissing me and rubbing my leg to calm me down. "It's gonna be fine."

The cop ran Jake's license and insurance, and I was about to shit a bulldozer. But Jake was smoother than a baby's butt. His congenial demeanor swayed the cop, who actually believed Jake's lame explanation for running the stop sign . . . after we had stolen blow from gangster dealers.

⌒⌒

The Camino Real Hotel has some of downtown El Paso's most luxurious digs. Jake requested a room, and my mind reeled, wondering what this guy whom I had only just met was getting me into.

As we rode the elevator to an upper floor, I noticed a bottle of Crown Royal in Jake's hand. "Where'd that come from?" I asked.

"Outta her ass," Jake said, pointing to my girl.

She smiled, leaned her head against my shoulder, and gave my arm a squeeze.

"Enjoy," he whispered to me. "I bet she's tight."

"You'll never know," she shot back.

The luxury suite with separate bedrooms and a hot tub exceeded my expectations. The girls began fiddling with the Jacuzzi's controls, and Jake called room service for two of almost everything on the menu. My inner supernerd reared his head again when I noticed that the TV had a video game console; I never had the time or money for video games, and the amenity held me awestruck. Though not for long.

I was spinning room drunk, but I couldn't take my eyes off my date. We talked about school, graduation, and the tribulations of life—a deeper conversation than I expected. When I noticed Jake in the kitchenette cutting lines of cocaine on the counter, my eyes grew big as garbage can lids, and my date laughed.

"Have you ever done coke before, sweetie?"

"Uhhhhhhh . . ."

"You are just too cute," she said, tousling my hair before straddling and kissing me.

Thus far, alcohol, sugar-rich treats, and poker formed the full extent of my vices—and even those came in relative moderation. So much temptation had never surrounded me like this before, and the beer, whiskey, and lust weren't helping.

Who the fuck is this guy? I wondered, thinking of Al Pacino's character in *The Devil's Advocate*. If he wanted to turn a complete square into someone who could never run for public office, he was succeeding. I was no Goody Two-shoes, but my past indiscretions were shits-and-giggles trouble compared to this.

What was I doing? I wanted to escape—and seriously considered it. It wasn't that far a walk from downtown El Paso to my car at UTEP. All I had to do was dash out the door and not look back. For the next five minutes, the angel and devil perched on my shoulders whispered opposing suggestions.

My date broke the tie. "Kiss me, Chris—and don't worry. It's only a bump. Not a lot for a beginner." She could have convinced me to rob a bank.

"Look, I don't—"

She tapped a small dollop of cocaine on her tongue and kissed me hard and deep. A second later a sensation unlike anything I'd ever experienced washed over me like a full sensory orgasm. I loved it. But at any moment I expected a SWAT team to fast-rope down from black helicopters, burst through the windows throwing flash-bangs, and haul us off to jail.

But there was no guilt. For the first time in my pathetically boring existence, I had thrown caution to the wind and gone wild—a little. For the next couple of hours we drank and talked and drank. Jake and the girls did lines, but I begged off. They made a few jabs—

"C'mon, cocaine is like bacon. It's great even without eggs."

"Just do one line. It'll make you harder than a marble statue."

At some point Jake and his date disappeared into one of the bedrooms, and I was about to chuck a lifetime of sexual caution out the window when my sexy siren beckoned me to the bathroom. She was sitting on the toilet, legs spread, pointing into the bowl. There was blood in the water.

"Sweetie, I wanna make love to you so bad. You're the kind of guy I'm looking for."

"But . . ." I pointed at the blood.

"Don't worry about that," she waved. "You'll earn your red wings."

"I don't follow hockey," I said.

"Huh?" She stared at me as if I were the village idiot.

"You know, the Detroit Red Wings. I'm from Alabama."

She nearly laughed herself off the shitter.

Jake stuck his head in the bathroom, startling both of us. "What are you kids doin' in here?"

"Nothing," she said. "I'm having woman issues."

Jake flashed me a thumbs-up. "Right on, Nutty. You'll earn your red wings."

I gave Jake a blank stare—and then it finally dawned on me.

"That's cool," he said. "I gotta get home anyway. Wifey thinks I'm in night class. You girls can keep the room and the goodies."

My date moved from the john to the bedroom, naked under the covers. She patted the empty space beside her. "Come back and cuddle with me, sweetie."

I smiled but didn't answer.

Jake pulled out his gangster roll, peeled off a few bills—cab fare for the girls—and tossed it on the floor. "See ya."

Waiting for the elevator, Jake looked at his watch, then slugged me in the arm. "Hell, it's only nine. Let's grab one more beer."

Ten minutes later we bellied up to Hemingway's, a hole-in-the-wall college hangout near UTEP. After a toast and a hearty swig, Jake asked: "Did you have fun?"

"Yeah."

"Too crazy for you?"

Hell fuckin' yes, I wanted to say. "Nah, just a lot of new stuff to process."

One beer turned into two, two turned into five, and we laughed our asses off rehashing the day, especially the look on the *cholos'* faces as we sped away from them.

Jake flirted with every chick in the bar. Cheesedick or not, this guy was damn good at swaying people to his side of the table. Figuring today's events were run of the mill, I wondered where he got the stamina. Were his confidence and bravado a product of the money, or was he just born with them?

Jake dropped me off at my car in the UTEP parking lot just as my night class was getting out. I was drunk, possibly still high, missing a sock, shirt stained, hair a mess, and heart racing. Fumbling with the key in the door, there was a tap on my shoulder. Wheeling around, I found myself face to face with my night class professor.

"Mr. Heifner, you weren't in class this evening."

"Something, uh, urgent came up," I said, hoping he couldn't smell the booze on my breath or the sin on my soul.

"Smells like it. You missed a test, one that counts as a third of your final grade. Bring a believable excuse to my office, and we'll discuss a makeup, which, as I'm sure you're aware, will be twice as hard."

Welcome back to reality.

3

Devil in Disguise

THE CORPORATE WORLD IS A COLD-HEARTED BITCH. HARDLY BREAKING news, I know, but it took me a couple of weeks to realize. Still, it was vastly superior to the life of a starving college student. A year and a half had passed since Jake had invited me to party with him. We both had earned bachelor degrees of business administration in finance, and I had moved back to Alabama, accepting a job as a staff accountant at a regional bank. After taxes and insurance, I took home $792 twice a month—barely scraping by—but at least it didn't require cracking a book.

For me to ascend the corporate ladder, most of the better-paying jobs required three to five years of experience or an MBA—or both. The college brochures don't mention that. So like all the other lost rats scrabbling around in the crazy maze, all I wanted to know was: *Who moved my fucking cheese?*

Jake called every so often to brag about his latest car, a threesome he had enjoyed, or renting a yacht for the weekend. On the latest call he talked about a trip he was planning—Hawaii or Costa Rica, he couldn't decide—and about getting into day trading. The guy was more scattered than sand in a windstorm, but scattered or not he led an exciting life. The most exciting part of my day consisted of deciding whether to wear tan- or stone-colored khakis to work.

Don't get me wrong, I liked my job, but why had I been in such a hurry to get out of college? After a few months of meager paychecks, nothing had changed: I was still broke and stuck in neutral. If one more clown told me, "You're a talented guy; be patient," I was gonna brain him with a tire iron and let Alabama house and feed me for the next twenty-five years.

But my friendship with Jake yielded some valuable intel: the source of his money. Turns out Jake was involved in an extremely dangerous and highly illegal endeavor: drug trafficking. Sometimes he tried to talk to me about the business, the nitty-gritty of it, but I didn't want to know. The less I knew, the better. But it was still fun as hell to hang out with the guy. Curiosity isn't always a virtue, so he filled a void of adventure that I had no desire to fill myself. Jake's plan was to party his ass off 24/7 and spend money like it grew on trees. I planned to do things the right way and squirrel away a tidy nest egg. Unfortunately, my way was slower than giant tortoises boning. Jake repeatedly tried to tempt me to the dark side, but I knew better.

At least, I thought I did.

At UTEP he always found a way to put money in my pocket. He once paid me three hundred dollars to buy him money orders totaling ten thousand dollars—a serious chore considering that at the time seven hundred dollars was the biggest order you could buy from the post office and three hundred was the max from a gas station . . . and I could only buy one at a time to avoid suspicion.

On another occasion, when one of Jake's underlings got busted at a checkpoint with a load of dope, Jake paid me two hundred dollars to call the poor sap's girlfriend from a pay phone and give her instructions.

I also made a small fortune by writing papers for Jake, not enough to buy a new car but enough to keep me in cold beer and hot grub. It wasn't honest work, but it didn't entail anything truly sinister or breaking a major moral code. Harmless, right? My days of begging lay behind me. I was legit now.

"Chris Heifner, management control," I said, answering my work phone on the first ring.

"Hey, honey, can you talk?" Missy asked. We met while I was in college and dated on and off for two years while I focused on graduating.

There was never any formal agreement between us, no declarations of love, but we enjoyed each other's company and had a ton of fun together.

Missy and Jake were always getting me to push the envelope and break the rules. I wasn't an angel, but most of it was harmless, no defense attorney required. They made me look at it as sport, solely for the sake of entertainment. While I hated Jake for it, I loved Missy for it.

A single mom with a five-year-old daughter, she toiled for her daily bread as a telemarketer. She had the sexiest voice I'd ever heard, and although singing was her true passion, telemarketing paid the bills. I hoped she would take an interest in something more dignified and stable, like teaching, but she had zero interest in school.

To her credit, though, she was the ultimate social engineer: beautiful, a good listener, a cover girl smile, and the most seductive demeanor you could imagine. With those qualities and her amazing rack, she could have sold spots to Dalmatians. No matter where we went—restaurants, concerts, hotels—she always talked our way into the best tables, seats, or accommodations. Office politics were new waters for me, and her ability to control a situation made her my lighthouse. Her guidance never failed; I just had to have the balls to follow it. I genuinely wanted my work to speak for itself, but office politics are the engine that pulls you up the corporate hill, so Missy's PhD in bullshitting proved invaluable.

"I'm a little slammed right now," I said. "Is there a problem?"

"Just call me when you get home tonight, okay?"

I wasn't worried; after all, there was nothing to worry about. She was safe and sound in El Paso, and I was searching for my pot of gold in Birmingham, Alabama. At worst her pain-in-the-ass mother was giving her crap again or, like me, she was having money problems.

The line rang again. "Chris Heifner, management control."

"Hey, Nutty, I'm gonna make millions in the stock market!" Jake said. "How do I open a brokerage account?"

I wanted to laugh. "I should charge you for my advice."

"Better yet, make me some money, and I'll pay you."

Beyond the brass tacks of opening the account, he was on the fence about starting with ten thousand dollars or twenty thousand. My checking account had forty-three bucks in it, and he was talking about playing around with more than five hundred times that.

How do people do it? Expensive SUVs and sports cars, nice homes with manicured yards—how much money did you need to afford a spread like that?

Dejected, I decided after work to splurge on a foot-long sandwich at Subway and a twelve-pack of cheap beer. Problem was, now I had to figure out how to stretch twenty-nine dollars for the next six days. Popping a beer, I called my woman.

"Hey, you wanted me to call you?"

"How's Alabama?"

"God, I love this place. I may be broke, but it's still a million times better than Hell Paso. I drive over this river my dad and I used to fish on every day, and it rekindles memories of the best times of my life. Next time I go back to El Shithole, it'll be in a box carried by six of my closest friends."

"So you'd never move back?"

Uh-oh.

A lump formed in my throat. "You know how I feel about that dust bowl. Why? What's going on?"

A long pause. "Are you sitting down?"

Oh no.

"Honey, just tell me."

"I'm pregnant."

The lump expanded into a boulder. I didn't ask if it was mine; I didn't have to. The time line fit. A month earlier my great-grandmother Laurencia, matriarch of my family and one of my favorite people on the planet, had died. I went back to El Paso for the funeral and stayed with Missy. We already know how I feel about condoms.

"I'm here for you," I said. "We'll figure this out."

We chatted some more about everything but her lump. It didn't matter, though—my decision was made. I loved Alabama. I had a million friends there. My mom and sister lived just up the road, and my stepdad, who'd adopted and helped raised me, wasn't too far away, either. It was great to be home. My job wasn't exactly filling my pockets with cash, but my quality of life made up for it: fishing, hiking, college football Saturdays, cookouts with buddies, and the occasional alumni party at my old frat house. I couldn't afford to bring Missy, pregnant, and her daughter to Alabama on sixteen hundred dollars a month. Hell, it would have been tough on double my salary. But an abortion was out of the question, and I couldn't bear the thought of having a child and not being a part of its life.

So back to Hell Paso it was.

Over the next few months, saving money proved next to impossible. My salvation came in the form of the forty paid sick days I received when I was hired. When I quit, that extra thousand dollars would be a godsend.

Everyone called me a fool for going back, but unlike them I saw the big picture: I had to pay the piper. This was about my child, not me.

"Told you not to mess with single mothers," said Kip, my biological father. "Now you're stuck, and if she ever wants to get rid of you, all she has to do is accuse you of molesting her daughter."

So much for encouragement. Kip was a real joy. An attorney full of trepidation, he saw nothing but tragedy and despair behind every door. Being around him made me realize that attorneys never build anything of their own. They tear things down or rubber-stamp the legitimate work of others. Funnily enough, Kip's son, my half brother, said the same damn thing his father said.

The twenty-one-hour trip back to El Paso was the shortest drive of my life. I was scared to death, focusing more on getting a job and explaining the situation to Missy's parents than the endless highway. Too many questions, too few answers.

⚊⚊

As I walked through Missy's front door, my eyes bulged at how big she had grown in the seven months since I last saw her. I gave her a huge hug, careful not to squeeze too hard. She put my hand on her belly. "Feel him kick. He's an active one."

"Wow!" I swelled with pride as the baby thumped beneath my hand. "What have your parents said?"

Her smile withered. "They're not talking to me."

"What a piece of work."

"Stop."

I always thought that vessels of the Lord were supposed to be beacons of goodness, catalysts for people to commune with their maker or some shit like that. Missy's parents were Christian pastors at a Spanish church, but apparently, they hadn't read that sermon. If I'd wanted to be judged and surrounded by negativity, I would have stayed put with Kip.

"Don't worry, things will be good in no time," I lied.

"I've got bad news. They cut my hours at work 'cause I've been sick with the baby and the bills are behind."

The lump in my throat came back—and it brought friends. "How much?"

"Nine hundred dollars."

Bye-bye, thousand-dollar cushion.

The next day, bright and early, I shot over to Jake's house. It still sucked to be back in El Paso, but I was looking forward to seeing him. If nothing else, one of his crazy *Guess what I did now!* tales would lift my spirits.

"What's up, champ?" he said, fist-bumping me.

"I need to use your computer."

"Don't get lost on the porno sites."

Jake's house was a zoo, people coming and going all the time. His wife, Sandra—a skinny, pretty Filipino girl he'd met while stationed in Hawaii—worked a lot; she liked to stay busy and have her own money. More leisure than labor, Jake farted around most of the time. Personal electronics weren't as common then as they are today, but their house teemed with them: cell phones, laptops, satellite television, big-screen TVs, dedicated Internet . . . he had it all. I didn't have any of it, not even a computer. Before, when I'd needed web access, I'd used the school's computer lab. Since I was no longer a student, that luxury vanished.

I blasted out cover letters and résumés while Jake worked in the yard—if you could call it that. He came inside, put on a porn channel for few minutes, made cheesy comments, then went back outside for a bit, repeating the routine for hours.

When noon rolled around, he fired up a joint. After a voluminous puff, he said, "You know what time it is, don't you?"

I knew damn well what time it was in Jake's world. "Yeah."

"You down?"

"Fuck it, let's go."

Every day at noon, like clockwork, Jake headed to the local strip club and blew his customary three hundred dollars. He left by four, grabbed a quick bite, and tried to beat his wife home. On rare occasions he picked up a girl and stayed out all night. I don't know how he got away with it or even found the energy.

"We gotta make a quick stop along the way," he said.

In Jake's world that could have meant anything, so I prepped for the worst. Imagine my surprise, then, when we pulled into the local Ford dealer's lot.

Jake jumped out of the piece-of-shit Camaro he was driving and threw the keys to the nearest salesman. The salesman threw another set back. Moments later we climbed into the nicest burgundy-and-tan extended-cab F-150 Special Edition 4x4 I've ever seen. It had full leather, heated seats, and every other bell and whistle.

"What the fuck is this?"

"My new ride," Jake said, fiddling with the stereo. "Signed, sealed, delivered. I'm just taking care of business."

"How much?" It was inappropriate to ask, but I had to know.

"Forty K."

Must be nice. The hurricane of financial failure was eroding my coastline, and Jake was surfing the waves. I needed to do something, but what?

"Don't worry, Nutty. I'll always keep the seat warm for you."

"Gee, thanks."

I wanted to take the truck to the sand dunes and test it properly, but Jake wasn't about to veer from his daily fix of boobs and beer, so we went to the Lamplighter, the same strip joint where I had my lap-dance cherry popped. Different girls worked there now, but the treatment remained the same. Resisting their advances was easier, though. I was living with Missy and had been there, done that.

"We need to talk," Jake said after a few pulls on our beers. "I might have work for you."

"Absolutely not."

"Suit yourself, but I'm always here if you need anything."

His stupid grin pissed me off. He knew I wanted to do things the right way, high horse or not. It had become a running joke with him to try to get me to go against my morals. I wanted to prove him wrong so badly that it hurt. I believed that hard work was the real key to success, not crime or luck. The way I saw it, he had already ruined his life, his wife's, his brother's, and a couple of his friends', and I wasn't about to let him suck me down with him. It meant flirting with disaster and setting myself up for a lifetime of ruin.

I didn't have all the details, but I knew the broad strokes: When Jake was a sergeant in the army, he was stationed at Fort Bliss in El Paso. Like him, many of his friends back in Kansas had an affinity for weed. Resourcefully, he realized that he could run loads back home and make respectable cash. As soon as he got his discharge papers, he did just that on a regular basis. From his strip-club connections, he found suppliers that gave him decent-size packages of dope—twenty to eighty pounds— and his illicit career took off. Simple as that.

One day Jake and his wife were driving back to Kansas to see his folks. Unbeknownst to his wife, Jake had hidden eighty-six pounds of pot in the car's rear quarter panel. A random check at a Border Patrol checkpoint on the outskirts of El Paso resulted in two felony drug trafficking convictions. Amazingly, they escaped jail time. Fines, community service, and probation were the sum total of their punishment. There was collateral damage, however. Jake's brother Eric, a captain in the army, was living with them at the time. The service booted him for "consorting with riffraff" or however they phrase it, although he may have been given the option of an honorable discharge. Unemployed and now damaged goods, Eric began running loads for his brother.

Now Jake wanted me to run them, too.

"Dude, I'm gonna find a job with health benefits," I said. "I'm gonna buy Missy a house."

"Whatever you say, chief!" Jake motioned to one of the strippers. "In the meantime, get another lap dance."

He pulled out a hundo and slapped it on the table, but I wasn't interested. I just wanted to drink, listen to the music, and think. There was a lot on my plate and a lot on my mind. It was a major change going from being a carefree bachelor to living with my very pregnant girlfriend and her five-year-old daughter. Even bedtime and trips to the bathroom had to be adjusted, but we committed ourselves to making it work. After all, what choice did we have?

We ate together, did family things together, and said our prayers together every night before bed. Still needing some "me" time, I alternated days hanging out with Jake and his computer and days being with Missy, who was happy to have me around. It felt good to be seen as a provider, but job interviews were scarce, and money was wearing thin.

Time flew, and Turkey Day descended. Jake and Sandra joined us for dinner. Jake said something smarmy about it working out because they were in town, but I think they were on probation and couldn't leave town. Either way, it was nice to have company; we weren't welcome at Missy's parents' house, and my grandmother always went away for Thanksgiving to visit other family.

We drank beer, told stories, ate turkey, and watched football. It was fun, intimate, and relaxed. But later that night Missy cried herself to sleep. Her parents' scorn had taken its toll, steeling my resolve to make everything right despite their judgmental tendencies.

With Christmas only days away, I still hadn't found work. Waiting tables or retail would have made me feel like an even bigger failure, but it turns out that I waited too long to try even that Hail Mary because, with Christmas looming, I wouldn't receive my first paycheck till after the New Year. Bottom line: We were fucked, and it was my fault for being stubborn. We were also flat broke.

Our apartment building's manager spotted me en route to check the mail.

"Excuse me, you're 705, right?"

Cue lump in throat. "Yes."

"I don't post notices of bad news during the holidays, but you're late on the rent. Again."

"Sorry. Missy usually takes care of that."

"I'm gonna have to give you an official notice on Monday after Christmas. Please make your account current. I don't like evicting people."

It hit me right between the eyes. When it came to taking care of my important responsibilities—like having a roof overhead—I was an obsessive-compulsive overachiever. I would have talked to Missy about it, but what was she going to do? More important, why worry her? It was my job. I was the man. The testicles proved it.

Getting evicted with a pregnant girlfriend and a five year old daughter was unthinkable. Where would we live? Her parents' house was out of the question, as was my grandmother's. I wouldn't be able to get work until after the holidays, not even as a busboy, and my paycheck wouldn't arrive until long after we'd been booted from our nest. My family wouldn't lend me money. A pawnshop would have been an option, but I had nothing of value. Up shit creek without a paddle, and the canoe had holes in it, too. So I did the only logical thing I could think of.

Jake was shocked to see me at the Lamplighter. "What are you doing here, Nutty? I thought it was a family day."

"You win," I said. "I need your help."

"Say that louder!"

Miserable prick. Rubbing salt in my wounds made him giddier than a Japanese schoolgirl at a Hello Kitty Convention. He was more concerned about being right than about right or wrong.

"You need to borrow money, don't ya?"

My intention was to borrow money and pay him back in installments. He had another idea. I stared at the floor.

"How much?"

"Two thousand dollars," I said without looking him in the eye.

"That's it?" he laughed. "Done! Now get a beer and a lap dance."

For the first time in my life, I felt truly defeated. Everything I'd ever stood for and worked so hard to achieve crumbled in a simple, albeit desperate request. That feeling of defeat increased when, later that night, Jake peeled off forty hundred-dollar bills and slapped them in my hand.

"Uh, this is four thousand dollars. I only asked for two."

"Merry Christmas, chief. But you owe me."

How was I going to pay him back? The money was in my hand, and there was no way in hell that I was strong enough to object. I considered returning the money, but we had no other options that didn't involve homelessness. If it were just me, maybe, but with Missy, her daughter, and the little one on the way, I couldn't take the risk.

Christmas came, and after paying the bills, I went nuts. Paul Bunyan would have been jealous of our Christmas tree. The room overflowed with presents. Each unwrapping elicited a cavalcade of smiles, hugs, and kisses. It could have been a hundred degrees below zero, but the feeling of watching them unwrap their gifts would have kept me warm for the rest of my life. Missy and I kissed under the mistletoe.

A few days later the phone rang.

"We need to talk," Jake said. "Get your ass over here pronto."

"On my way."

His tone sounded different, but he had bailed me out, so off I went. Maybe he would let me pay him back over time, but who was I kidding? Even at two hundred dollars a month, it would take forever with a family to support.

"How was Christmas?" he asked when I arrived.

"Great."

"You're gonna ride with me to Ruidoso tonight."

"Uh, okay."

During the two-hour drive to New Mexico, he laid out my repayment plan. "We're going to meet a guy I know from Kansas and collect some money. Tomorrow we'll deliver a package to him, and this whole ordeal will be done with."

He was telling me, not asking. And what ordeal? I stared out the window, pondering my options, but I had none. I owed him. At the very least I'd have a story to tell my grandchildren about the time that Grandpa flirted with the devil. But even more important, my debt would be repaid ricky-tick.

We pulled up to the Inn of the Mountain Gods Resort and Casino, and Jake peered into a white Cadillac Escalade with Kansas plates. Making our way to the room, he seemed unnerved—which unnerved me. But I wasn't there to do a deal; I was just an observer, Jake's backup.

A nondescript white guy in his fifties met us at the door, looking down the hallway before letting us in. Jake put on his gregarious country boy affect and huddled with the guy in the corner, laughing and carrying on like they were old buddies. After a few minutes the guy handed Jake an envelope, and we rushed back to Jake's truck.

"What the fuck was that about?"

"This," Jake replied, handing me an envelope stuffed with thousands of dollars. "The plan's changed. You're driving to Kansas." He gave me a pit-viper stare. "You ready to do this?"

There wasn't any room for a lump in my throat because of the fucking boulder that now resided there.

"I don't know."

"Take four thousand dollars out of that envelope."

It barely dented the stack.

"You do this tomorrow, and that's your bonus."

My eyes bulged. "What?"

"Put it in your pocket. See how it feels."

I didn't need a cheap parlor trick to know it would feel fucking orgasmic. I already knew my answer to his question. Every man has his price, and mine was eight thousand dollars. Tomorrow was going to be the first day of the rest of my life. I hoped the rest of my life would last longer than tomorrow.

4

Smuggler's Blues

HE SOUNDED LIKE A FUCKING IDIOT.

During the two-hour drive back from Ruidoso, Jake tried speaking in code on numerous calls, but his wording was so moronic and nonsensical that the people on the other end kept making him repeat what he was trying to say. For example:

"Nutty's gonna deliver a C-note of tiles to E in the home state in twenty-four clicks."

Translation: I was taking one hundred pounds of weed to Jake's brother Eric in Kansas tomorrow. The only reason I knew was that Jake had already told me—in English. Otherwise, I'd have been as clueless as the mope on the other end of the phone.

In between Jake's idiotic calls, he divulged his entire drug trafficking strategy.

Rule number one: Only deal with people you know.

Two: Only clean-cut white people drive the loads.

Three: Cash basis only. Never use credit; "that shit will get you killed."

I sat in rapt attention, waiting for number four. It never came.

That's it? Holy shit, Jake's master plan was as strategic and complex as a game of Chutes and Ladders—and I was entrusting my life to it. What the fuck was I thinking?

"When we get home, gimme about three hours, then meet me here around eleven-ish." He handed me a scrap of paper with an address scribbled on it.

This had to be a bad dream, but pinching myself proved that it wasn't. Undignified accountant to Cell Block D in one fell swoop because I couldn't find a real job. But, Jake reassured me ad nauseam, there was nothing to worry about. But if there was nothing to worry about, why the hell was he paying me eight thousand dollars?

The lure of quick and easy cash proved too strong to resist. So I rationalized it, convincing my superego that everything would be okay. I was too clean-cut, too polished, too smart, and too lucky to get caught. Only idiots got pinched, right?

I went home to hide my cash and exchange my small Nissan pickup—no place to hide the drugs—for Missy's Honda. She knew I was up to something but didn't ask questions. Relieved to have some money in our hands, she just smiled.

At eleven I circled the destination block three times, looking for suspicious activity—not that I'd even know if something was suspicious—before sacking up and parking.

Jake's truck was out front—otherwise, I would have stayed in the car—so I knocked on the door and waited. A million questions ripped through my mind: What type of evil lair was this? How intense would security be? Did I need a secret code?

A fat woman in a Kmart-issue terry cloth bathrobe answered the door. Five or six little kids were running around the house behind her.

"Is Jake here?"

"Follow me," Kmart said and led me through the cheaply furnished home to the garage.

Older kids were fiddling on a computer in the kitchen, and some hideous, greasy meatlike foodstuff was bubbling on the stove. The entire mess of a house smelled of cigarettes and dirty dogs.

My rotund tour guide opened the door, and the overwhelming stench of pot hit me full force, nearly giving me an instant contact high. In the two-car space sat hundreds of shoebox-size packages of weed. In a house full of kids.

Sitting at a table with two other guys, Jake was getting stoned while wrapping more packages of pot. He motioned to his associates. "You know Richard and Byron, right?"

Decent guys, as far as drug smugglers went; I had met them once before. Richard, who owned the joint, was fortyish and butt ugly—quite possibly the lab-crafted lovechild of Gene Simmons and Roseanne Barr. Byron, mid-twenties, was a skinny but handsome mustachioed Mexican who used to belong to a gang. Richard had married one of Byron's sisters or cousins. They laid tile by day—the source of Jake's idiotic tile code—and moonlighted as stash-house sitters and drug traffickers. Byron was also using his back-in-the-day gang-banger connections to help Jake find product. Richard obviously needed the money; I wouldn't have let this shit within a thousand yards of my family.

They were using their own proprietary method for packaging the dope and hiding its smell: a mixture of gelatin, motor oil, and suntan lotion smeared between layers of Saran Wrap. They called it a wrap party (har har). I called it moronic; all the pot they were smoking was tainting the outside of their carefully wrapped packages, rendering their deception methods totally useless. But this was a one-and-done deal for me, so I kept my mouth shut. They had already filled two large Army surplus duffel bags, which were ready to go. Where the rest of it was going, I didn't care, nor did I ask questions.

We chatted and joked for a few minutes. They were feeling me out, seeing if I was up to the task. I passed. Apparently, the bullshitting techniques that Missy had taught me for office politicking worked across multiple platforms. Who knew?

The irreverent chitchat stopped as we got down to business.

"There's your stuff," Jake said, pointing at the duffels. "I'm not gonna tell you how to drive or what route to take, just get it to Wichita in the next day or two. Check into a hotel, and then call this number." He repeated the digits, making me memorize it. "That's Eric's number. Coordinate with him, and he'll give you the money. Bring it back to me. Only I know the amount. Every dollar you're short, you're gonna owe me."

"No prob, I got this," I said coolly, fake smile and all.

Jake broke into a goofy little dance he always did, rubbing his hands together, looking like a tweaked-out miser on meth. "I knew you were the motherfucking man!"

I lifted the duffels—much heavier than they looked—carried them to my car, and threw them in the trunk.

I couldn't get away from that fucked-up scene fast enough. I had a hundred pounds of pot in my car, a destination, and little else. Driving straight home, I observed every traffic law as if I were taking my driver's test. I must have checked my rearview mirror a thousand times. Bullets of sweat were pouring off me, and I hadn't even really done anything yet. It was almost midnight; what if some dumbass drunk driver hit me? How would I explain the trunk full of dope? What if I got a flat tire or hit a DUI checkpoint? What if my car broke down?

Eight thousand dollars was beginning to seem cheap.

My apartment at the time was near the newly built Federal Justice Center, which housed the DEA and FBI. As I passed it, I laughed at the irony. I was trafficking dope in their backyard. Only in America, people.

I backed the car up to a wall a good distance from the apartment, hoping no one would break into it, hit it, tow it, or do anything to bring any kind of attention to it. For good measure, I peed on the back bumper, hoping the stink of my urine would mask any residual odor.

In bed with Missy, I tried to sleep, but my mind raced with a multitude of *what ifs*. I stared at my sleeping future wife, wondering what I had gotten my family into. I hated myself for the predicament I was in, but I also hated Jake for doing this to me. Why couldn't he just be a friend and help me out rather than not give a shit about my carefully planned future? I couldn't believe that I had that poison in my car. But it would be over soon enough. I prayed for God's forgiveness and the protection of my family.

At four in the morning, a nightmare about getting arrested woke me up. Rather than try to go back to sleep, I decided to hit the road. It was December 28, 1999, a day I will never forget—the day I sold my soul to a green-eyed Kansas devil.

The toughest part of the trip was going to be passing the Border Patrol checkpoint outside El Paso, so I threw my skis and boots in the Honda's front seat to look like all the other ski bums heading up to the mountains. In addition to looking for illegals, Border Patrol checkpoints have snared more than a few drug traffickers, and I didn't want them to add my name to their list. I even wore my ski jacket.

I skipped coffee that morning. I was already nervous and didn't want to sweat profusely or give myself an aneurism. Kissing Missy and her daughter as I made my way out the door, I said a silent prayer that the day would end quickly and uneventfully. As I got on the road, a deep sigh heaved my lungs, my body knowing that I was taking those drugs and all they represented away from my family.

Never again, I thought to myself. *Never again.*

Driving out of El Paso was the loneliest feeling in the world. It was dark, there was nobody on the road, and the insanity of my decision put me into panic mode.

On the open highway I wanted to pull over and run out into the desert, getting as far away from that stupid car and its payload as humanly possible. I actually considered doing that, but that would have been even dumber than driving the load in the first place. I tried to think the scenario through in every way possible, but I had nothing for reference. It all came down to: Big idiot drives small car with big load of illegal drugs on delivery mission. 'Nuff said.

Jake's entire strategic trafficking premise centered on his belief that clean-cut people—that is, clean-cut *white* people—could get away with anything. His experiences thus far had proven the theory. Jake, his brother, and his friends from Kansas had all been mules. Only one guy other than Jake had been pinched—the guy whose girlfriend I called to give instructions to, it turns out.

Apparently, the mental tater tot wore a suit and tie through the BP checkpoint after partying into the wee hours the night before. He looked disheveled as a bum and healthy as a cancer patient. Sick, rumpled, nervous guys in suits tend to draw suspicion from even the greenest of border agents, let alone those with experience, so off to jail he went. But so many of Jake's runners made it through unscathed, which comforted me. John— Jake's best friend, who had followed him to the army after high school and was best man at his wedding—had made numerous runs and hundreds of thousands of dollars. So why weren't they driving? And why did Jake want me to work for him so badly? Every time my nerves calmed, nagging questions roiled them up again.

I took a route that would have taken me toward Ski Apache, one of the big ski resorts. It would be just like the numerous other times I had passed through this checkpoint, where they saw my skis and waved me through without a word. *Thank God I'm white,* I kept thinking.

After forty-five minutes, the lights of the checkpoint came into view in the distance.

Game on, Chris. Be as cool as the other side of the pillow.

Pulling up, I rolled down my window. "American," I said with a grin.

"Where ya headed?" the agent asked.

"Skiing."

"How are the conditions?"

Thank freakin' God I had checked the snow report. "Horrible—but I gotta get my fix, even if it's dirt and rocks."

The agent stared me down.

Did I do something wrong? Does he know? Oh, fuck, he knows! I'm screwed. My life is over. I'm—

"I'm jealous. Have fun, man," he said and waved me on.

Yes! I did it. I fucking *did* it!

Less than a mile later, the thrill of my small victory faded, and the dread of what I was doing returned. Every cactus, bush, and passing car was a cop coming to get me. Then I thought back to my conversation with the BP agent. There shouldn't have *been* a conversation. Way too close for comfort. I slapped the steering wheel and started yelling at myself in the mirror.

"Idiot! What were you thinking?"

Jesus, I was freaking out. But I calmed down and got my head back in the game. At my first gas stop, I called Jake from a pay phone.

"How ya doin', chief?"

"I'm in jail," I said. "Bail me out, or I'm ratting on you."

Dead silence. Realizing that joke may not have been such a smart idea. . . . "I'm kidding. Piece of cake. I'm the man."

Jake breathed a deep sigh. "You *are* the fucking man!"

"Call you when I get to the home state."

"Yeah, buddy!" he said and hung up.

Jake was more hyper than a toddler with ADD on uppers. I played it cool, but I was losing my mind. I would've called Missy, too, but I didn't want her to worry. Out of sight, out of mind. I hoped.

Later that day, when my emotional juggernaut came to a head, I started crying—bawling. *I am such a bitch. I'm not cut out for a life of crime.* My own disgust with my sissy behavior made me sack up and get hold of myself, though. To soothe my frayed nerves, I started playing mental games.

The first game was Pretend I Wasn't Here. Become a robot. Do the job, no emotion. This wasn't really happening—just a bad dream. There's some psychobabble term for it, but dissociating myself from the situation worked like a charm. I steeled myself to the task and began thinking straight again. My keen eye observed everything, soaking in the situation. I didn't know then, but the ability to operate like an automaton would soon become a very valuable skill.

The second game was Create a Drug Trafficking Business Plan. Business was what I knew, what I studied. Might as well apply my knowledge, right? Now you see the overachiever in me. Turns out that, too, would have a significant impact on my drug trafficking future—only I didn't know that at the time. There wasn't supposed to be a drug trafficking future.

The miles slowly ticked by and, unlike my twenty-one-hour drive from Alabama to El Paso, which seemed to pass in minutes, this twelve-hour, 900-mile journey to Wichita took ages: 100 miles. 145 miles. 175 miles. 190 miles. *Jesus H. Titty-Fucking Christ!* The scenery passed as if from a jailhouse window; it wasn't touchable or appreciable, just a sad tease. This wasn't just boring—it was torture.

Every gas stop became an adventure as I looked around to see if I recognized any cars, which meant I was being followed. Paranoid delusions convinced me that everyone was my enemy, all of them trying to put me in jail. Navigating my way through Amarillo and Oklahoma City, I cursed other drivers when they did something stupid, like follow too close or cross into my lane without signaling. Didn't these insensitive assholes realize that I was just a good guy trying to get out of a bad situation and their idiotic antics could seriously fuck that up?

In Wichita, at the end of the trip—or so I thought—I went into a Taco Bell for my first meal of the day. Nerves had made me forget to eat. In front of me a young black thug, an obvious nickel-and-dime drug dealer, was bragging to the cashier about how he was going to buy her this and that. I just wanted to order and get to my hotel, and this show-off wouldn't shut up. Finally, my turn came, and I put in my order.

"That'll be $5.48," said the teenage cashier.

I fumbled in my pocket for change.

After a bit the thug stepped up beside me. "I gotcha, I gotcha," he said, pulling out a fat wad of ones and fives.

This fucktard was drawing way too much attention to himself. Normally, I wouldn't care, but the car I was driving had a hundred pounds of dope in it . . . so it was a big fucking problem!

"Thanks, but it's cool," I said, still checking my pockets. "I've got money here somewhere."

"Nah, it's all good. I'm a king in the game, bro. I got you covered."

This yahoo had no idea that I had enough pot in the trunk of my car to cover his game for five years, but I said thank you and got the hell away, grabbing a table in the back. Just as I was about to dig into one of my tacos, cops walked in.

Pure amateur, the thug bolted. The cops of course reacted out of instinct and followed him, stopping him by you guessed it *my car*. I wanted to rip that douche bag's head off, but instead, I ate and ignored the scene outside while the cops ran his name for warrants. I was worried they'd see my Texas plates and get suspicious . . . because the only reason that cars with Texas plates came to Kansas was to deliver drugs, or so I imagined. What would they think of the skis and gear in the car? We were far from any mountains.

The cops finished their business with the thug and walked back into Taco Bell. I passed them walking out, and we nodded at each other. Once again I thanked God for being white.

I made my way to the nearest motel, debating what name to use. Ultimately, I went with an alias with a Kansas address since they didn't ask for ID. Using an El Paso address was obviously out of the question.

Sitting on that shitty motel bed, trying to relax and watch TV, I called Eric and waited . . . and waited . . . and waited. I was so close to ending this nightmare, and this knucklehead was standing in the way of my goal. As I was flipping through the channels for the hundredth time, the phone finally rang.

"All right, boyee, where you at?" Eric asked.

I was literally a sitting duck. I didn't know what to expect. I was relying only on the fact that this was Jake's brother.

Forty minutes later, Eric knocked on the door. I was expecting someone cooler than a cucumber, but Eric looked more nervous than a sheep on a cliff's edge cornered by shepherds on Viagra. Hadn't he done this before?

"How's it going?" I asked.

"Good, man, good," he said with Jake's country-boy charm and slapped a thick wad of hundreds in my hand. "C'mon, follow me."

I followed him through Wichita traffic. Now, not only did I have drugs in my car, I had a hefty chunk of cash on my person, too. This was beyond stupid, and I was beginning to question Eric's street sense. It didn't take long to figure out that the guy was dumber than a box of rocks as he weaved in and out of traffic like a bat out of Satan's asshole. If I had owned a cell phone, I would have chewed his ass out something fierce.

At his trailer he made me back up to the door. I popped the trunk, he grabbed the bags, and away they went. Neither Eric nor I wanted to talk. It was over, and I was gone.

I've done some crazy shit in my life, and some of it would put hair on the chest of an X-Games athlete, but nothing has topped the rush that washed over me when that first load of herb was finally out of my possession.

But as I headed back to the motel, my paranoia raged. What if Eric told people I had money and sent them to rob me? What if the cops had been waiting for the transaction to occur before busting me? What if Jake decided that I was untrustworthy and decided to have me clipped?

I didn't return to the original motel. Instead, I got back on the freeway and headed south. I would have driven back to El Paso if I could have, but a twenty-four-hour round-trip drive, considering the emotional roller-coaster I'd just been through, really would have been insane.

I drove to the first motel I saw. My mind and body hummed with an odd concoction of complete exhaustion and absolute victory. Drop-dead tired, I felt the blood surging through my veins as if I'd received a double shot of adrenaline. To this day I don't remember where I stayed, but it was the most restful sleep of my life.

Thirty-seven hundred dollars. That's what Eric handed me. I counted it over and over, wondering how much he was supposed to give me. I thought it would be more, but fuck it. My job was done. The next day I was still experiencing an indescribable emotional high. Now I had enough money to tide us over until I found gainful employment in a position worthy of my time and effort. It was the easiest eight thousand dollars I've ever made. Too bad I couldn't find a legal way to earn money like this consistently.

On my way up to Wichita, I took the most direct route. On the way home my route took me through places I've never been, including Roswell, New Mexico, which has fascinated me ever since the supposed UFO crash. The scenery was beautiful. I was happy, smiling, singing, on top of the world. I had survived the stupidest decision of my life, and I was ready to enjoy every moment of it from here on out. I was *never* going to do this again—obviously.

Across the Panhandle, myriad Texas state troopers pulled over everything in sight. I wondered if they were looking for a *supervillain* like me. I mean, a hundred pounds of pot was some heavy shit, right? But the coppers couldn't catch me now; I was the Gingerbread Man! At a gas station three state trooper cars pulled up, and the officers walked in. We were all standing in line together, so I asked the nearest lawman why there was such a heavy patrol presence today.

"Drug interdiction task force," Johnny Law replied. "We pick a road and check everyone on it thoroughly."

"Thank God. Drugs are ripping apart the fabric of our nation. You should just pull people over and search their stuff regardless of what the law says."

The cop's mouth curled into a giant shit-eating grin. "That's exactly what we do."

"You can search my car if you want," I said with a chuckle. "Where were y'all yesterday?"

"We were gonna do 40 East, but a couple guys called in sick," he said, eyeing me suspiciously.

"Oh. Well, have a nice day." My balls receded into my stomach. That's the road I was on. I didn't realize how close I'd come. But I was still on Everest, looking down on the rest of the world. I'd had a great Christmas, still had a decent chunk saved up, and I owed nobody anything. Now if I could only find a fucking job.

As I approached El Paso, driving through the same lonely darkness I had departed in, I knew that good things—hell, *great* things—were on the horizon.

Little did I know.

5

Hate It or Love It

FEARS FLOATED NERVOUSLY IN THE AIR.

It was Y2K eve, and Missy, her daughter, and I were ushering in the new year from Tom Lea Park, a scenic overlook of downtown. Just across the border lay El Paso's Mexican cousin, the city of Juarez. We hugged and counted down to midnight, my mind whirling in anticipation that world domination—or at least regional ascendancy—was imminent . . . or so I thought.

Missy and I prepared for the birth of our son. Still not talking to her parents, we did what we could to manage on our own. We bought new furniture, rearranged the apartment, organized the kitchen, and hosted a few showers. Despite her repeated warnings about how much work it was to have a baby, I remained firmly in denial. I didn't know what I didn't know. But the stars had aligned, and for once the compass of my life was pointing in the direction I wanted. No time like the present, right?

While driving back from a quick but much needed weekend getaway in the mountains, I was already envisioning a return trip. "We should come back up and get a cabin again in a couple weeks," I said.

She looked at me like I was crazy. "The baby's due in a couple weeks. We won't be doing anything for months after that. This is going to be *a lot* of work."

"All right, then."

"I'm serious, Chris. I'm nervous."

"Then that settles it. Let's get married tomorrow. I don't want my son being born out of wedlock. Maybe that'll settle your nerves." I pulled off the road and looked her in the eyes. "I love you, Missy, and I want to be your husband and fix all your problems."

The very next day, Missy, her daughter, her sister, her one-year-old nephew, my grandmother, and one of my grandmother's friends, a nun, and I—a motley crowd—hopped through the courthouse from judge to judge, looking for someone available to marry us on short notice. Finally, we stood in front of the justice of the peace on January 10, 2000. Holding hands, trembling like nudists in a meat locker, it was hard to know who was more frightened. Missy's beautiful face betrayed abject terror, her swollen belly bulging beneath her blouse. I for one never envisioned getting married in khakis and a polo at the courthouse.

"I do marriages, but I don't do divorces," His Honor Sam Paxson said gruffly. "You kids better understand that."

"Yessir," said everyone in our group, more than a little intimidated.

The next day I went over to Jake's. "Guess what I did yesterday."

"You jerked off. Twice."

"No, you fool. I got married."

"Aww, congratu-fuckin'-lations!"

I changed my schedule around, making it a job to use Jake's computer every morning to look for one. When he went to the strip club, I shot back across town to be with the family. I had been to a couple of temp agencies and interviews, but I couldn't close the deal. Finding a decent job seemed all but impossible, but the comfort of not being broke or desperate combined with my desire to pay Jake back and fly right spurred me on. Eight thousand dollars was hardly a fortune, but it was nice to have choices.

"Find a job yet?" Jake mocked, surfing the porno channels.

"Find a soul yet?"

Rejection letters filled my inbox each day. All those years of waiting tables or playing poker to pay the bills didn't exactly prepare me for the corporate world. And my nine-month stint as a staff accountant really didn't bolster my résumé.

"Come work for me," Jake offered. "I need a regular driver. I don't have anyone I can rely on."

"What about John or Byron?"

"John's a drunk that can't drive more than six hours without stopping for hooch. Byron looks too gangster. You'd be the shit."

"I like the money, but I can turn my situation around legally."

"Whatever." Jake returned to his porn as I dialed yet another temp agency.

"We can get you nine dollars an hour for account reconciliation; however, it's a forty-five-mile drive from your address to their office," said the booker, who sounded like a teenage girl chomping gum.

"Can't you get me a commissioned sales job somewhere?"

"Sorry, but I need to fill this one position."

"I'm glad you're putting your needs in front of mine," I said, slamming the phone down.

"That's how you do it!" Jake shouted, pumping his fist. "Fight the power!"

"How 'bout I make you eat this phone?" I snapped, in no mood for his jagoff commentary.

"Go ahead and try," he said smarmily. "I'm strip-clubbed out and headin' to the mall. Wanna go?"

"Sure."

We hit Cattle Baron, a local steakhouse, for lunch. Eating filet mignon and sipping a cold one, Jake gave me an impassioned speech about making it in the world by any means necessary: lie, cheat, steal. Nice guys finish last and all that jazz. He believed firmly that giving your loyalty to a company only to retire with a plaque, a gold watch, and a meager pension was for fools.

"Look around," Jake said. "How many of these corporate drones in here are happy?"

"They look happy to me."

"Fuck that shit. Make money any way you can. Answer to no one. *This* is the life, not that."

"Shut your cake hole. I just wanna eat—and lunch is on me. I owe you one."

But damn if he didn't make a convincing argument. I was beginning to doubt my desire to be in the corporate world. Maybe my talents were too big for a cubicle. I loved the freedom I had, and I loved how having money made me feel.

Jake and Sandra were becoming regular fixtures in our lives. Despite the friendliness of it all, Jake was serious about business, and he was courting me hard. The prospect didn't scare me. Having broken through the fear threshold by doing it once only made me more knowledgeable about the process.

Jake gave me a tutorial on how he ran his organization—little more than a group of buddies endeavoring to make money. Really, there was no planning or structure. Everything that Jake, Eric, John, and Byron discussed was anecdotal and haphazard. Now that their trafficking club included me, they told me everything without hesitation whenever we got together.

"One time," said Jake one night, while kicking back and relaxing in his hot tub with Byron and me, "I picked up an eighteen-hundred-pound load in a van from a guy in the lower valley and noticed two state troopers following me everywhere I drove. I freaked, parked at the Lamplighter, and went inside. I called the guy I got the shit from, and his son came and got the van and raced back to Mexico."

"Why didn't the cops get them?" I asked.

"The cops are dirty, too, bro."

"Whatever," I said in disbelief.

"Seriously. It happened once before with those guys. We had a nine-hundred-pound load, and the cops made no attempt to hide that they were following me. I freaked, pulled over, left the van, and took a cab home. I called the guys from a pay phone, then got my car. I came back to check it every few hours, but it eventually disappeared. They said they watched the cops take it, but no one was ever arrested. We reported the van stolen and never heard word one about it. Explain that."

"The cops took it and sold the shit themselves," Byron said.

"So the second time, the guys decided to run the load back to Mexico and start over," Jake explained. "I stopped buying from them. Too much heat."

"The cops have never looked for you?" I said.

"Nope!"

"Shit, everyone in these two towns is dirty and has a story like this," said Byron, and he was right.

My uncle Jimmy served time for trafficking, and Uncle Charlie hid a million dollars in my grandfather's house. Everyone in El Paso has a story about some family member in the narco biz. It's even more common than high school hero stories.

"Remember when Raymundo hid all that money in the bushes at Wienerschnitzel?" Byron asked.

"Yeah," Jake laughed. "Or when John got a flat and some cop helped him change the tire with a load in the trunk?"

Their stories went on for hours, all shits and giggles. They were romanticizing the life for the benefit of the part of me that saw an opportunity to make a ton of money quickly, which I wanted to use to open a proper business back in Alabama. If I had one good year, I could put away two hundred thousand bucks and coast. The endless rejection letters and pathetic employment offers were pushing me in that direction, too.

Just over a week later, the day after my birthday, I was eating leftover birthday cake for breakfast. Not exactly the food of champions, but I was hardly a winner, so it fit.

"Instead of hanging out with your *friend* today, could you take me to the doctor for a checkup?" Missy asked.

"Sure. Saddle up, fatty!"

She pinched me *hard* as we walked out the door.

In the waiting room, looking at all the other preggos, I'm certain I wasn't the only one thinking about where to eat lunch. Everything appeared normal as the nurse performed the checkup, poking and prodding my wife as though she were a used car at the mechanic's. Then the nurse called over another nurse. They checked and rechecked the fetal monitor, each time giving each other a serious look. Then the doctor came and huddled with the nurses, speaking in hushed, concerned tones while scouring the results.

"Congratulations!" he said. "You're going to have a baby today. We're calling the hospital now, and they're readying a room for you."

"But the baby isn't due for three weeks!" I said.

"Due-schmue, it's coming today." Missy had started having minor contractions, and each time she did my son's heartbeat slowed, which meant the umbilical cord was pinched. They needed to induce labor immediately.

I nearly had a heart attack, but that was nothing compared to what Missy endured.

My lovely wife spewed an unending stream of furious profanities and ghastly bodily fluids. Childbirth isn't beautiful; it's disgusting. Surviving it is beautiful. I held her hand with eyes clamped shut.

After almost eleven hours of labor, my son entered the world screaming—something he hasn't stopped doing yet. Nurses counted fingers and toes and did the required medical procedures while the doctor finished with Missy. I wasn't sure what to do other than not pass out. My wife was still making noises like a broken tractor on a bumpy road, my son was wailing like an ambulance siren, and I was trying to hide in plain sight. Then, from the corner of my eye, I saw the nurses lock their gazes on me. I tried to avoid their piercing stares, but they marched over.

The nurse thrust my son into my gut like a football handoff and congratulated me. The fear that swallowed me at that moment was indescribable. He was so small, so fragile. I was afraid of dropping or hurting him, and I couldn't wait to give him back. It didn't help that he was still screaming his swollen little head off.

"Talk to him," one of the nurses commanded.

"Yeah, talk to him," echoed my wife and her mother, who were speaking again. Marrying her daughter nine days prior helped grease the wheels of forgiveness, but having babies got them turning.

"Mr. Heifner?" another nurse urged.

I caved and smiled down at the little booger. "Hey, buddy, what are you doing?"

His crying ceased, and everyone in the room stopped to see what had happened. I was shocked myself. I didn't think he'd respond to anything other than a boob.

"Hey, buddy, it's your dad," I said, confidence building. "What's all the fuss about?"

"*Ooooooooooooo . . .*"

I couldn't believe it. My minutes-old little kiddo was cooing at me and trying to open his eyes. It blew me away.

The feeling didn't last, unfortunately. Life quickly became an endless parade of annoying visitors, cheap gifts, and sleepless nights. The bills picked up their pace, and that nice little cushion of money was only going to last another six weeks.

Jake and Sandra came to the hospital and then to the house to bring a gift and check out my stinky little bundle of joy. While the women talked, Jake and I went outside.

"How does being a dad feel?"

"Amazing!"

"As good as being a kingpin?"

"They don't compare."

Fundamentally, nothing had changed in the last few months; that eight thousand dollars was just a Band-Aid. That temporary feeling of accomplishment turned out to be little more than a cruel flirtation with success—and my problems were mounting.

"I've got an offer for you," Jake said. "Run a bag up to that friend we met last month at the casino, and I'll pay you 4K."

"Fuck, no!"

"Nutty, it's a gift. The checkpoint will be closed tomorrow from midnight to six."

"How do you know?"

"Didn't I tell you?"

"No."

"That's 'cause I didn't want you to know." His trademark line.

A two-hour drive for four thousand dollars? Fuck. The simplicity of it was hard to fathom, but it meant another two months of time on my side.

In robot mode, borderline unconscious, I passed through the closed Border Patrol checkpoint at five the next morning.

"I'll be damned," I said aloud. Jake was right.

This time I was cooler than dry ice, no paranoid delusions. I drove, fiddled with my CD player, drank my usual morning OJ, and ate an Egg McMuffin. At the casino I handled Jake's buddy like a seasoned pro: We met by his Escalade; I threw the duffel in the back, shook his hand, and smiled as he handed me thirty-seven hundred dollars.

"Jake told me to tell you that you were three hundred dollars short on your last trip, but now you're paid in full," the old guy said.

I didn't say a word, stewing for the two-hour drive back to El Paso. I went straight to Jake's house, hoping to catch him before his daily strip club ritual.

"How'd it go?" he asked.

"What's up with that three-hundred-dollar bullshit?"

"That's how it works."

"Whattaya mean, 'That's how it works'? Eric only gave me thirty-seven hundred bucks. Call him."

"I got a better idea. Are you ready to step up to the big leagues?"

"What the fuck are you talking about?"

"Run a load to Memphis. Two days' work, twelve grand. I'd hire John, but the drunkard's on one of his benders."

There was that lump in my throat again, but it had changed. It had become a lump of excitement. Twelve thousand dollars for two days? We were talking Gordon Gekko money now, or so I thought.

"Man, I don't know," I said, playing coy. "I would only pay John eight thousand. You're getting a bonus. Think about it. It's almost noon, and I gotta run. Special business today. Call me tomorrow with your answer."

My family was $3,700 richer, but again nothing had changed. We didn't have health insurance or a nest egg. Hell, I still didn't even have a job. I had made $11,700 in less than a month, but that was little more than hand to mouth for a family of four. My children were going to need a lot more than that.

Something had to happen, and it had to happen soon.

6

Mo' Money, Mo' Problems

SOMETHING HAPPENED, ALL RIGHT.

I hit the PANIC button and became a drug trafficker. Wanting and needing but never having had become too much to bear. Broke, I went for broke: corporate lackey to criminal conspiracy in an instant. Hail, Mary—here goes nothing.

Rationalizing my decision, I planned to get out if (a) I spotted trouble, or (b) I got caught. Because Jake had filled my head with such shit about my not having any priors, which meant that getting pinched would yield little more than a slap on the wrist, I actually believed that I had made an intelligent decision. Talk about screwed up.

Being a drug mule was anything but a typical day's work. Danger permeated every load, every trip. Amazingly, though, all that preparation to run a Fortune 500 company one day, in a warped and twisted way, actually paid dividends. My new career also required me to think on my feet and maintain hypervigilance. If I was going to do this, I was going to do it right.

During the run to Memphis, I hit the Border Patrol checkpoint at about 6:00 a.m.

"American?" an agent asked.

"Born and bred."

He waved me through.

No problemo, I thought, forgetting that a state trooper task force could lie just around the bend. I could break down, get into a wreck, or get pulled over. Dropping my guard meant getting pinched, so I vowed never to take anything for granted.

The miles ticked by faster this time, and though I handled the heaviness of the situation much better, the stress still made me sick. Monitoring speed, the car's vitals, mirrors, and the road kept my mind constantly occupied. There was no room for error. It made me wish I had a chase car to run interference and help me if an accident or breakdown occurred.

But a potential problem nagged at my gut: Jake and his crew had failed to pull the spare tire first and put it on top of the load. The load weighed more than 250 pounds—serious weight if I got popped—so a flat would send me up shit's creek.

Richard and Byron shot me dirty looks as I left Richard's house, pissed that they didn't get a shot to run it. But my mind had already focused on the thousand-mile drive to Texarkana.

Drug trafficking isn't as glamorous as it seems on *Miami Vice*. After navigating Texas and the sprawling zoo of the Dallas Metroplex, the sight of a motel on the border was an oasis to tired eyes. I rented a room, stowed my luggage, and made a quick trip to McDonald's, my stomach growling like a caged tiger. A greasy burger and some even greasier fries soothed my frayed nerves. At midnight I pulled back into the motel parking lot . . . surrounded by cop cars.

"Sir, what are you doing here?" a cop asked, shining a Maglite in my face.

Byron or Richard had ratted me out, payback for not getting to run the load. Shit.

"Sir?" he barked. "*What. Are. You. Doing. Here?*"

"I'm, uh, staying in the motel."

"Why didn't you just say so?" He clicked off the Maglite. "Please enter your room, and do not leave or let anyone in."

It took a moment to realize that they weren't there for me.

"Sir, do you understand?"

"Yessir, officer. Got it."

51

I backed my car into a spot and made my way to my room on the second floor, which gave me a front-row view of the hullabaloo. Cops had fanned out around the property, their beams scanning the darkness. Apparently, a fugitive was loose in the area. After watching for a while, I tried to get some sleep, even though a mob of police was literally outside my door.

Three hours later, when I woke up and peeked out the window, Johnny Law had left. Anxious to get the hell out of Dodge, I took off after little more than a nap, stopping at a gas station a few miles outside town to fill up. What I didn't see—until it was too late—were the dozen marked police units from various agencies parked in back. The line for the can was a law enforcement convention.

"Damn, guys," I said, chill as an arctic wind, "doesn't the toilet at the barracks work?"

Several cops laughed. The others stared at me as if I were holding a see-through suitcase filled with cocaine, assault rifles, and body parts. I cracked another joke, and everyone laughed. Maybe I should have taken drama classes instead of finance. Fuck all those thespians in Hollywood. My life literally depended on this one-take performance while those Tinseltown tough guys got meaningless multiple takes.

As my turn to use the facilities drew nearer, I noticed that a few of the vehicles were marked as K9 units and some of the officers were exercising their dogs. *Fuck me with French bread. Please don't go near my car,* I prayed.

In the can I pissed in a trough with two officers talking about how they were going to kick ass at their roadblock. Luckily, they didn't look down, see my hand shaking like a leaf, and arrest me for being a pervert.

Back on the road to Memphis, sweating bullets, I began to wonder if twelve thousand dollars was worth the years that all this stress and anxiety had taken off my life. Pulling into the Gold Strike Casino, south of Memphis, I checked into a room and called my contact, a black guy named Larry.

"I'm here," I said.

"All right, boy. Where you wanna meet?"

I suggested the parking garage for safety's sake. "Fourth level, gray Honda Accord with Texas plates."

"See ya in twenty," he said and hung up.

I went early and waited. A security guard pedaled by on a bike, and I immediately regretted my choice of location. Too late now, though. A couple of minutes later, Larry—like a short Derek Jeter without the looks or money—pulled up in an old Ford Escort with a ten-year-old riding shotgun. *What the fuck?*

"Yo, man, this my son," said Larry, who had long, straight hair and a pimp swagger and fancied himself a smooth talker.

"Uh . . ."

"It's cool. Let's just do this and get gone."

Larry took the duffels and tried stuffing them into the back of his car. A ridiculously tight squeeze, he had to rearrange them several times before they fit. Then he laid some money on the front seat of his car.

"Here ya go, man. Give this to Jake."

The cash covered the entire front seat. It was going to take more than two hands and a shovel to get it all. I walked back to my car to grab the plastic bag I was using for trash. When I turned around both, Larry and his son, obviously spooked, had their hands in their pockets as if they were both about to draw on me.

I played it cool and scooped the bills into the bag, which felt like it contained a bowling ball instead of cash.

"When ya leaving?" Larry asked.

"Tomorrow morning."

Larry winked, and I instantly realized that he might have been fishing for info so his cronies could rob me before I blew town. The hundred-thousand-plus payment along with the load he'd just received would make a damn good year for him. Dammit. Shouldn't have said that.

"I got some fly girls workin' for me," he said. "Want me to send ya one? . . . or two?"

"Sure, man, I can stay an extra day. But I'm exhausted. Let's party tomorrow night. I'll call ya tomorrow, and we'll set it up."

Walking through the casino with a plastic-bag fortune felt beyond exhilarating. In my room I quit counting at seventy-five grand, counting out my twelve thousand—plus a three-grand insurance policy in case Jake got screwy with the numbers again—and separated that from the rest of the loot.

There was a legit chance someone would try to rob me tomorrow, so I put the money in the room safe and filled up my car. The plan was to leave at 5:00 a.m. and not stop until the car was driving on fumes, just in case anyone followed. Larry could keep his skanky hookers.

Driving money proved even more stressful than driving a load. I had heard that money smells like dope, and K9 units would hit on it faster than a truckload of Purina. Losing a drug load, while bad, wasn't the end of the world. Pinched loads happened and were factored into costs. Losing a money load meant losing your life.

So here I was again: neck deep in shit without a real plan.

Back in El Paso I stopped at my house first to drop off my cut.

"Honey, grab my toiletry kit and hide it. It has money in it," I said to Missy.

Naturally, she grabbed the wrong bag. Her eyes bulged when she saw what was inside. "What's this?"

"Jake's cut."

"Jake's cut of *what?*"

She understood my *You sure you wanna know?* look loud and clear. "You're right, I don't wanna know. Just don't do anything stupid. Your son needs you."

"I got it. It's all good."

We stared at Jake's cut. He had paid for the load in advance, so this was his profit. Eighty thousand–plus.

The wheels of Missy's mind were spinning. "Do we have to give it to him?"

God, I love this woman. "Yes."

"This would change our lives. Let's run with it."

She didn't know the details, but she wasn't naïve. She had seen the drug business firsthand through family and former boyfriends. She loved me, in part, because she knew I did things the right way and because I was going to be someone someday.

"I gotta go," I said, pecking her on the lips.

Jake needed his money as quickly as possible. He still had to pay Byron and Richard, and I didn't want their cut in my hands.

He greeted me at the door with a hero's welcome, dancing around like an idiot for a few minutes as he spirited away the cash. Apparently, I had passed the test and had become part of his inner circle. We popped a few cold ones and jumped into his hot tub, just what the doctor ordered after four tough days of driving.

"How come you didn't tell me I was bringing money back?"

"That's just how it worked out," he said.

"Shouldn't I get a bonus? Everyone gets paid for money trips."

"We'll worry about it later."

He got a free trip out of me—my risk, his reward—but I had also taken out a three-thousand-dollar insurance policy against this kind of bullshit, and I wanted answers to other questions.

"What's the deal with that Larry cat? He brought his son to a drug deal, and I think he had a gun."

"Larry or the kid?"

"Both."

"Doesn't surprise me. He's got, like, a dozen kids, and I guess he's startin' 'em young to keep it in the family." He took a big slurp of brew. "So, you ready to taste some *real* success, champ?"

"Sure," I shrugged, sliding down the slippery slope. "Whatcha have in mind?"

"I want you to be my right-hand man. You're someone I can count on, someone I can trust. Like I already told you, John is a bed-shitting drunk. Byron isn't a big-league player, and he sure as shit ain't a big-league thinker. And my brother won't follow instructions. You got the skills, Nutty. Plus, you *hate* this business. That means you'll stay smart and on your toes." He gave me a dead man's stare. "So, you in or not?"

Before I realized it, my lips were moving, and words were coming out of my mouth. "Fine. Bring it the fuck on."

"*Yeah, motherfucker!*" Jake roared, banging his beer against mine. "That's what I wanted to hear! Next load'll be in a few days."

Out of the frying pan, into the fire. Suddenly, all I wanted to do was spend time with my family and get my affairs in order, a subconscious just in case.

I had never seen this kind of cash before, let alone had it, and I wasn't sure what to do with it. I had only ever had a checking account, and that was usually in the red. The IRS and other agencies monitor large transactions, especially deposits, so there were lots of questions and zero answers. Ultimately, I wound up hiding money all over my house and my grandmother's—places you'd never think to look, places *I'd* never think to look—like some cracked-out squirrel. During runs I constantly created mental checklists to pass the time, keep my mind occupied, and deal with my newfound success.

The first checklist got my house in order. Cell phones at the time were the size of toasters, and not everyone had one, but I bought a matching pair and surprised Missy with one. She wasn't going to drive around with my kids without a lifeline. I also started shopping for cars. She drove my Nissan pickup with the baby seat while I used her Honda to mule, which might implicate her in my shit if I got caught.

"Welcome to Pep Boys," the service tech said. "How can I help you?"

"I need an estimate on tires, brakes, oil change, new radiator, tranny service, and a brake fluid flush. I don't want premium parts, warranties, or bullshit. Just do me right, and don't waste my time," I said.

"Yessir!" said the tech.

Then I had the car detailed, treated myself to some much-needed new clothes, and started looking at new furniture for the house—including a big-screen TV.

Three weeks after the birth of our son, Missy was still struggling with postpartum depression. I wanted to help, but changing a diaper—let alone anything more significant—scared me to death. Depression had eroded her patience, and we stood at a stalemate. So I foolishly threw myself into my work, not understanding the gravity of the situation.

My plan was to learn everything I could about trafficking and laundering. But Jake had a plan, too. He began introducing me to his contacts. As we drove into Mexico the next morning, I said a solemn prayer because Mexico is Mexico. With cowboy justice, only the strong survive.

"Remember this route, Nutty. You'll be coming back."

"For what?"

He double-pumped his eyebrows silently as we drove through the *Campestre,* the richest neighborhood in Juarez. We pulled up to a palatial residence that could have taken pride of place on MTV's *Cribs,* and my jaw went slack. Laptop case in hand, Jake led the way as I all but drooled at the exquisite home. He rapped on the wrought iron front door, and a bodyguard—submachine gun slung across his thick body—answered.

Jake and the bullet sponge exchanged handshake hugs, and we were led into a gorgeous parlor off an expansive formal living room. Sculpted stone and polished marble shone everywhere. Beneath colorful artwork, an insanely hot maid dusted a long mantel above a cave-size stone fireplace. A few minutes later a Mexican guy in his early twenties with short, spiky hair like a pro soccer player's came bouncing down the central curling marble staircase.

"Jakey, *mi amigo! Que paso?*"

"Adan, this is Chris. Chris, Adan."

The decadence of his house was still distracting me as we shook hands. It was all picture perfect except for an ugly-as-sin red leather sectional couch in the living room—which probably cost as much as an Asian family, but damn, it was heinous.

Joining Adan on the hideous couch, Jake opened his laptop case, revealing a mess of cash. Adan began counting out the money but soon noticed my wandering eyes.

"Do you like my house?"

"Gorgeous."

"What do you think of my couch?"

"My honest opinion, or should I lie to your face?"

Jake groaned as he closed his eyes and scooted away from me. Adan and I stared at one another.

Then the narco boss burst into laughter. "I fucking hate this couch, *too!*" he roared and slapped the leather so hard it sounded like a gunshot. "My girlfriend made me pay fifteen thousand dollars for this piece of shit!"

The smokin' hot maid brought us icy Tecates with limes and salt and a crystal pitcher of chilled tomato juice on a huge sterling silver platter, and we carried on like old friends. After a while the bullet sponge returned to take the money and stash it.

"Let's go eat," Adan said, getting to his feet. "I want him to meet Guerro." Despite being only Taco Bell proficient in Spanish—I can order food, find a bathroom, and get laid—I knew that Guerro (pronounced *wear-o*) means "blondie."

"Let's rock and roll," said Jake.

In the trafficking biz you never trust *anyone* completely. I had driven, and with six hundred dollars in my pocket if I needed to ditch them, I could. But taking my car instead of Jake's also made me suspicious. My mind swam in circles considering all the variables. This business was going to make me old and gray before I hit thirty—if I lived that long.

We pulled up to another huge, megadollar house. A gold AMG Mercedes 600 SL—one of my favorite cars on the planet—sat out front, complete with custom rims and dual TVs. I was peeking in the window when three guys bounced out from the lavish home's front door. The guy in front had to be Guerro. Pale, beanpole thin, and handsomely sinister, he wore snakeskin cowboy boots that probably cost more than my college education.

"Guerro, this is Jake and Chris, the new guy," Adan said.

After scrutinizing me Guerro said, "You like that car, man? You can have it right now for 20K. Just pay me later. I got it as payment from some *myates* from Chicago, and I hate the color gold."

That car was an orgasm on wheels. I was tempted—but I wasn't stupid. Owing them money allowed them to get their hooks into me.

I needed to keep my options open, to be able to walk away clean at a moment's notice.

We spent the rest of the day partying like rock stars, bouncing from restaurant to bar to bar. I never ate so much good food or drank so much top-shelf tequila in all my life. The four of us plus a contingent of bodyguards made quite a spectacle moving from location to location, getting royal treatment wherever we went.

For instance, parking spaces? Nope. We pulled up to the front door, parked in the street, and left the cars there. Women followed us everywhere—most hotter than the summer Sahara—and various people came and went, taking care of business tableside, Mafia style. I still didn't know how to act, so I acted like I belonged.

"When you bring money," Adan said to me, "bring it to me or my brother, Jose. You will meet him next time. No one else, *comprende?*"

"Yessir."

"And be *very* careful. I've already had two couriers killed. You are not safe until you get to my house."

It felt like I'd swallowed a cement mixer.

In Mexico people disappear all the time, and the police don't give a damn. Risky business and warnings aside, these guys genuinely seemed to like me. They treated me with respect and made me feel welcome—that is, until Adan got drooling drunk and his mood turned sour.

He took my face in his hand. "How do I know I can trust you? You've partied with us all day but haven't touched a thing."

He was right. I hadn't done coke with them like Jake had, and I was blowing off the girls, too, a move that reeked of dishonesty in his book. I motioned for the bullet, a small device for snorting coke. He loaded it, and I took a monster hit. There's no way you can fake that. That first stripper I partied with a few years ago had probably saved my life.

"Sorry to offend you, Adan. I just got married, and I have a newborn son. Just trying to be a good dad, that's all."

"I was there," Jake added. "He's a good-lookin' little fella!"

"No shit!" Adan smiled. "I like you, my friend."

The peace didn't last, though. One of the girls at the table started yelling at Guerro in Spanish. Everyone in the bar stopped to look at the commotion, but a bodyguard quickly quelled the situation by grabbing her by the hair and dragging her out the back door.

Her vicious removal took only me by surprise.

"What's gonna happen to her?" I whispered to Jake.

"You don't wanna know."

These guys didn't fuck around.

On the way back to El Paso, stuck in the line at the bridge for two hours, Jake got out to piss in traffic four times. "You better rest up," he said, climbing back into the car. "You've got two big loads comin' up in the next few days."

"Two?"

"Yeah, you're gonna run one through the checkpoint, then Byron's gonna run it the rest of the way to Memphis. Then you're coming back, loading another car, and going to Kansas."

Don't get me wrong, the danger was exciting, but the emotional roller coaster had overloaded my system. A fever started digging into me as I drove Jake back to his house, wondering what would kill me first: Adan, the police, Jake, or the stress? At least I wasn't going to die broke.

A few days later Byron rented a car that I drove through the checkpoint to Van Horn, Texas, about a hundred miles outside El Paso, while Jake followed in his wife's red Acura.

"You okay, man?" Byron said as we exchanged keys in the bathroom of a McDonald's.

"Yeah, just a fever."

"You look like death."

"Don't worry about me," I said, knowing he cared more about my appearance than my well-being. "Look, Jake's only paying you fifteen hundred for the Memphis run, but I don't think that's enough, so I'm giving you fifteen hundred out of my pocket."

"Wow, I don't know what to say."

"Don't say anything; just have my back one day."

"You know it."

We hugged, and Byron hit the road to Memphis while Jake ferried me back to Hell Paso. Jake was screwing Byron royally—and even bragged about it on the trip back. He had budgeted ten grand for the load to Memphis and was paying me eighty-five hundred to drive it past the checkpoint.

"Why are you paying Byron so little?" I asked.

"Fuck him. He's expendable."

"He's been loyal, got you all your hookups, and helped introduce you to the people that *keep* introducing you to the right people."

Jake waved me off. "That's the life of a mule, Nutty. I'm not training *you* to be a mule. I'm training you to be a trafficker."

Just like that, my career choice came sharply into focus. Too sick to argue on that long drive—freezing, shuddering, dripping with sweat—I realized that trafficking was every man for himself, and I had damn well better chuck any romantic notions of loyalty and allegiance out the fucking window.

It was time to come up with a new plan, and fast—but first I had to get my sick ass to Kansas for another ten grand.

7

Hotel California

Less than two months after my indoctrination into the dark and dangerous world of drug trafficking, I had become a seasoned smuggler making fifty thousand dollars a month—a hard way to make an easy living that made going straight unthinkable.

Ever the overachiever, I treated my narco work like a real job. I bounced out of bed every morning and did anything to be productive, including developing my own contacts. Worse, I began scheming to run my own trafficking organization. Jake's approach was reckless and, for lack of a better word, unprofessional. The longer I worked for him, the more of a risk it posed. If I wanted my time in the biz to go smoothly and as safely as possible, considering the arena, I had to hit and run—get in, get out. The stakes were too high otherwise.

Putting in more than eighty hours a week with Jake left my family life in shambles. Missy was desperate for a break from the kids or at least a little help. She didn't appreciate the lengths to which I was going to provide for us, which solidified my realization that this triumph could only ever be temporary. I had better keep getting while the getting was good. I pleaded with her to trust me and to hold down the fort for a few more months, but she always preferred living in the moment to delayed gratification. She understood my methodology, but her sanity was on the brink. Angering her was a risk I had to take.

In the Lamplighter with Jake, I tried a tactic he had never considered: I talked with the girls. For him the strippers satisfied carnal needs and little else. For me they became a source of information. I tipped big and often, encouraging them to share what they knew. Turns out that many of their repeat customers were dealers or otherwise involved in the game. Those players routinely talked shop to peacock for the vixens, and the girls gave me a who's who of El Paso's narco realm, from the heads of operations down to their customers.

"That guy sells many of the girls coke," said one stripper while sitting on my lap, discreetly pointing to an older man across the club. "He works in Juarez as a plant manager. I think he brings it over the bridge in small amounts using his company car and E-ZPass."

"Him? He looks like a perv."

"He is." She motioned to another man. "That guy drives an eighteen-wheeler. He runs pot in rotting fruit loads. Dogs can't sniff it. But he's small time, only fifty pounds at a time."

"I can't believe these guys tell you all this stuff."

"They like to brag, and I'm a good listener, just like you, sweetie." She pointed to a table of young guys across the room. "Those guys sell meth. The one on the left is from Iowa and has friends in Denver, where he takes a lot of trips, probably to deliver. I think they make it in Mexico."

"I wonder how they cross it."

She smiled. "He hires us."

Bells went off inside my head: money and safety combined. Front a load financially and pay someone else to drive it. I could buy a pound of pot in El Paso on the US side for $225 and sell it anywhere else in the country for $600. If transportation costs $50 per pound, that's $325 per pound profit. Multiply that by a hundred, two hundred, or three hundred pounds, and you had a potential profit of a hundred grand for a weekend's work. *Sick!*

"I'd drive for you," she offered. "You're definitely the smartest one I've met yet." She nuzzled my neck. "And the cutest."

"I'm no narco," I lied. "I just like hearing the stories."

"Yeah, right," she said, kissing me on the cheek.

I already knew Adan and Jose, so supply wasn't an issue. I just needed to snag a route or make a connection that needed me to deliver. A few loads, and I'd be ready to retire.

All of this may sound neat and clean, but the drug business is a cold, mean, ass-kicking bitch. Not only do you have to stay one step ahead of the police, but you have your fellow criminals to consider as well. Whoever said there's honor among thieves never worked in the drug trade. Sometimes you got money for your efforts, sometimes you got a gun in your face and a calm "Fuck off." You had to find people whom you could trust—easier said than done in organized crime. If you got fucked over after delivering a load, you couldn't sue for nonpayment. You could kill someone who screwed you, but Jake had a theory about that.

"Carrying a gun will just get you more jail time," he said. "If you commit murder, the cops will *never* stop hunting you, but they'll forget all the loads you ran."

He was a child genius in his way. After a few months I conjured up a million different ways to run his operation better and more efficiently. But he took no interest in my suggestions. Because nothing bad had happened so far, he thought nothing bad ever would. Apparently, he didn't remember the RICO Act from the biz law class we had together, which basically said that I was a coconspirator and subject to criminal penalties for everything he did from here on out. His mistakes could be paid with flesh from my ass. Actually, as time wore on, it thoroughly annoyed him that I even had an opinion. You'd think he might appreciate my dynamism. Not a chance.

February was spinning by like a top on nitrous. While I juggled business, family, and deteriorating health—stress and crazy hours constantly making me sick—Jake was planning what amounted to a company retreat. At the end of March, he wanted to take everyone to Telluride on his dime to ski and womanize. It was all he could think about. There was still serious business to handle, though, so I kept my head on straight and stuck to my plan—as well as I could.

Running a fever for the fourth time in six weeks, I checked myself into the emergency room for the second time in as many weeks. It felt like an elephant was standing on my head in a freezer.

I wouldn't let Missy or the kids visit me in the hospital because I didn't want them to catch whatever I had. So I lay alone in the bed crying like a baby, certain that my illness was karmic payback for my sins. Sick as I was, though, I still had obligations. When my cell phone rang late one night, I knew it was bad news even before I checked the caller ID.

"Hello?" I sounded like death warmed over.

"Wassup?" said Adan.

"I'm sick as a dog."

"Tequila will make you better."

Just the thought made me gag. "No. It won't."

"Sucks for you. Bring me my money tomorrow."

Click.

Fever, headache, aches, and pains beat death any day. I called Jake and told him to get a packet ready. For money runs like these I used his street bike, a Suzuki GSX-R1000, essentially a rocket on two wheels. Doped up after two days of hospitalization, I got the money and the bike and took off for Mexico. My head was floating in a fog, and ninjas were using my body for kicking practice—but I had no choice.

A twist of the throttle sent me across the Bridge of the Americas. Why did Adan want the money now, I wondered, pulling up to a stoplight. Did he have debts that needed settling? Were the authorities closing in on him and he wanted to get out before they got him? A glint of sunlight reflecting off a shiny object snapped me out of my thoughts.

Holy shit! Someone in the car next to me was pointing a gun at me, ordering me to give him the money—around $150,000.

Too sick to be scared, I acted like I was going to comply. Then I popped the clutch and twisted my wrist as far as it would go. The powerful bike lifted onto one wheel and rocketed across the intersection, narrowly avoiding crossing cars. Illness muted my reaction as I raced to

Adan's house. In fact, it may have saved me. *Fuck you* was all I could think. *Catch me if you can, and bring me a goddamn aspirin.*

In the Campestre Adan had more security around than usual. I didn't care. I just wanted to get back on the bike, speed home, and go back to bed. But as bodyguards were forcing me into an SUV, I remember thinking, *If they're gonna kill me, I hope they do it quick and put me outta my misery 'cause I really feel like shit.*

In the backseat a pretty girl in her mid-twenties grabbed my arm and jabbed an IV needle into it. I was too weak and confused to stop her.

"We're going on a trip," Adan said from the front seat. "I wanna show you something. I know you're sick, but don't worry. We checked your hospital charts so we could give you the right medicine." He patted my knee. "Just relax and enjoy. You'll be okay."

Warmth spread through my body. I pointed at the IV. "What's in it?"

"You don't wanna know," Adan smiled.

He was probably right. It looked like a morphine drip, but whatever it was made me high as a kite and damn glad to have it. The girl took great care of me: ice packs on my head, blood pressure checked frequently, hand-fed ice chips . . . all while being bounced around in the back of an SUV speeding to God knows where. At some point I fell asleep. . . .

Night was falling when I woke up. We were driving down a dirt road festooned with potholes before pulling up to a blazing campfire. I got out to pee, and my nurse followed with the IV bag.

"This is my airstrip," Adan said proudly, pointing at a stretch of dirt that disappeared into the darkness. "Welcome to Copper Canyon." A lunar landscape receded into the pitch black.

"Beautiful."

Copper Canyon—actually, a group of canyons in Mexico's Sierra Tarahumara that are larger and deeper than the Grand Canyon—lies approximately six hours from the US border. I had heard about it but never seen it. It's well-known in the trafficking world because, during harvest season, pilots flying loads from southern Central America through Mexico usually land around or in it. Narcos often joke that they need to hire an air traffic controller for the season.

"I've been keeping tabs on you," Adan said. "You talk to strippers, you ask questions. You want to do your own business." He pinned me in an icy stare. "You think you're smarter than Jake."

A statement, not a question.

"Uhhh . . ."

He smiled. "I agree with you. But be smart. And be swift, my friend. I might have work for you, but I need you to see my operation so you can send a message to my connections on the US side. We will discuss why later."

I began to understand. He was trying to expand, too, but first he had to prove that he had the chops to operate at the next level. He clearly trusted me more than Jake. Sick as it sounds, I was honored.

We set up camp and ate fajitas with freshly killed goat—the best I've ever had. Seriously, Anthony Bourdain would have licked a dick for a bite. After eating we sat around the fire, and Adan and his men sang *narco corridos*, drug story songs. I never went to sleep-away camp, but if I had I imagine it would have been something like this . . . without the drug dealers, of course. My nurse spent the night in the tent with me, never leaving my side. She ran her fingers through my hair, calming me, and eventually, I passed out. I never did find out what was in that IV bag, but I felt like a million bucks the next morning when I awoke—to the sound of airplanes and chaos.

Two old shit-bucket Cessnas—one held together by wire and duct tape—were coming in for a landing. The first made a textbook touchdown, but the other broke its nose gear on impact and veered into a ditch.

By daylight the runway was nothing more than a long dirt strip carved into the side of a mountain on the edge of the canyon. The majesty of the vista was inspiring—apart from the plane that had just crashed of course.

Men hurried to both planes and began unloading them, each filled beyond capacity with bales of pot. Adan refused to let anyone help the injured pilot in the crashed plane until his men had removed the load.

When they pulled the pilot from the wreckage, my nurse became his nurse. What shocked me more than dope outranking human life was seeing Mexican soldiers loading the pot into military trucks. The Mexican army was in on it! Adan ordered them to take it back to Juarez, then told the pilot that he should be shot for crashing his plane.

After the commotion Adan walked back and threw his arm around me. "Let's eat breakfast, my friend."

This guy was *not* my friend. He'd cut my throat in a blink if it improved his business. But I cozied up to him, even though his Dr. Jekyll–Mr. Hyde personality was starting to scare the bejesus out of me.

◦—◦

The drive back to El Paso gave me time to do some soul searching. Less than two months' work had netted over a hundred grand—but where was this headed, and how would it end? Not liking the obvious conclusion, I decided to take some time off. I was committed to a couple more loads and meetings, but after that it was vacation time.

The first day of my self-imposed sabbatical was glorious. Jake and his wife hosted my family and Byron's for a cookout, one of many group gatherings that also included kids' birthday parties, dinner parties, and more. My break couldn't have come at a better time, though. Not only was Missy giving me dirty looks from inside the house, but Jake and I had been getting on each other's nerves, too.

The biggest problem was that he ran his business capriciously, hinging on impulse. He promised me twelve thousand dollars for running a load but then only gave me eighty-four hundred. He did this to everyone. But every time I brought money back, I skimmed a little insurance policy to cover these losses. Guys with less *cojones*, like Richard and Byron, got shafted.

His tactics were idiotic. In the underworld only money can guarantee loyalty. Jake laughed out loud when he screwed over his underlings. He joked about it to me all the time. Because the money was so good—even the money that they actually got—everyone wanted to run loads. So what did Jake do? He doled out runs to favorites based on emotion. Someone could squeal at any moment and throw us all under the bus. It was a powder keg ready to explode. I had to say something.

"Why do you play that shortchanging game with us, Jake?" I said at the cookout. "Don't you realize how hard this work is?"

"Hey, hey, hey . . . *relax.*"

"Last time I was in Memphis," I interrupted, "they unloaded the car at Larry's cousin's house in the hood. When I got out of the car, they yelled, 'Get yo' ass inside, white boy! Don't let no one see ya,' 'cause I obviously stood out like a sore thumb. They even stole my spare tire when they unloaded the car."

"He owes me two hundred thousand, but it's all good," Jake said. "Just buy another spare."

"Not when *you're* shortchanging me!"

Jake laughed.

"Larry tried to pay me right there," I continued, "but I made him bring it to the casino and pay where it was safe. I wasn't gonna get robbed in South Memphis in front of his house. I know how those people think."

"Smart, smart, let's just figure this out later and drink now," Jake pleaded.

Frustrated, I agreed. My beer was getting warm.

Staying home all morning with the family for the first few days felt weird. I was so used to bouncing out the door at the crack of dawn that I didn't know what to do with all the free time. I decided that the best way to keep busy and help my family was to spend money. When in doubt, change it up—drastically. I bought new couches, a new TV, an antique rustic armoire, new kitchen appliances and dinnerware, an expensive painting, a new grill, a new car, and a wedding ring.

"Missy, call your fam-damily, and tell them to pick this shit up, or I'm throwing it away," I told my wife.

"But I've spent years getting some of these things."

"If it ain't new or nice, it's *gone.*"

I was getting rid of money like it was radioactive a thousand dollars at Target, four thousand at the furniture store, nearly twenty grand at the car dealership. It felt great to stomp into each place like I owned the joint, point at something, pull out a wad of cash, and watch the salesmen jump like hungry fleas fighting over a wet hound.

Money can buy you happiness. It can also buy you swagger. If my car broke down, I didn't give a rat's ass. Hell, I could afford to have it *airlifted* to the nearest mechanic. Neither Missy nor Jake appreciated my newfound strut, but it had taken over. The only way out was straight ahead, full bore, with no consideration of slowing down. Either that or die. I hoped the fuck-ton of cash I'd just spent on a new Dodge Intrepid and a wedding ring would assuage Missy's growing hate for my neglect. She needed to be in good spirits when I unveiled the full thrust of my master plan.

Trinity, the stripper, introduced me to someone who introduced me to someone who had a cousin whose babysitter knew a guy who needed product, and he wanted to meet me. Problem was, the meeting was taking place in Sin City. Being mistaken for a narc would get me killed, so I quickly ended my vacation and headed over to the Lamplighter.

"I need you packed and ready to go in an hour," I said to Trinity, tickets already in hand.

"Go where? I have to work."

"Vegas. I already paid your stage rent with your boss. Let's go."

I didn't have to tell her twice.

In Lost Wages a superstretch limo picked us up from the airport and took us for a joyride up and down the Strip before bringing us to the Mandalay Bay, where an enormous suite awaited.

My contact, Trey, proved elusive—he was probably checking me out—so Trinity and I lived it up for a few days, maintaining image. We dined at the Stratosphere's Top of the World restaurant, took a night helicopter tour of the Strip, and did some serious shopping. I wanted to rent a Ferrari (seven hundred dollars an hour), but without a credit card the clerk wouldn't accept a cash deposit, no matter how much I offered—and I offered *a lot*. But the best part of the trip was an aerial tour of the Grand Canyon on a private chartered plane.

Despite the perks of this big-money lifestyle, the stress of it all still weighed on me, and I could feel myself getting sick again. If that wasn't enough, Trinity was falling for me, even though my interest in her was mostly professional. We had plenty in common, I showered her with attention and gifts, and I liked her as a person. It certainly didn't hurt that she was smoking hot, and she even said all the right things.

"Leave your wife. I'll make your friends my friends and your enemies my enemies."

That's some seriously deep shit from any woman—but I loved my wife despite all the difficulties we'd been having lately. Missy and I had known each other for years and dated casually, but we really didn't *know* one another. The shotgun marriage and trying living situation made it almost unbearable. We nearly hated each other: I couldn't understand why she didn't see the value of my efforts, and she couldn't understand why I wouldn't settle for mediocrity.

Trinity prancing around stark naked in our lavish suite didn't help. Other less driven men might have acted differently. Granted, Trinity's good looks and schoolgirl charm were hard to resist, but she was young and immature. If she were older and wiser, maybe I would have jumped ship. Who knows? But I sure as shit wasn't going to leave my wife and children for a glorified teenage femme fatale.

As I walked into the House of Blues at Mandalay Bay, my phone rang. It was Trey. We agreed to meet at a bar on the other side of the casino. A gangsta in his late twenties, he had a swagger that reeked of *My shit don't stink*. Two bald thuggish bodyguards who looked like they enjoyed committing bodily harm for breakfast accompanied him.

"Took you long enough to get back to me," I said.

"Been followin' you," Trey said. "I like yo' style."

"So let's talk business. Delivery timetable is twelve to thirty-six hours. I expect payment in full every load, which you'll pay directly to me."

"Fine. But I still don't trust you. Let me and my boys have a run with your girlie, and it'll be cool. You can have one of ours in turn."

My blood began to boil. "What?"

Trey opened his hand to reveal a pill. "Slip her this, and take her up to yo' room. We only need an hour, and we won't be too hard on her. We'll even clean up when we done."

If I'd had a gun, I'd have emptied the clip.

"No fucking way."

Trey shook his head. "It's a deal breaker."

"And you're a fuckin' nigger!" I roared, fully expecting to be stabbed and/or shot.

That was the exact moment in which I realized that I didn't have the heart to be in the drug biz. I was trying to make illegal money without any victims, but that's not how it works. There's no empathy; no compassion; little, if any, respect; and there are always victims.

That was the beginning of the end. Adan and Jake and the other slimy fuckers would have hawked Trinity out like a coupon dinner to make the deal, but not me. Byron deserved his proper cut. The pilot of the plane needed medical attention first. Trinity trusted me to get her home safe. I had already betrayed myself for a huge pile of cash. I wasn't about to compromise my ideals for a drug-dealing rapist scumbag.

Raging like an inferno, I walked back across the casino to the table where Trinity was waiting. She was almost glowing, her breasts bursting out of her blouse, her long brown hair cascading over her shoulders, her huge beautiful brown eyes fluttering.

Then she saw the look on my face. "Everything okay?"

"It is now."

I *hated* her at that moment. She'd made me realize that I had a heart. Thank God we were heading home in a few hours. Otherwise, I might have done something that I would have regretted—enjoyed, no doubt, but regretted.

In the limo back to the airport, she put her head on my shoulder and whispered, "I love you."

Sigh.

In the terminal, sitting at our gate, my fever spiked with a vengeance right on cue.

"Are you gonna be okay?" she asked.

"Yeah. I just hope the DayQuil kicks in."

"I wanna talk to you about the future," she cooed.

It suddenly occurred to me that, for the first time in my life, I hadn't considered the future. I had been living in the moment—loving it—but it was slowly tearing me apart.

Time to get my shit together.

8

Changes

WHATEVER I'D SAID IN MY SLEEP MADE MISSY BURNING-BED ANGRY. I vaguely remember dreaming about Trinity and walking with angels, looking for her so they could help claim her soul. Beyond creepy. My fever had hit 103.

During our layover in Phoenix the day before, my fever skyrocketed, and the NyQuil wasn't cutting it, so I ingested several over-the-counter remedies. I didn't remember getting in my car or going to Trinity's apartment, just that I woke up thirsty as hell, freezing my ass off.

I left to get a Gatorade and debated going to the hospital, but I must have gone home instead because the next thing I knew Missy was punching me in the chest, yelling, "What the *fuck* did you just say?"

I've never been blackout drunk, but I'm guessing that's what it feels like. It had been more than twenty-four hours since I'd returned, and I was still sick as a dog. Time to hit the emergency room. Again.

I barely made it to the check-in desk before collapsing. Riding in a wheelchair to my room, feeling sorry for myself, I had no clue that Trinity was also in a hospital across town, feeling even worse.

The day after we got back from Vegas, she was supposed to go to South Padre Island with her ex-boyfriend, his sister, and one of her sister's friends for spring break. The ex fell asleep at the wheel, rolling the car, and throwing everyone out, killing his sister and her friend.

"Mr. Heifner, do you want to die?" the ER doctor asked.

Huh?

"You don't eat, you drink too much, you rarely sleep, and you wonder why your body hasn't beaten this pneumonia."

"Pneumonia?" I rasped.

"Yes, you have pneumonia. Eat more, drink less, and take these antibiotics, or you will die!"

Translation: I was an idiot with a death wish.

Then I remembered my moment of clarity in Vegas: time to make some changes. Life is short, and everything was dissolving into one big pool of quicksand. I had only been married three months, and I had seen more shit in the last few weeks than in my entire lifetime. I was done.

Done.

Home from the hospital, I cornered Missy, who still wasn't speaking to me.

"Missy, I'm sorry. I've been horrible. I tried to do some things for us, and I made some bad decisions. I don't want to get into it right now, but please, work with me. Work with me to make this—make *us*—work. We can do it."

"I feel like I don't even know who you are."

"*I* don't even know who I am. I need to find the old Chris again."

"How? You're so far up Jake's ass—"

"Sweetie, you don't know the half of it. Let me just get the Telluride trip over with, and when I get back it'll be nothing but us. Okay?"

She sighed. "Okay."

She didn't trust me, and I didn't blame her. She was home alone every day with a newborn and a five-year-old while I was gallivanting with creeps from the drug world. But this was the quick exit I had envisioned, and I was determined to clean up my mess. It began with Trinity.

There was no friggin' way I'd let her or her friends mule for me. If I didn't have drivers, there was no sense in pursuing a route. My trafficking organization came to an unceremonious end before it even began. As much as I hated to do it, I ended my friendship with Trinity, as well. The lines were blurring, and the temptation was growing.

A few days later a call alerted me to her presence in the hospital.

"How are ya, kid?" I said, giving her a cheap bouquet of flowers from the hospital gift shop.

"I've been better. No broken bones or internal injuries, so I guess I got lucky."

"I guess you did."

An awkward silence.

"Well, I can't hang around," I said. "Hospitals give me panic attacks." I was lying, but it was my only out. "I just wanted to check on you."

"You'll be back giving lap dances in no time," said Jake, whom I'd brought along as a buffer.

"I know your rent is due, so I'll pay it for you," I said. "Just get well, okay?"

"Next time I see you, I'll tip you good," Jake added.

She gave a confused look as we left the room, but this was good-bye, a clean break. Besides, I couldn't take another Jake-ism. I needed to mend the fence with him—I wanted a graceful exit, but I also didn't want to burn a bridge. Taking him out to lunch, I fed his ego all it could swallow and laid the groundwork for my departure from his crew.

"After Telluride I'm gonna take some time to focus on Missy and the kids, so don't give me any loads, okay? Not for a while. Plus, you gotta appease John and Byron."

"Yeah, I do," he said. "You're so right. I'm on it."

Telluride lay just over the horizon, a few days away. To ground myself I called old friends and roommates, fraternity buddies, random classmates, and even an ex-girlfriend or two to see what they'd been doing. Most were living large; all had jobs they seemed to enjoy and were climbing life's ladder. They talked about buying condos and houses, how happy they were in their relationships, what they believed the future held. When they asked how I was doing, my heart sank.

"So where you getting all your money from?" asked Chris, my old supervisor from the bank. "On second thought I don't wanna know."

"I'll never forget the last bit of advice you gave me," I said.

"Tell me. I forgot."

"It doesn't matter what happens . . . deny, deny, deny."

"I've got new advice for you," he said. "Remember the movie *Wall Street?*"

"Of course. Greed is good."

"Yeah, well, remember what the old stock trader said: 'A man looks in the abyss. There's nothing staring back at him. At that moment, the man finds his character, and that is what keeps him out of the abyss.'"

Why did everything magically seem to work out for everyone else? Sure, I made a small fortune during my sixty-day experiment, but that wasn't something of which to be proud. In the real world my résumé was still online and in the hands of placement agencies far and wide. No one had even contacted me lately.

A mileage sign on the way to an all-expenses-paid trip to the premier Colorado ski resort made me realize the insanity of my choices. I had traded security for hedonism, and the thought of five straight days of sugary mountain powder combined with five straight nights of drunken debauchery seemed like the perfect farewell to the criminal life I was happily leaving behind.

Jake, John, Tracy, Byron, Eric, and I caravanned in two cars from El Paso. Everyone took turns driving and switching cars. Jake's brother Ryan and a couple of his friends from Kansas were also meeting us there.

John, the infamous drunk, kicked off the trip by pouring half a bottle of Seagram's 7 into a Styrofoam cup filled with ice and finishing every drop. The drive into Colorado, winding and twisting through the mountains, was truly stunning, but John's drunken commentary ruined most of it. Every time we stopped he fell out of the car, flopped face first into the snow, pissed himself, stumbled into other cars, or some combination of the four. No wonder Jake had trouble trusting him to run loads.

Tracy, an Asian-African mix, liked to play the badass but had decidedly more bark than bite. Jake's biggest problem with Tracy was ego—he drew too much attention to himself—a definite no-no when it came to drug trafficking.

Once in Telluride, we stopped at Smuggler's Blues. I played the Glen Frey song on the jukebox while we drank and chuckled at the coincidence.

Jake rented us rooms at a posh resort; the suite had an outdoor Jacuzzi, my favorite amenity, adjacent to a picturesque running creek. Skiing conditions were perfect, though forgetting to use sunblock my first day on the slopes gave me a nasty case of raccoon eyes that lasted for the rest of the trip.

John, our token drunk, caused chaos wherever he went: grabbing the wrong skis, returning the wrong boots, wetting his bed once or twice and possibly the couch. He was a total mess but never stopped drinking. Eric, my roommate, played comic relief for the group, his antics like a four-year-old's. Off in his own world, doing his own thing, Eric didn't have a bad bone in his body. I could never figure out how he became an officer in the army. Tracy actually turned out to be a cool guy, though at times he could be stubborn and demanding. He also nearly flipped our rental car by doing a high-speed U-turn on a snowbank.

With many great memories forever etched in my mind, I was thankful that Jake not only had the foresight to plan it but the generosity to bankroll it. Relaxed and recharged, I was ready to get back to El Paso and start my life anew.

Eric, John, and Tracy had made different plans to get home, which left Jake, Byron, and me for the return road trip. I was looking forward to a relaxing drive surrounded by magnificent scenery, but Jake had other plans. With us careening at ninety mph down a twisty mountain road, that relaxation quickly morphed into sheer terror.

"Hey, man, slow down."

"Naw, man, let's get home," Jake said, pushing the gas even harder.

"Dude, c'mon. I wanna enjoy the ride."

"Nothing will happen."

We were doing a hundred on a road where half that speed would have been dangerous.

"Seriously, Jake, I have kids to think about. So does Byron. Slow the fuck *down*."

Byron was sound asleep in the back.

"Relax, I got this," Jake said.

"Byron, wake the fuck up, and say something!" I shouted.

"Huh?" His eyes blinked open. "Uh, yeah. Right. Slow down." He fell back asleep a moment later.

When Jake didn't, I'd had enough.

"Jake, you fucking idiot! *Slow. The fuck. Down!*"

He slammed on the brakes, and the car slid off the road onto the shoulder. We both flew out of the car in a flash, grabbing each other's shirts and rolling around on the snow-covered ground.

Byron—now fully awake—jumped out of the car and tried to play peacemaker. "Guys, *chill the fuck out!*" he yelled.

Amazingly, we listened. Jake and I stopped fighting, stepped back, and without saying a word got back into the car. Moments later we resumed our way home again; this time Jake obeyed the speed limit. *Even more reason to jump ship,* I thought. At that moment I was done with Jake and just wanted to get home safely.

When the Telluride trip ended, the plan was to spend the next two months being Mr. Perfect Family Man. My body had different ideas, however. Sick yet again, I determined to relax, heal, and avoid stressful situations like the plague that I was fighting. Turns out that wasn't enough.

"Missy, take me to the hospital," I said one afternoon.

"Why? What's wrong?"

"My chest feels funny. I think I'm having a heart attack."

Kids in tow, we rushed to the ER. During the ride, my chest pain increased; I was extremely dizzy and having heart palpitations. My eyes went wonky, too: I was seeing flashing lights everywhere. Even though I was sick and felt like I was having a heart attack, I had a difficult time explaining that to the admitting nurse.

Everyone with a medical degree gave me a skeptical look—until they hooked me up to an EKG. Next thing I knew they were giving me nitroglycerin. Ironically, Jake and the drug biz hadn't killed me, but a bum ticker almost did.

After a litany of tests, the doctor diagnosed the problem as pericarditis, an inflammation of the heart membrane. On my last ER visit, someone apparently had given me the wrong antibiotics, and the streptococcus infection moved from my throat into my chest cavity. As a precaution the doctor ordered an angiogram to check out my heart. That went wrong, too. During the procedure they discovered—the hard way—that I am allergic to iodine. The nurse freaked out and knocked over a tray laden with supplies as she rushed to get the necessary meds to stop the reaction.

Later, in recovery, the doctor looked at my records in astonishment as I stared at the semicomatose old people in the room.

"How the hell have you been functioning for the last few months?" he asked.

"Honestly, I don't know."

"You must be one tough mother," he said, grinning. "I'm going to have a couple other doctors come look at you. It's not every day we get a twenty-seven-year-old pericarditis patient requiring an angiogram."

Story of my life: special—but for all the wrong reasons.

When I recovered and was discharged from the hospital, Jake felt sorry for me, also wanting to atone for his jackassery in Colorado, so he paid me well to take a quick ride with him to Memphis to pick up money from Larry. A quick and easy score.

He was supposed to collect a hundred thousand, but Larry only offered sixty. At first Jake ignored my pleas to take the cash. Larry had some badass jailhouse punks with him, but Jake was posturing like a bigger badass. The smart move was to take the sure thing now and make up the difference later. Jake should have relented, but of course that didn't happen, and Larry blew off Jake the rest of the trip. Jake spiraled into a crater of self-pity and hate, all directed at me for giving him an I-told-you-so lecture.

He dropped me off at the Little Rock Airport and told me to find my own way home. So much for fixing my problems, but at least I was free of the anchor to which I had tied myself.

Ecstatic to be home, I changed my first diaper, proudly not passing out. Watching the kids while Missy went to the store, I was equally proud that

I didn't die from fear. If there was such a thing as a phobia of watching children, I had it—but I vowed to face it head-on.

Neither of the kids was in school, so we all took a vacation to Vegas. The trip started as an Easter weekend jaunt and ended up with us bouncing from casino to casino chasing cheap room rates for an entire month. We had an amazing time.

Months flew by, and in July I thought about visiting my mom in Florida so she could meet her new grandson. The situation between Missy and me wasn't great, but it hadn't deteriorated, either. We were a work in progress. How was it possible for us to date for two years and not learn anything about one another? After living together a few months, however, our different values had become glaringly obvious. I was a stressed-out neat freak, and she was a carefree ball of organized chaos. I had to be on time for everything; she was constantly late. I was a talker; she was the silent type. I was ultraaggressive, she was passive-aggressive. Our commonalities were minimal, our differences many. But she was my wife and the mother of my children, and though there were times when we wanted to kill each other, we still loved each other. That had to count for something.

I still hadn't secured gainful employment, but you wouldn't know it from the way we lived. We took numerous trips, but a cloud of worry was starting to creep into the back of my mind. The money we had left, about forty thousand, would last only another eight to ten months—*only* if we stopped splurging. It was time to focus on getting a job that not only paid the bills but that I genuinely liked. I was terrified that I might fail.

The months of travel had made my soul happy and gave me the opportunity to reconnect with my wife and kids, as well as avoid Jake and his temptations, but it had also jaded me. Finding something legit with a paycheck that could compete with trafficking was going to be borderline impossible.

I considered playing poker professionally. It had paid for our trip to Vegas, but making a career out of it, knowing my weaknesses and craving for action, would prove a stepping-stone to disaster.

That's when the idea of day trading hit me. Also a form of gambling, yes, but playing the market instead of the felt had more cachet. It would take more cash to get started and do it right, but the potential reward outweighed the risk. Since Jake was still rolling, maybe I could convince him to play the market with me. I had made him money in the past, trading his accounts, so perhaps that was enough to get him to trust me with fifty or a hundred thousand. I decided to pay him a visit.

"Holy shit, am I seeing a ghost?"

"Whatever," I said, playing it cool.

"Seriously, I don't know whether to hug you or kiss you."

"How 'bout neither. I've got an idea."

There was that look in his eyes, undoubtedly stemming from the look he saw in mine. I gave him my best sales pitch, laid out my trading strategy, and explained how I would implement and back test it. It was comprehensive and solid, but Jake wasn't buying.

He shook his head. "Nope."

"Why the fuck not?"

"'Cause I can invest $40,000 in a load and make $140,000 guaran-fucking-teed. There's no guarantee to this."

"But a load can get popped."

He folded his arms and shook his head again. "Nope."

It was like talking to a child. He never saw the big picture. Hell, often he didn't even see the *small* picture. I wanted to choke him senseless for being so shortsighted and pound foolish. But there was no sense in trying to explain anything to him. When you argue with an idiot, the idiot drags you down to his level and beats you with experience.

"But I've got an offer for you," he said.

"I'm afraid to ask."

"I've got a load going to Kansas. I'll pay you a hundred dollars per pound. It's two hundred pounds, so that's twenty Gs for the load."

He had always paid by the pound and always understated how much the load weighed. But I never called him on it, nor did I ever say anything about his stiffing his mules when bringing money home. Some trafficking consortiums paid upwards of 10 percent of a money run's total because, believe it or not, it was actually more dangerous.

"Nope," I said, mimicking him.

"C'mon, that's a lot of cash for a quick two-day round-trip run." He clapped a hand on my shoulder and gave me a forlorn look. "John and all these other fuckers are pissing me off. I need you, Nutty."

"Let me sleep on it."

That much money was a hefty sum; plus, I could probably grab another ten grand from the pile when I brought the cash back, more than enough to visit my mom in Florida and start my own little Wall Street empire. Then Jake could go fuck himself five ways from Friday.

If you're gonna be a bear, be a grizzly, I thought.

I was in.

———

The rental car trunk was stuffed full of weed. It was my last load. This final run, a financial home run, would set me up nicely. Perversely, I even considered beating myself ugly with the car's tire iron, telling Jake I got robbed, and stealing the money—around $150,000—but ultimately decided against it.

Nothing about the trip felt routine, even though I had made the Wichita run several times without a problem. Something felt wrong. Actually, *everything* felt wrong. The car felt wrong. The air I breathed smelled wrong. I felt wrong. A superstitious bastard, I would normally have heeded these feelings and changed my route, switched cars, or even pulled over and rented a room somewhere until the feeling passed, but I wanted to get it over with, so I pressed on.

Cops kept popping up in the damnedest places—places I had never guessed they would be. My gut told me to stop and sleep at a passing motel, but I overrode the instinct and told myself that if I hurried up this six-month walk on the dark side would all be just a strange but happy memory.

Just west of Amarillo on I-40, state troopers and sheriffs' cars were driving through the median, pulling over anything with wheels. It took a second for me to realize that I had hit one of those rolling roadblocks where they pulled over anything they wanted for whatever reason they cared to give. The fear suddenly was overwhelming, like seeing a great white shark blasting up at you from the depths.

Breathe, breathe.

I was in a new Buick Century rental and driving the speed limit. A dry-cleaned suit hung on the rear hook. I was clean-shaven and groomed, wearing khaki shorts, sandals, and a polo. A briefcase on the passenger seat made me look every part the businessman on a road trip. Nothing to worry about, right?

I checked my mirrors and the car's vitals and made sure my balls hadn't receded too far into my body cavity as I passed the police cars sitting in the median à la *Smokey and the Bandit.*

Breathe, breathe.

Amazingly, nothing happened. I passed through the checkpoint un-scathed. The angels were on my side, a gift for quitting the biz. Even though I had already promised myself that this was my last load, I vowed the same again—just in case God didn't hear me the first time.

Unfortunately, that's when I spotted them. Two specks in my rearview mirror were getting closer and rapidly.

A sheriff and a trooper had peeled out of the median with the urgency of organ transplant couriers. Gumballs flashing, sirens blaring, they were approaching hard and fast. I figured something had happened ahead of me and they were going to fly by. I hoped there would be an exit before I reached the mess that had spurred them into action.

I braced for a high-speed fly-by, but the trooper tucked in behind me, his Ford Explorer nearly ramming my bumper, while the sheriff's car pulled up alongside and slammed on his brakes, scrubbing speed to remain dead even. Both cops motioned for me to pull over.

Fuck.

9

H to the Izzo

THE STATE TROOPER WALKING UP TO MY CAR WAS PART OF A K9 UNIT, with TASK FORCE emblazoned on the hood of his SUV. *Fuck, fuck, fuck.* The sheriff, a rotund country bumpkin, remained in his car on this exceptionally hot July day.

"License and registration," the trooper said.

"Sure, no prob," I said, fishing out the documents. "Just outta curiosity, what are you pulling me over for? I wasn't speeding 'cause I had the cruise control on."

"Where ya headed?" he asked, ignoring my question.

"Wichita, for a sales meeting. A waste of time for something that could've been handled by phone."

"Uh-huh, hold on."

He strode back to his car as I patted myself on the back for staying calm. I could talk my way out of this. But the minutes he was gone felt like hours, and my confidence wavered.

"Mr. Heifner," he said when he finally returned, "you were doing seventy-three in a sixty-five, but I'm going to let you off with a warning."

What? *No fucking way!* I wanted to scream at the lying pig; my cruise control was set at 64. "Thanks. I appreciate it."

"Are you on probation, Mr. Heifner? My computer says you were arrested in Virginia for marijuana possession."

"Excuse me?"

"Yes, in 1999."

"Sir, I've never been arrested in my entire life. I've never been to Virginia, and I don't do drugs. I'll gladly submit to a drug test right now. You must have the wrong person."

He shrugged. "That's what the computer says."

"How can I say that I don't believe you without being disrespectful?"

"Step out of the car."

We walked around to the back of the car. I leaned against the trunk and tried to look relaxed but annoyed—not hard considering that was exactly how I felt.

"Exactly when were you arrested?"

"Officer, I told you, I have *never* been arrested."

"Tell you what, just let me look in your trunk, and you can be on your way."

Alarm bells sounded inside my head so loudly that I was afraid the cop could hear them. *Stay cool, Chris.*

"Look, normally I'm as cooperative as a kid in a candy store, but I really don't appreciate this. I wasn't speeding, and you pulled me over anyway. Then you called me a criminal, and now you want to search my car. If I remember college correctly, I have the Fourth Amendment right to protect myself from unlawful search and seizure."

My little speech went over like a lead balloon.

"Stand back," he said. He stormed over to his SUV and pulled out his dog—a freakin' German Shepherd puppy, six months old, tops. Puppy or not, I still prayed that Jake and his brainiac crew had packed the stuff correctly.

Walking around the car several times, the dog didn't do a damn thing—a sniff here, a sniff there, nothing else. My guts in knots that Houdini couldn't escape, I chatted with the fat sheriff who finally decided to exit his vehicle. Then the trooper yanked the dog's leash with enough force to cause the puppy to yelp.

"That's a hit! We're lookin' in your trunk."

Frozen in disbelief, all I could think was: *What the fuck?*

The sheriff grabbed my wrist as the trooper popped the trunk.

"Well, well, well, lookit what we got here."

The world slowed to a pregnant snail's pace as the multi-hundred-pound load revealed itself. Before I knew what hit me, the sheriff slammed my face down on the hot, black hood of the trooper's unit. The flesh on my cheek sizzled as he twisted my right arm behind my back, then my left, and cuffed me.

My prayers to be spared turned to prayers for a tornado to descend from the cloudless sky and destroy everything in its path, including me. When no tornado came, I prayed for angels to whisk me into the heavens. I'd rather take my chances with St. Peter than these fucking cops.

They took me to the nearest patrol station and paraded me around like a trophy buck mount fresh from the taxidermist. They were so proud of themselves, but what had they really accomplished? Potheads are anything but menacing. Sure, some of them are less than model citizens, but they're all ultimately harmless. It was a huge waste of resources to stop me. They should have been looking for *real* criminals—criminals who robbed, raped, and murdered. Of course, I was lashing out. I wasn't ready to accept the full responsibility of my actions.

After the impromptu show and tell—dragged from office to office, posterized as the day's catch—the most bass-ackward hillbilly cop, who just happened to be the station commander, cornered me.

"Do you wanna talk, boy?" he asked.

"For the safety of me and my family, I want an attorney," I replied respectfully.

"Let's go for a walk."

The tall redneck unlocked my cuffs and led me outside. My load of pot was neatly stacked. It looked impressive.

"Go stand beside it." He gave me a not-so-gentle push on the shoulder.

When he tried to snap a photo, I started to walk back into the station.

"Get your ass back over there by the pot."

I did as I was told once again, but I put my head down and my hands behind my back, pretending they were cuffed.

"Stop that!"

After a few minutes they finally gave up trying to take a posterity picture and walked me back inside. They placed me in a holding cell alone where I gathered my thoughts and figured out my next move. That's when I noticed a sentence scribbled in pencil on the back of the cell door: *You are here because you are stupid.*

Ain't that the truth.

The arresting trooper took me to Potter County Jail in Amarillo for booking. En route I berated him on the social injustice and inefficacy of the drug war. It wasn't the smartest move, but I needed to lash out. My screed made him feel like shit, to the point he was almost apologetic, but you can't unring a bell. And my bell was definitely rung.

Potter County Jail, a converted aircraft hangar at the airport, is a complete shithole. It has your usual booking and processing areas, but the cells were separated into twelve bunk-bed areas with six metal four-stool tables bolted to the floor, along with a few crappy toilets and showers. Instead of bars it had a thick wall of glass so the jailers could view their miscreant pets. Imagine a dingy human aquarium chock full of dregs.

The beds were hard, the food was gross, and there was absolutely nothing to do for the entire day—no books or even TV. My options consisted of cards, dominoes, and uninspiring conversation with twenty-three of the biggest idiots I had ever met. Some of those morons had been in this can for years. How in the hell does this constitute rehabilitation? How are these people supposed to reacclimatize to society upon release? This was easily one of the most fucked-up places I had ever seen—and I was now a part of it. Jesus, what did that say about me?

My first call was to Jake, who was understandably angry, but pinched loads and drivers are a part of the game. We already had an agreement in place: If I got popped, he'd bail me out and pay for the attorney. There was only one attorney to handle my case: Gary Joel Hill.

Hill was a legal god. However, he couldn't do anything until bail was set, so I had to twiddle my thumbs for a few days until arraignment.

The next call was to Missy, a call I dreaded more than anything. When she answered, I blitzed-spoke, getting everything out before she got a word in.

"Missy, I'm in jail, but you'll be fine. You got that extra thousand dollars from Jake today that he was supposed to give you for me passing the checkpoint, right?"

Silence.

"Missy?"

"I didn't feel like driving across town."

"Why don't you ever listen to me?"

Click.

And just in time for me to go back to my cell. Great.

As the jailer tossed me into my cell, he said aloud, "Possession, pot. Two hundred fifty pounds." Talk about an introduction.

The days crawled by like a crippled tortoise through molasses. The jail wasn't dangerous, just boring. Nothing but endless banter with mindless degenerates who believed they were victims of society. I almost wanted to get shivved to escape the monotony.

Dumb as they were, the other guys were surprisingly friendly. They even had a prayer circle every night.

"Come find God with us," said the inmate leading the prayer.

"I'm sure when you get out you're gonna want me to find drugs with you, too, right?" said the other guy who also skipped them. "Shut the fuck up, hypocrite."

I laughed, but inside I wasn't laughing. Jake didn't want to bail me out, and he also wanted my Intrepid as repayment for the confiscated load—which wasn't part of the deal. After three days, I still hadn't been arraigned. Missy, God love her, took matters into her own hands, though. I don't know what she said to Jake, but next thing I knew Gary Hill was on his way to Amarillo to save my sorry ass.

I was arrested on Monday. On Thursday morning, they took me and others to a video-conference room for arraignment. Via grainy video feed and staticky audio, yet another fat redneck spoke to us. I hoped my boyish looks and otherwise clean record would help.

First up was a white trash couple. The judge read them the riot act for having a highly toxic and highly flammable meth lab in the same house as their kids. He set their bail at forty thousand, and I smiled; mine surely would be lower. I had thirty-five hundred dollars' worth of credit, so anything less than thirty-five thousand and I'd slap the 10 percent bond on my credit card and vamoose, a free man.

"Mr. Heifner, how do you plead?" the fat judge asked.

"Not guilty."

"Bail is set at one hundred thousand dollars."

His words hit me like a wrecking ball.

"Your honor, with all due respect, I didn't endanger children or manufacture a poison like meth. I—"

"Shut up, or I'll *double* it!"

Suck-monkey. I hoped he choked on a Twinkie.

On the way back to the human aquarium, the ugly female component of the white trash couple—who had flipped me off when I made my appeal—asked, "Hey, what did you do to deserve such a high bail?"

"I chopped off the heads of a white trash couple who had a meth lab."

The sheriff's deputy escorting me whacked me in the back of the leg with his baton.

Later that day my savior arrived. In a dual-telephone, Plexiglas-separated visitor booth, Gary Hill was waiting on the other side. I had never been so happy to see a lawyer in all my life. He asked a few questions, then told me to call the office.

When you're incarcerated, every phone call is an exercise in futility. You have to call collect, and a prerecorded message says, "This is a collect call from [name], an inmate at Potter County Jail. Do you accept the charges?" Imagine listening to this every time you had to call your employer, wife, or lawyer. Missy cried about how much she missed me on each of our several daily calls. Gary Hill's secretary, Donna, on the other hand, comforted me like almost no one else in the world could—that is, when the jail didn't turn off the phones for the rest of the day every time they did a prisoner transport, which sometimes occurred at 10 a.m. Were they expecting prisoners to coordinate their escapes via monitored phone calls?

Gary hired a local attorney, a former prosecutor, for five thousand dollars to do a bail reduction, and he had it cut down to twenty-five grand. It had been a week already when I got the good news—and not a moment too soon. I could handle hot, unconditioned air; boredom; disgusting food; even talking to a bunch of misguided miscreants. What I couldn't handle was the unknown: What was going to happen next?

They took me to the front of the jail for out-processing and gave me back my luggage. In a dressing room they let me shave, brush my teeth, and shower. After that, anxious to get any trace of the stink of incarceration off me, I dressed in the nicest clothes I had packed. Putting on my Rolex, I walked up to the jailer to be released—the same asshole who had hit me with the baton. He gave me an odd look.

"How did you afford a hundred thousand dollars?" he asked.

"I don't have time to explain it to losers."

He turned so red I thought his mustache was going to burst into flames.

"We'll see you again," he said snidely as he stewed and unlocked the door for me.

"Tell your wife I said hello," I said, chuckling as he reddened even more.

I had the taxi stop at the first gas station we encountered after leaving that shithole. The Diet Dr Pepper and brownie I bought tasted like a gourmet meal and made me feel somewhat human again.

As the prop plane ascended, the jail came into view, and I wished the plane had bombs beneath its wings for a proper farewell. Calling the stewardess over, I asked if they had beer on the flight.

"Yes, however, this is only an hour flight, and it's lunchtime. Technically, I'm not—"

"Miss, I've had a horrible week, worse than horrible. Could you please bring me two beers, any kind, even stale warm ones, before you serve anyone else? Please."

"Sir, really, I—"

I pulled out a twenty and pressed it into her hand. "*Please,* and keep the change."

She saw the desperation in my eyes, and a few moments later there were two ice-cold cans of Bud on my tray. Neither lasted more than a minute.

In Dallas, still shell-shocked, I had a few more beers to dull the pain. How did all the commuters flitting around, seemingly happy, do it? How did they get so lucky, how had things worked out for them? It was self-loathing at its finest, but at that moment I felt entitled to complain.

"Ten dollars for a freaking beer!" said the businessman on the stool beside me when he'd heard how much I gave the flight attendant.

"I would have paid a hundred," I said.

"That bad, huh?"

"Don't ask," I said as I signaled the bartender for another. "What do you do?"

"Computer sales."

"Good gig?"

"Yeah, I got lucky. Met a girl at a bar one night; she liked my style and hired me 'cause she had an opening at her company. We got married a year later. It's been perfect. I'm so lucky."

I wanted to punch his fucking lights out.

"So what do you do?" Mr. Luckier than Shit asked.

"Time," I said. "I just got out of jail for drug trafficking, racketeering, and about a dozen other violations of the RICO statutes."

Without saying another word the guy grabbed his jacket and laptop case and took off. Go figure.

———

At the El Paso airport Missy was waiting in our car with the kids in the back. I got in without saying a word and kissed my children. The way they felt, the way they smelled I nearly burst into tears, but somehow I held it together. Missy and I shared a look but said nothing. As we drove off I knew nothing would ever be the same.

First stop was Gary's office to assess the damage.

"I need $32,295," he said.

"Jesus, I don't have that kind of money. Jake said he would pay for it."

"Fine. Give me seventy-five hundred tomorrow, and I'll take care of the rest."

He scared me to death, but Gary Hill was a legend. I would have sold my soul to him on the spot to get out of that jam. I trusted every word he said. If I've learned anything in life, it's this: When your back's against the wall and you need someone in your corner, you get the best you can find and let him do his job.

I was beyond scared straight. The thought of spending years in that dingy human terrarium with nothing to do but accessorize a demeaning orange jumpsuit was terrifying. The pathetic structure, the inability to choose my meals, the lack of positive stimuli, the thought of my family suffering—it was all unbearable.

In the grand scheme seven days in jail is not the end of the world. But lock yourself in a fetid bathroom for a week, and see how you react. Going to jail isn't supposed to be a leisure trip, but the process was so humiliating that it's no wonder most criminals never recover emotionally or become productive members of society after doing their time. I was facing two to twenty; my only hope was for leniency.

Missy and I hid our dirty little secret from everyone. There was a family reunion to attend, then a trip to see my mom in Florida. Both helped me focus on us, the now, not what might be coming. The possibility of being dragged away from my family for two decades made me try even harder. She was still hesitant—and I couldn't blame her—but I vowed to regain her trust if it was the last thing I ever did.

She had it worse, though; she had to make excuses to both our families about my weeklong absence, then hide the stress of the sentence hanging over our heads. She had started talking to her family again after our son was born, but they still judged her, so there was no chance that we would tell them. I wasn't going to tell my family, either. Some secrets are worth keeping.

And some aren't.

"I'm late, Chris."

"Late for what?"

"My period."

Did she just say what I think she said?

"I thought it was the stress of you being in jail, but I think I'm pregnant."

Just when I thought things couldn't get any more stressful. . . . On TV couples happily glow at the test results when they find out they're pregnant. We just sat on the couch and silently stared straight ahead.

I had to confide in someone. So of all people I told my biological father, filling him in while we stopped in Houston en route to Florida to visit my mother. He was my flesh and blood. I hoped he'd have kind words or sage wisdom. I desperately needed a pick-me-up. No such luck.

"You're a fucking idiot, Chris. Do you realize what could happen?"

"I know."

"I can't believe you're so dumb. Didn't you think about your family?"

"I know."

My biological father is an attorney who I'd never retain. He thrives on fear, but there's no fight in him. I wanted the old "I'm by your side" speech, the kind I'd have given my son. Instead, he called my half brother and grandfather and spilled the beans. After that I never heard from them again. So much for that long-lost family I had always dreamed of. Now it was just Missy, my kids, me . . . and Hell Paso.

Despite the fear of the unknown, life returned to normal. The trip to see my mom took us three weeks, detouring through Alabama on the way home, and when we returned to El Paso, it was as if nothing had ever happened. I even started looking for a job again.

When Jake asked me to meet him at Pitchers, a quiet bar at the Marriott, I knew it was a bad idea, but part of me missed the guy and the craziness surrounding him. It surprised me to see John and Eric with him. Even more surprising was their demeanor: nervous to the point of untrusting.

"How ya been, Nutty?" Jake said.

"Yeah, how ya been?" John echoed.

"Been good?" asked Eric.

I leaned back in my chair and smiled wide. "I've been great."

"We wanted to have a talk and check up on you," said Jake, more sinister than sincere.

I laughed. "Look, guys, I know what you're thinking. Before you say anything else, I'm great—really. Life is great. Missy is pregnant, and I just want to focus on my family and get away from this business. I made a mistake, but I'll keep my mouth shut, and if Gary can't get me off, I'll do my time."

The cocksuckers shared a look before breathing a collective sigh. They didn't even congratulate me about Missy or offer to help with the legal finances. They only cared about whether I'd rat them out.

"If you hadn't been speeding, it wouldn't have happened," Jake said. "You'd still be rolling."

Fuck you, I thought. I'd told Jake the entire story, cruise control and all, but he didn't believe that the cops would pull me over for no reason.

"Just admit it, Chris, or else I won't help you with Gary's bill. You were speeding, right?"

I folded my arms across my chest and looked him dead in the eyes. "I already told you."

"Do you want my fucking help or not?"

"How long you gonna beat a dead horse?"

"Just tell me you were speeding."

A long pause. John and Eric looked back and forth between us as if they were watching a tennis match.

"I'm not gonna help you if I don't know the truth," he said.

More silence.

"Well?"

A million thoughts raced through my head, including smashing him in the face with my beer bottle, but not only would that not accomplish anything, worse, I'd be wasting good beer.

"Fine, I was speeding."

"I knew it," the self-righteous prick smiled.

And then they left.

Words cannot convey how supremely pissed off I was. They had no clue what loyalty meant. But I did. I was loyal to a fault. But fuck them. They were out of my life.

Being out on bail is like hanging by a string. Walk the straight and narrow and you're fine. Screw up just a little, even something stupid like a disagreement over a parking spot, and your bail could be revoked in a heartbeat. I played the role of family man to a T. I went to church, praying diligently while I was there, and looked for a job like my life depended on it—which of course it did. Unbelievable as it sounds, things really were great. We worried about the future, of course, but life turned around. After six exhaustive interviews—two with the district manager, one with the branch manager, and three with the senior broker—Merrill Lynch welcomed me onto their team as a stockbroker trainee.

I'd never been happier. I wore a suit to work each day, had my own parking spot, health benefits, business cards, and a top-shelf real-world education about the financial markets. My BBA in finance was finally helping me do something more important than balancing my checkbook.

"I love that a secretary answers for you when I call your work," Missy said. "What time will you get back today?"

"The plane lands at seven. We can eat dinner after."

"Good. I'll be your dessert."

Every two weeks Merrill Lynch flew the broker trainees from the El Paso office to Albuquerque for training. We caught a morning flight, trained, ate lunch, and flew back the same day.

Boarding the flight home, I settled into my seat and motioned for the stewardess. "Listen, sweetie, I know it's only a forty-five-minute flight, but I had a long day and really need a beer. The second we lift off, could you bring me two Bud Lights?" I pressed a twenty into her hand while loosening my tie. "Keep the change."

The guy beside me tried to make small talk.

"What do you do, buddy?"

"Stockbroker," I said.

"Cool. How'd you get that gig?"

"I got lucky."

10

Somewhere I Belong

AFTER PAYING GARY HILL MY PORTION OF THE MONEY, I HADN'T HEARD anything about my case, but I was in good hands. He thought he could get it dismissed, and I believed him.

When I was in college, I had two fascinations: playing poker and playing the stock market. One made me money, while the other was untouchable because of money.

A better than average poker player, I can read people solidly, which meant a consistent couple of hundred dollars each week, ground out at low-limit hold 'em tables at Speaking Rock, the local casino. It wasn't going to get me on *High Stakes Poker*, but it was decent money for a college student.

As much as I enjoyed playing poker, I'd have parted with fingers and toes to play the market. The two have a lot in common, and a solid comprehension of statistics and probabilities will pay big dividends in the long run for both. I never had enough scratch to play the market, but for as long as I can remember I've read everything I could get my hands on and followed all the fluctuations and indexes. Before I was muling for Jake, he let me handle his brokerage account for a few days during the dot.com bubble, and I made him a quick five grand. As a reward the fucker shut me out of his account and used the profits to go to Hawaii. I should have known then what kind of person I was climbing into bed with.

The Merrill Lynch world fit me like a glove. I loved the job, the people, the environment. The position required me to be there at 7:00 a.m., but usually, I arrived early to study the markets and get up to speed on the business news of the day. I had a neat little computer system where I could listen to *The Squawk Box*, a morning conference call on which Merrill Lynch analysts gave their predictions for the day, while watching CNBC. I also had access to all the information available on the broker system.

After the markets opened I studied for the Series 66 and Series 7 exams, which everyone insisted were difficult, yet my practice exams gave me near-perfect scores. The rest of each day I spent learning about the company's financial products and how best to sell them via estate planning, retirement planning, or asset protection. It wasn't work—it was entertainment.

Aside from paid training, trips to Albuquerque, and gourmet coffee in the kitchen, there were weekly catered visits by mutual fund reps, lavish corporate events, free tickets to local attractions, and innumerable other perks. Missy and I enjoyed delicious steak Diane dinners at the company Christmas party, complimentary tickets to UTEP basketball games, even lunch with a state senator. My biggest worry was what color suit to wear or whether my power tie looked powerful enough.

She was due in March, and it was a relief to both of us finally to have first-rate health insurance. The Christmas presents I bought came from properly earned funds. We kissed under the mistletoe and toasted our happiness with spiked eggnog on New Year's Eve.

I should have known it was too good to last.

"Fill this out, then give it to the other trainees," said Troy, my branch manager, handing me a form.

"Yes, sir. What is it?"

"It's a U4, a background check from the SEC."

"No prob," I said, my heart tripling its pace.

After reading the form, though, I realized there was nothing to worry about. It asked about convictions, and technically, I didn't have any. I answered truthfully and greased by. A disclaimer on the form stated that if anything changed I was required to notify both my employer and the SEC immediately. Fair enough. Easy breezy, free and clear.

Jake and I talked sparingly, but I wanted no part of his business or lifestyle. There was no reason to rock the boat.

All those flights to Albuquerque earned me a free ticket. A few days shy of my birthday, I took Missy on a surprise weekend trip to Vegas. It was her first time on a plane. She squeezed my hand so hard during takeoff and landing that I thought she was going to break it.

In Sin City we shopped and ate to our hearts' content and saw an amazing show at the Mirage. When we got back to El Paso, she squeezed my hand again.

"Are things always gonna be this good?" she asked, looking into my eyes.

"I think so, sweetie. Remember those lucky assholes we used to hate? Now those lucky assholes are us."

She kissed me, and it was the best kiss of our lives.

Going to sleep that night, I felt big things were coming for us—and I was right.

That's when the shit hit the fan.

At home there was a letter from Gary Hill's office. I had been charged with a felony, and my court date was set for April 6. Some of the legalese in the letter confused me, though, so I had my biological father call Gary.

"Son, you've screwed the pooch," said Kip afterward. "Hopefully, he'll get you a good deal."

"What does this mean for my job?"

"Don't know. You'll find out tomorrow when you talk to your boss."

I wanted to choke him through the phone. Needing real answers, I called Gary myself.

"Gary, what's the story?"

"Those dumb fuckers don't know what they're doing. I told the DA I'm gonna whoop his ass. But don't worry, I'll get you a killer deal."

"I'm afraid this might sink me."

"Keep your head up, Chris. You're a good kid. You'll figure it out."

Even if he had lied to appease me, that's exactly what I needed to hear. Why couldn't Gary Hill be my dad?

It was a criminal offense not to inform Merrill Lynch or the SEC, though, so, tail between my legs, I told my boss the next day.

"I've been charged with a felony. Drug possession. It's a long story, and I don't want to say anything that might jeopardize my defense. Let's just say I was just in the wrong place at the wrong time. But I'll do whatever you want—I'll even submit to a follicle test. I'm gonna beat this."

"I'll see what I can do," Troy said, "But I gotta send it to Legal."

"I understand. You gotta do what you gotta do." I looked him in the eyes. "Will you fight for me?"

"Absolutely."

"This will all shake out in April. If it's okay with you, I'd like to continue my training, and Legal can make a decision after that."

"I'll see what I can do."

The next morning, huddled in my office, staring at the computer screen, I wondered how long it would take for Legal to make their decision. Turns out I didn't have to wait long.

"How's it going?" Troy asked, walking into my office.

"Give it to me straight," I said.

"You are no longer employed by Merrill Lynch and must leave the premises immediately."

I didn't blame them, but I wish they had given me a chance. I wanted to play ball their way, but their way was the highway. I didn't have the balls to go home and face Missy. Instead, still in my suit, I went to the casino. At a hold 'em table, a player whom I recognized recognized me back.

"Where have you been?" he said.

"Working," I said flatly.

"You look like a defendant in that suit."

"You look like an asshole."

I was up five hundred bucks when my cell phone rang around 5:00 p.m.

Shit.

"I called the office," Missy said. "You weren't there."

"We need to talk. I'll be home in twenty. Be prepared for bad news."

I would have preferred to stay at the casino all night—not because I wanted to play poker, but because I wanted to avoid the inevitable confrontation—but I cashed out my chips and went home. I didn't want her to go into labor, but I had to forewarn her.

She heard everything: the letter, Gary's plan, my dad's advice, how Merrill Lynch responded. It crushed her. My job at Merrill Lynch was as much her dream as it was mine. The defeated look on her face tore me in half, but I wasn't about to give up. I couldn't; too many people were depending on me.

With no other options for bringing in decent money legally, I played poker every day like my life depended on it—which it did. I stayed focused, reminding myself that I was at the felt for survival, not recreation. I made money every session.

After a month of playing, I had pulled in almost forty-five hundred dollars, which made it easy to decide not to quit playing cards until the deck turned against me. The best part? Missy saw how hard I was working to provide for us and supported me wholeheartedly. Instead of berating me for losing the job at Merrill Lynch, she championed my efforts, finally giving me that boost I had craved so desperately.

"My husband, the professional poker player," she said proudly.

"Maybe it's a sign," I said. "Maybe God wants me to play poker for a living. One big tournament win, and I could bank a million dollars. That'd be enough cash to set us up and let me play the market."

"I'll support whatever you do," she said, squeezing my arm.

"Imagine, retiring before thirty, with all these fucked circumstances, all because I won a big poker tourney."

Obviously, I was trying to repress my pain and look on the bright side, but Jake constantly joked that I got canned. At least he had the good sense not to talk to me about working for him again.

Amazingly, everyone was more supportive than expected. Even my grandmother, who never said anything nice about anyone, had a few kind words. But her praise didn't alter the fact that I was a semiprofessional, low-limit player with a pregnant wife and two kids, going on trial for felony drug possession. Still, I wasn't scared yet—at least not on the surface. Until the day I started to question whether God Himself had it in for me.

Arriving at Speaking Rock, I parked my car in the lot and walked into the casino through the front entrance. As I made my way to the poker room, a security guard intercepted me before I could enter.

"Sir, you can't go in there."

"Why not?"

"The State of Texas has shut down portions of our gaming operations."

"What?"

"The poker room is temporarily closed. That's all I can tell you."

I was ready to jump in front of a bus.

On March 15 my daughter was born. All of Missy's family and even my grandmother came for the event. I was sitting in the hall, holding my overactive toddler and talking to Missy's daughter when I heard my baby girl's first scream from the birthing suite. My trial was only weeks away, but the only thing in the world that I wanted was to get my little screamer with a full head of hair home. Still scared to death of babies, I determined to try harder this time. Then my phone rang.

"Good news," Gary Hill said.

"I need it. I'm a father again."

"How many is that, boy?"

"Three."

"Well, I kept your ass outta jail and got you a sweetheart deal. Six years deferred adjudication, fifteen hundred dollars' fine. You could probably get off the probation in two years. Whatcha think?"

"No community service?"

"Nope. Enjoy all your free time."

"If you think it's good, so do I."

I had hoped for an outright dismissal, but beggars can't be choosy. I made the drive to court in Amarillo via the same route as the day I got popped. If only I had trusted my gut. I was *never* going to set foot in Amarillo again after this.

The courtroom looked nothing like I expected, nothing like what you see on television; it was more like traffic court. The many people in the courtroom looked like the same type of dirty denizens I had met in jail, wearing blue jean shorts and tank tops. Ignoring the signs outside the courtroom forbidding such attire, they sat there looking as if they'd die if they didn't get their nicotine fixes. I wore the same blue suit I was wearing on the day Merrill Lynch fired me. It classed me up even more than many of the attorneys, which meant I stuck out like a sore thumb.

Fucking Amarillo.

I expected to powwow with Gary before being called and have him coach me on the finer points of whatever I needed to say, but he was late, which added to my stress. When he finally came in, two other people were with him, all sharply dressed.

"Just follow my lead," he whispered.

Like I had a choice.

He walked up to the court clerk and whispered something in his ear; he in turn talked to the judge. Apparently, my adjudication was going to be handled exactly like traffic court, alphabetically, but Gary wasn't prepared to wait, and he had the clout not to.

"I have just received word that Mr. Heifner's attorney's private jet is waiting on the tarmac, and he's asking to be heard first on the docket today," the judge announced to the courtroom, his voice dripping with sarcasm. "If no one objects . . ."

Beyond embarrassed, I looked around, expecting to see glaring faces aimed in my direction, but the assembled dirtbags were too busy playing with unlit cigarettes or mumbling among themselves.

"So be it," the judge said with a shrug. "Mr. Heifner, please stand."

After being sworn in I answered a bunch of questions required for my plea agreement. Gary stood beside me and shook his head yes or no to guide my response. It was over before I knew it. I was now a ward of the great State of Texas.

Gary shook my hand, and his entourage spirited out of the courtroom, leaving me standing there like a doomed gladiator in the center of the arena. My heart was pounding so hard I could barely breathe. I didn't know whether to be afraid or happy. My trial was over, but it felt as if everything was just beginning.

The bailiff directed me to an attractive young woman, my first step in the probation process. Dressed sharply in a smart suit, she was absolutely gorgeous and probably as young as I was.

"Your attorney put on quite a show," the sexy probation officer said.

"I guess that's included in his fee," I replied sheepishly.

The ringing in my head had subsided enough to allow me to realize that the young probation officer was making eyes at me—a possible felon.

"I might be free around 12:30 if you want to get some lunch," she said.

If it helped my situation, I would have in a heartbeat, but not knowing where the boundary lines lay, I decided against it. My past actions had enshrined me as a genius at complicating things. I didn't need that here. I just wanted to get home and drink myself into oblivion.

"I'd really love to," I said, "but I've got a flight to catch, and I just want to get away from this place."

"I understand. Maybe next time. Now you need to go downtown, where they'll process you and tell you what you can and can't do."

I had to report in once a month on a scheduled appointment date in El Paso, even though I was on probation in Amarillo. I also had to pay seventy-five dollars a month to the probation office in Amarillo to cover my supervision fee (forty dollars) and payment on my fine (thirty-five dollars).

I couldn't associate with other felons or probationers. I couldn't drink or go to a bar. Owning guns or weapons was prohibited. I couldn't travel out of town without permission. Bottom line: short leash. It was a long fall from Merrill Lynch to the life of a probationer, but there was no time for self-pity or shame: I had three kids to protect and nurture. The struggle was just beginning.

11

Meant to Live

LIFE OFFICIALLY SUCKED.

The warning from my former bank supervisor, parroted from *Wall Street*, when Charlie Sheen's character was arrested, kept playing over and over in my head. Money was also thin and dwindling fast. I didn't have a spending problem; I had an income problem. Finding a job—*any* job—was proving harder than a dyslexic trying to read Chinese. My ego hurt, my body hurt; hell, even my soul hurt. I didn't want to eat or drink. I couldn't get out of bed in the morning. Sleep was my only escape.

Have you ever been charged with a felony or deferred adjudication? Check. Have you ever been convicted of a misdemeanor or felony? Check. I knew exactly what this meant for my employment hopes.

No one wanted to be my champion, not even my wife. Turns out there really are people who like to kick a dog when it's down. Despite feeling as though a cinder block was hanging from my jaw, I held my head high. I entertained the idea of law school and even aced a few LSAT practice exams. But the Texas bar recently had changed the rules regarding admittance qualifications: If you had a deferred adjudication, no admittance to the bar and therefore no admittance to law school.

Then my previously trouble-free Dodge Intrepid began to break down. You name it, it went wrong. I was even in a minor fender bender on the drive home from Amarillo. I was convinced the car was cursed because I'd paid for it with drug money. The deathblow to the Intrepid—and my psyche—came when Pep Boys repaired the stripped oil pan and their shoddy work blew the motor. They refused to admit fault, and I was left with a pricey lawn ornament. The car wasn't cursed. *I* was.

"What can I do to make Pep Boys fix my car?" I asked my biological father. "No local attorney will take my case."

"Write a letter," Kip suggested.

"To who? And what would I say?" I threw up my hands in disgust. "You're an attorney. Haven't you handled something like this before?"

"Yeah," he said. "But it's a simple matter."

"For you, maybe," I grumbled.

He didn't take my case.

Missy had finally patched things up with her family, so we spent a lot of time at her parents' house. On the way over for a cookout, she made a confession.

"I told my parents."

"I thought we agreed not to tell anyone," I said.

"I was looking for some support because of all these ridiculous problems we keep having."

"Did you get it?"

She looked out the window. "No."

"I'd sure as hell love some support, too, starting from you."

"Let's just drop the subject."

Lovely. I was walking like Daniel into the lion's den, except I didn't believe I'd be saved. Truth is, I was dying for guidance. Given that her parents were pastors, I would have listened to anything they had to say if framed in the word of the Lord—a prayer circle, a confessional, even an exorcism. But instead of enlightenment or encouragement, all they gave me were thinly veiled criticisms and sarcasm. Apparently, unless you're a winner, everyone hates you, including Jesus.

Part of my new, thick-skinned plan involved taking jobs I detested. The first, in June 2001, was selling cars at Westway Dodge. I was a decent salesman, selling two cars my first day, but I was a college graduate . . . selling cars. I didn't have a problem with the job. It's just not what I planned to be doing, and the commission structure was almost impossible to decipher. I was positive I was going to get screwed.

At first I thought the worst part of the job was going to be the dealership's location: directly across the street from Merrill Lynch, giving me a daily dose of the happy little world I longed for. But I was wrong. Listening to customers gush about their solid financial situation and about their perfect lives proved even more infuriating.

Our money had officially run out. I couldn't afford to eat lunch every day. Staring at the soda machine at work, I tried to will myself a Diet Coke. Unfortunately, my telekinetic powers also failed me, so I stole chips from coworkers' lunch bags to keep from slipping into hypoglycemic shock.

Then there was the heat. Walking from the cool, air-conditioned dealership into the steaming hot lot in the middle of a June heat wave to greet customers was brutal. Several trips to retrieve keys took brutal to another level. I had never wanted a job that made me sweat, but as I never seemed to get what I wanted, that's exactly what I got. Walking customers into the showroom, my curse was about to rear its ugly head yet again.

"Whatcha say we get out of the heat and go over some basic info in the comfort of the air-conditioned showroom?"

"Sure, no problem," the customer replied.

The dealership felt like a sauna, and my fat customers immediately started bitching.

I motioned them to a table. "Please have a seat right here while I go see what's up with the A/C."

At the sales tower the sales manager was staring at his computer screen, looking bored.

"Hey, what's up with the air-conditioning?" I asked. "My customers are complaining."

He gave me a "fuck you" stare. "My name isn't 'Hey.' It's Sal."

"Excuse me?"

"You heard me. Refer to me as Sal, or go home for the rest of the day."

"I apologize. My customers are eager to buy a car, and I was just trying to figure out why it's a hothouse in here."

His stare intensified. "Do you wanna go home?"

"Excuse me?" I repeated, totally confused.

"I told you to call me Sal."

I looked at him blankly. What I wouldn't have done for a Scottish claymore.

"*Sal*, what's wrong with the A/C?"

"Better," he smiled. "It's broken. Won't be fixed for three weeks."

"Yeesh. Sal, it's the middle of summer."

"Tough it out."

"Sal, the customers are gonna hate this."

"Then sell quickly."

Our idiotic conversation lasted only a minute, but in that time my customers had left. My brisk sales pace morphed into a trickle. Who wants to suffer through tedious negotiations in unbearable heat? The salesmen were screwed.

With no customers, I stood around with the other salesmen and swapped stories. A few were also felons, some even from the narco biz. Most were drunks. All were losers—me included.

"What did you do before this?" one of them asked.

"I worked there," I said, pointing to Merrill Lynch across the street. "I bet their fucking A/C works."

"Yeah, right," the salesman said, waving me off. "You're a fuckin' liar. If you worked there, how the hell'd you wind up here?"

They all laughed at me.

Good question, and one I had no desire to answer. With sales dried up I'd become nothing more than a minimum wage lackey. The thought of suicide danced in my head. Dead end, no hope, no support, no future. If it weren't for my kids, I probably would have done something stupid. Their existence saved me, but that didn't stop me from wishing I were dead.

Going to the probation office was mortally embarrassing. I had driven Jake there many times, silently laughing my ass off on every trip. Now I was sitting in that room, reading the inane informational posters, surrounded by small-time criminals who made a career out of being pathetic.

When I met with my probation officer, I always turned on the prom-night charm; after all, he had the power to put me away. Thankfully, my PO wasn't a hard ass but a charming older guy, an attentive listener who realized that people made mistakes. The guys in jail had told horror stories about some POs, but from our first meeting I knew I'd get along with mine. If I befriended him, maybe I could keep him from doing those annoying in-home and at-work visits. Sell it now, and maybe he wouldn't need to check up on me later.

"Mr. Heifner, you obviously don't belong here. What happened?"

"Life didn't work out for me."

"How do you mean?"

"My brother also worked at Merrill Lynch, and he was also fired, but only because he didn't make his quota. He got another analyst job, and that didn't work out either. He was on his third job in three years, having problems in sales again, with one foot out the door, but God, luck, and timing saved him."

"How's that?"

"My uncle was banging this chick, and she got my brother a job with her company. Bigger salary and commission. This one worked out for him. Not to mention, he met a great girl along the way with a fantastic career. They lived happily ever after."

"Lucky him."

"Yeah, and unlucky me."

My PO chuckled. I didn't.

"I see it all the time," he explained. "People are victims of their own circumstances. But there comes a point where you have to draw the line and define your circumstance." He looked me in the eyes, his stare unwavering. "Where is your line going to be, Mr. Heifner?"

"I don't know."

"Give it some thought. I believe in you. Things will get better. Just stay away from bad people and bad influences. You're a winner, Chris. I can see it."

I had nearly the exact same conversation over the phone with my Amarillo PO when I checked in with her. She also believed in me and lavished considerable praise. Talk about irony: The only two people who encouraged me were my probation officers.

Staying away from Jake, a condition of my probation, was easy. I didn't have a car to drive across town. Missy had our only car and ferried me to and from work. More pathetic irony: working at a car dealership and not having a car. But pathetic was the story of my life, chapter and verse.

That's not to say I didn't wonder what he was up to. I hadn't eaten out in months, much less had a decent night out, so the thought of him living the high life lay beyond my mental pain threshold. I could only imagine what new car he was driving or great trip he was taking. But it was over. *We* were over. Unfortunately, it looked as though Missy and I were also coming to an end.

Lying on the couch one night—my son and baby daughter in my spot in bed—a thought popped into my head about the future, *our* future. I walked into the bedroom and tried to discuss it with Missy, but as usual that didn't fly.

"I wanna draw a line in the sand," I said.

"You wanna *what?*"

"It's an expression. I wanna define my life once and for all and fight for something better." I choked back the tears that had suddenly overtaken me. "For us."

She rolled her eyes. "You are definitely the woman of this relationship. You talk too much. Just get a good job. It's simple. I'm tired of defending you. Everyone thinks you should do more."

"I'm dying every day from the heat of that hell hole. What more can I do?"

She shrugged and returned to watching television. Everything I said after that went in one ear and out the other. She didn't believe in talking through problems. She wanted results, not the process.

One small victory came when the mechanics at work proved that Pep Boys had blown the motor on my car, and the car shop agreed to make me whole. But that only happened after an unrelenting letter-writing campaign to the Pep Boys CEO and board of directors. My literary Hail Mary caught their attention, but they said it would take months.

Wonderful. But results nonetheless. Which galvanized me. I had to get better results. I had to quit the hellishly hot stealership.

The next few months were hand to mouth while everything degenerated into an even bigger mess. I slept on the couch. Friends and family avoided me. I bounced from job to job. Donating plasma to the local blood bank for twenty bucks a pop became a necessity. I couldn't even afford to drink.

Missy spent most of her time at church or her mom's house, saying our home was too depressing. I went with her occasionally, but my presence caused tension, so usually, I stayed home, sat on the couch, and watched TV. Then one day, as I helped her unload the kids from the car, she helped me break through my wall of depression.

"Are you gonna get a steady job or just continue being a loser?"

"I'll get a job if you could support me for once."

"I will support you, Chris, but you have to give me something to support."

It was just what I needed—a loving kick in the ass.

"I think I can get on at Circuit City."

"Then do it. Thanksgiving is next week."

My first day was Black Friday, thrown to the wolves. Sales were commission based, and if I hustled I could earn decent money. But on the busiest day of the year, I didn't have a clue what I was doing, and no one had time to help me. A few good commission checks came in, though that hardly gave me a hard-on for retail.

My coworkers thought I was a pathological liar because, during breaks, I talked about my past life. They figured that, since I was busting my ass hawking laptops like them, none of what I said was true. Clearly, I didn't fit in. It was almost as bad as Westway Dodge, but at least I didn't have to go outside.

My newly bolstered confidence sagged again, and I withdrew from everyone and everything. Life seemed pointless. At work dealing with customers became a monumental challenge. I didn't want to make eye contact, and my voice came out in hushed tones.

Missy, on the other hand, was fairing much better. She had both family and church as a support system, along with a job she loved: show choir director for a local private high school, Loretto Academy. She had an amazing voice and constant opportunities to sing. I pleaded with her to give some of them a shot, if only to help provide for our family, but she always rebuked me. Her reasoning sounded unlike anything we had discussed before, which meant someone clearly had her ear and was putting ideas in her head. My dreams were decaying, and with three mouths to feed and three growing bodies to clothe, it was becoming unbearable.

Then, a rare celebratory night during Thanksgiving vacation came back to haunt us. She was pregnant again. If the financial burden of three kids was painful, four was going to be pure agony. We had already outgrown our small two-bedroom confines, and now there was going to be another person in the mix. I couldn't have made a bigger mess of my life if I tried.

The camel's back finally broke just after New Year's 2002. Coworkers had made crass comments about my family that soured my mood. Desperately wanting to quit, I tried to discuss it with Missy, but she blew me off.

"Why the hell can't we discuss this?"

"Because that's your fucking *job*," she barked. "Now leave me alone!"

It triggered the mother of all arguments. We threw dishes alongside every imaginable expletive. The pent-up animosity between us erupted into a cataclysmic scream-fest that everyone in our neighborhood heard. Before long there came a pounding on the front door, followed by: "Police. Open the door."

Two cops were standing there, one average size and the other short and frail, maybe five-five and 125 pounds soaking wet.

"What's going on in here?" the little one asked.

I gave the standard domestic squabble response: "Nothing."

He looked to Missy, and recognition formed in his eyes. He cocked his head sideways. "Don't I know you from somewhere? . . . Missy?"

He led her to the other side of the house while his partner grilled me. From the corner of my eye, I could see Micro Cop repeatedly touching her arm and laughing.

In high school Missy was voted almost every "most" you could think of: most charming, most beautiful, most friendly. On top of that she was an athlete and head cheerleader. It never surprised me when we ran into guys from her past that she said they had crushes on her. Another of those enamored hard dicks, this gun-toting pipsqueak was practically humping the air as he talked to her.

After listening to our versions of what had transpired, the cops allowed me to gather some possessions and go to my grandmother's across town. Once there, I figured the whole situation had blown over, but shortly after I arrived, there came another loud knock at the door.

"Police. Open the door."

What the fuck?

Two new cops.

"Mr. Heifner?"

"Yes."

"Please come outside."

"I discussed this already at my apartment. They let me leave."

The cop produced his cuffs. "I'm placing you under arrest for family domestic violence."

My face couldn't have registered more shock if you'd stuck a cattle prod up my ass. I tried to ask questions naturally but didn't resist and got in the patrol car.

"What exactly am I being charged with?"

"Sir, you'll have to ask the officer that handled this. We were just told to pick you up since you're in our jurisdiction."

As I went through booking, all I could think was that my probation was going to be revoked. This bullshit charge was going to put me away for twenty years. Finally allowed my phone call, I dialed Missy.

"Missy, they arrested me. *What. Did. You. Say?*"

"Nothing. I just caught up with an old friend."

"Well, I'm on probation, remember? That fucking midget could send me to jail for *twenty years*."

I hung up before she could reply. I didn't want to hear her response. I sat in the holding tank, numb, mind spinning, no clue what would happen next, surrounded by putrid orange walls, drunks sleeping off their buzz, and thirty or so other geniuses coming off their highs, barfing in the toilet.

The monumental failure of my life had reached an all-new low.

12

Blurry

"Heifner," the jailer called.

Sitting on that concrete floor, I knew I'd be stuck there for a while. There was no way I could explain this to either of my POs. They were going to revoke my probation, I was going to be convicted of a felony, and I was going to do serious time. But I wasn't pissed, just defeated because I didn't know how to recover. I was twenty-eight and had had a good run, but now it was over.

"*Heifner!*"

My brain dropped back into gear. When I looked up the jailer was standing inside the cell's doorway. *Time to get my jumpsuit,* I thought.

"What's next?" I asked as we rode down to the lower level.

"You tell me. You got bailed out."

Huh? Who the hell cared enough to bail me out?

It was 6:00 a.m. as I walked from the El Paso County Jail in downtown El Paso to Apodaca Bail Bonds. Shuffling up to the counter without a dime in my pocket, I assumed I'd be walking home.

"Sign here, here, and here," the counter girl said, indicating lines on a form. "An explanation of our terms and conditions are in the paperwork. Make sure you read it."

I grunted and scribbled my name.

She handed me a crinkled twenty-dollar bill. "Your grandmother left this for cab money."

A crotchety old woman who loves to complain, my grandmother still loved me enough to spring me from the pokey. My heart swelled. The moment I got to her house, I crawled into the guest-room bed and hid under the covers. It was the loneliest feeling in the world: I had no money, no one to talk to, and the entire weekend to think about what I was going to tell my probation officers. There was also a temporary restraining order preventing me from seeing Missy or my kids for 120 days. Probation revocation hearings would surely happen before the TRO expired. Would I ever see them again?

The day in bed morphed into days. I didn't eat, watch TV, or go to work. I slept and hid; 2002 was off to a fan-fucking-tastic start.

After a week of being a bedridden zombie, I pulled a 180 from intelligent. I called Jake.

We hadn't spoken in months. When he answered the phone, music was playing in the background, which meant only one thing.

"Nutty? *Nutty!* I can't hear you. I'm at Tequila Sunrise. Come on down!"

I bolted out of the house like my ass was on fire. Hanging around Jake and visiting a strip club broke at least ten of my probation rules, but I didn't give a fuck anymore.

The bouncer summoned Jake because I didn't have five bucks for the cover. Jake paid my freight, and a few moments later I was tableside, sipping a cold beer. It felt glorious.

"So whatcha been up to?" Jake asked.

"I just got out of jail."

He nearly spewed his brew. "What for?"

"Domestic violence."

"I always knew she was a typical Mexican," he frowned. "I'm sure she deserved it."

"I didn't touch her. It's bullshit."

"Even so."

"There's a restraining order, too. I can't talk to her or the kids for months. It might fuck up my probation. I don't know if she's on my side or not."

"Call Gary."

"I don't have any money."

"For what we paid on your drug case, he should handle it for free."

I nodded. "Tomorrow."

"Byron got arrested for domestic violence, too." Jake started laughing as though it were funny. "I went to his house to pick him up, and Sandra and him were going at it like cats and dogs. When the cops came, he lost it. They put him in the car, and he started kicking the windows, so they hogtied him."

"What were you doing while this went down?"

Jake started laughing again, harder than before, nearly choking. "Nothing . . . I tried to calm him down . . . but he wouldn't listen . . . so I got a beer!"

Yeah, hysterical.

But in a flash my mind-set changed—if you can't beat 'em, join 'em. Then, interestingly enough, my luck changed, too.

Pep Boys had put a new motor in my car, but they blew that one up, too. They put a second motor in, which ran hot, but they gave the car back to me and said it was fine. I fired off more threatening letters to their corporate HQ in Philadelphia. One day my phone rang at 7:00 a.m., waking me from a dead sleep. It was a conference call; on the line were some of Pep Boys' big wigs.

"Mr. Heifner, why won't you accept the car?" somebody asked. He introduced himself, but still half-asleep, I forgot who he was.

"Because it doesn't run right," I replied groggily, still waltzing with the sandman.

"But we put a new motor in it."

"And you tore the wiring harness, which is now being held together with zip ties. I don't think that's safe or Dodge-approved, do you?"

No response, but now I was fully awake.

"That car was less than two years old when I took it to you guys. Now it's unsafe. I've been without it from April 2001 to January 2002. I want the car back in perfect working order, and I want compensation for the loss of use."

"Mr. Heifner, the purpose of this call is not to talk settlement."

"It is now. My father is an attorney. We've given you more than enough rope to hang yourselves while documenting this entire process. I'll take the car right now, but I want eighty-five hundred dollars in my hands tomorrow for loss of use and to repair your errors. If you don't accept these terms, my demands will double as soon as I hang up the phone."

"Sir, we have been more than accomm—"

"No, you have been more than *incompetent,* and my father and I let you. Dare me to hang up. I'll take this to court, and I feel lucky. Do you?"

I was bluffing, of course. I had talked to over a dozen attorneys, my father included, and none would take the case. But Pep Boys didn't know that.

After a long pause, "Mr. Heifner, we're sorry for the inconvenience. You'll have a check tomorrow."

Yahtzee! That cash would get me back on my feet, and I could worry about the car later.

Doing mental cartwheels, I dialed Gary's office.

His secretary answered. "Law office."

"Hi, Donna, it's Chris Heifner."

"Hello, Chris!" she said, enthused. "I heard you've had some hard times lately. But it will get better. I believe in you."

"Thanks, Donna. You've always been the best."

"My pleasure. Now let me transfer you to Gary."

"I talked to your wife," Gary said. "She's lost her goddamn mind. She's pissed as all hell at you, but I think it's because y'all have had some shitty luck. She'll calm down, and I'll get this dismissed. You're a good kid. Relax."

"I want to talk to my kids," I pleaded.

"Listen to me, son. Do *not* violate that restraining order. Do you understand me?"

"I understand," I said, simultaneously elated and deflated.

Gary and I spoke with my POs. They were disappointed, but they gave me a reprieve, albeit with a stern warning.

"You need to get the case dismissed, or it will cause problems with your probation," said Joyce, my Amarillo PO.

I had a little money, an attorney I trusted with my life, and I could look people in the eyes again. It was the slow season at Circuit City, so

I put myself on the schedule less and hung around Jake more. It seemed the more time I spent with him, the more good things happened to me. Bizarre. I play it straight and narrow and get screwed, but I play it wide friggin' open and everything's aces. Adding to the insanity, I made a new friend while playing Hearts online.

I wasn't trying to meet another woman. My life didn't need additional complications. But sometimes things happen, and the coincidences were too spooky to ignore.

Tosha was also on deferred adjudication. She had gotten popped trying to drive a load across the Bridge of the Americas into the States. Her story was as long and complex as mine, and it felt great to commiserate with someone who had lived the highs and lows of the narco biz. Her jogger's build, large breasts, curly brown hair, and killer smile also happened to be my type. But what made her so captivating was that she also was a college grad who had found bad luck at every turn. She had earned her MBA and was planning to teach at a community college in Albuquerque while figuring out her next step.

I broke probation and made several trips to the Duke City to have drinks with her, which also violated her probation. It was the best therapy: Listening to her stories, failures, and problems made me realize I wasn't alone.

But I was still married. I hadn't spoken to my wife in a month, and I was facing twenty years in jail. It's not like things between my wife and me were peachy before the TRO. I slept on the couch. We didn't talk much, and when we did we usually fought. We didn't spend much time together, either. It was painfully obvious that our marriage still existed because we were stuck with each other to raise our children. Sure, we shared some great moments, but they were few and far between. As far as I was concerned, Missy and I were done.

I needed a woman in my life. Tosha could have filled that void easily. But the joy I felt simply being friends with her made me feel incredibly guilty. The guilt so overwhelmed me that it made me wonder how I could possibly be a good father as a divorced parent. My children's needs always came before mine, and divorce wasn't going to change that. What kind of father could I be with a combative ex-wife and a strict visitation agreement?

At Tosha's urging I started studying for the GMAT so I could enroll in grad school and earn my MBA. I figured I'd be off probation and my case dismissed by the time I graduated, making it that much easier to land a job—or at least harder for my bad luck to screw everything up again. Also, I could live off the financial aid in grad school. Not the wisest move, but it was a move forward. First I had to get the domestic violence charge dismissed, though—the linchpin on which everything hinged.

I was still living with my grandmother, hadn't seen my kids in months, and was suffering at Circuit City, but it felt like things would work out. Tosha was succeeding, so why couldn't I?

I was in the shower one day when my grandmother yelled to me. "Chris, there are some men here to see you!"

"Who?"

"I don't know, but they look like cops."

Still wet, I threw on boxers and a T-shirt and made my way to the front of the house. Two men were waiting for me in the den. Both were wearing jeans, cowboy boots, and button-down shirts. One held a cowboy hat. They flashed their badges, introduced themselves as law enforcement officers. One worked for the Texas attorney general's office, the other was with the Department of Justice (DOJ), in the Drug Enforcement Administration (DEA).

Uh-oh.

"Chris, we want to talk to you about Jeff Andes," the AG cop began.

"Uh, okay."

"Specifically, we want to know about his drug operation," said the DOJ cop.

"And what you were doing with him the other night," AG added.

I did my best to look confused. "Excuse me?"

"We know you've been running around with him lately." A pause. "Again."

I shrugged. "He's my friend."

DOJ nodded. "So what can you tell us about him?"

"Other than that he's my friend, not a whole lot."

"You ran drugs with Jeff, right?" said the AG cop, trying to pin me down.

"Look, guys, my case has been adjudicated. I'm on probation, and I will defer any and all questions about it to my attorney, Gary Joel Hill."

The DOJ cop put up his hands to signal that he came in peace. "Look, we're not here to bust your balls, but we know you violated your probation by hanging around Mr. Andes and going to the bars and strip clubs with him."

His statement felt like a sucker punch to the gut. "I would love to help you guys, but I have nothing to say."

I figured I'd be questioned about drug trafficking immediately after my arrest in Amarillo, but nothing ever happened. Back then I was prepared to deal with an interrogation, but I didn't expect one now. I was on probation and in violation of it and had domestic violence charges pending, so their visit made me paranoid near to insanity. Still, I tap danced around their questions until they finally gave up.

"Mr. Heifner, don't tell Jeff about this meeting," AG said. He handed me a business card, as did the DOJ cop. "Here are our cards in case you change your mind."

"Thank you. I'll think about it. Be safe."

The only thing I was thinking about was calling Jake immediately. We had been through tough times and had our issues, but Jake bailed me out of jail, paid for my attorney, and had been a good friend when I needed one. Loyalty was a virtue I was proud to have, especially when most others didn't. Jake needed to know that he was under investigation by the big dogs. I could see all the angles, which meant I was on the hook, too, via the RICO statutes. Also, my trafficking case had only been adjudicated in state court. I could be charged under federal statutes at any time.

My calls to Jake went unanswered, so I hit the road, frantically searching for him high and low. For the cops to show their hand by talking to me meant the hammer was gonna fall—*soon*. We needed to circle the wagons and take drastic measures.

Jake was at home, outside, watering the plants.

"Why the fuck aren't you answering your phone?"

"I was busy. Where's the fire, Charlie?"

"We need to talk. *Now!*" I hustled him inside and pulled out the business cards. "These guys just paid me a visit."

I laid out the entire conversation and recommended that we speak to Gary together, along with Byron and the rest of the crew. I explained how I saw the government playing their hand and how I thought we could beat them. Then I promised my undying loyalty to our friendship, even though I didn't think I had to. This was Uncle Jake, after all. He and Sandra had attended all of my children's births. Our families had spent countless time together doing everything imaginable.

I hadn't worked with Jake in almost two years, and even though we didn't talk shop, it was my understanding that he had seriously expanded his business and was making a *ton* of cash—much more than I could have imagined.

To my amazement Jake wasn't the least bit concerned. "Relax. Nothing's gonna happen."

"What the fuck do you mean, '*Nothing's gonna happen*'?"

"If they were gonna arrest me, they already would have. They got nothin'."

"C'mon man, how foolish can you be? They knew what we did the other night, for chrissakes."

"It'll go away. Trust me."

"If it doesn't, are you gonna pay my attorney when the case goes federal?"

Jake laughed. "Nope, you're on your own."

Well, fuck me with a fire truck. This was by far the most irrational logic I had ever heard in my entire life. Why didn't he want to investigate further or at least consult Gary? This was naivety in its purest form.

I stormed out. He wasn't just gambling with his freedom—he was gambling with mine, too. His empire was pulling six-figure profits every month, and he couldn't afford to throw ten K at an attorney if I went down? What a cheap bastard. Here I had just pledged undying loyalty to him and his organization, and he still gave me the cold shoulder. Fucking prick! Even if you removed the money and loyalty from the equation, paying for my attorney still made smart business sense: It guaranteed my silence and protected his ass. How could he not see it that way?

My only option was silent desperation: keep my mouth shut and head low and pray that when all this blew up—a week, month, or year from now—that none of the shrapnel hit me. I had done my duty as a friend. Against the express wishes of the authorities, I had warned Jake. Now all I could do was wait and hope he came to his senses.

———

The next morning was another gorgeous spring day in the Borderland: clear blue skies, mid-70s, light breeze, the kind of day that made me love life. Pondering my day's leisure activities while enjoying a relaxing shower, I had just finished working up a thick, frothy lather when a strange sound from the den snapped me into danger mode.

Wet, soapy, and naked, I wrapped myself in one of my daughter's oversize Barbie beach towels. Armed with a plunger—the nearest plausible weapon—I crept down the hall. At the corner I squirreled up my courage, raised the plunger, and peered into the den.

"Wassup, Nutty?" hollered Jake, sprawled on the couch, overpriced sandals up on the glass coffee table.

Jake often came over unannounced, so his presence didn't bother me. It was the second man in the room who chilled me to the core. In a lived-in leather motorcycle vest, he had an unruly mane of black hair, a week of scruff, and wild eyes that screamed of meth or gak—probably both. He was standing beside a bookcase, leering at framed photographs of my wife and children like a cannibal contemplating his next meal.

"Forgive the intrusion," Jake said, motioning to the man, "but I wanted you to meet Hank."

"What's up?" I said, my voice cracking in barely repressed fear. I lowered my weapon of minimum destruction and stepped into the den. They burst into laughter.

"What were you gonna do, Nutty, smother the intruder with your Barbie towel?"

"Nah, I would've just dropped the towel and scared him away with my anaconda."

The cemetery silence that followed confirmed my worst suspicion.

"Sit down, Chris," Hank commanded, pointing to the chair beside the couch.

Hank plopped down beside Jake, his eyes never leaving mine. They leaned forward, as did I—monkey see, monkey do—and Jake pinned me in a malevolent stare. That I was practically naked, dripping soapy water everywhere while being told what to do like an insolent child—in my own home, no less—suddenly became the least of my worries.

"Chris, remember when the DEA and the Texas attorney general talked to you yesterday?"

"Uh-huh. They sat on that same couch and also came when I was in the shower. People should start making appointments."

"Shut the fuck up and listen," Jake snarled. "Hank's my insurance policy, just in case you decide to be Chatty Kathy with them. I would really hate for something tragic to happen to you or your family."

Hank jerked a thumb at the photographs. "Three kids, right? Play ball with the authorities, and I'm gonna make you watch me shoot 'em one . . . by one . . . by one. Then I'll do your wife, too. Maybe have a little fun with her first. But that's not all."

I don't know about you, but when someone starts talking about killing my kids and raping and murdering my pregnant wife, calm and nonchalant go to the back of the bus. My guts were being sautéed in napalm.

"When I'm through with them, I'm gonna take you into Mexico and work on you for a few days. When I get tired of torturing you and hearing you scream, I'm gonna stuff whatever's left of you in a fifty-five gallon drum and set you the fuck on fire."

Hank was no wordsmith, but he got his point across. Time slowed to an imperceptible crawl as I tried to collect myself. That's when I noticed the patch on his leathers; he wasn't faking membership in one of the nation's most ruthless motorcycle gangs. He wasn't a big guy, but his lean, chiseled muscles; numerous shank scars; and many inartistic tattoos suggested that he'd been to prison—more than once.

"Jake, hold on a sec," I said, trembling like a Yorkie in a room full of pit bulls. Time for an Oscar-winning performance. "I came straightaway and told *you* what was up. Don't you remember?"

"Yeah, I remember."

"Well, doesn't that count for something?" I said in the most nonthreatening tone I could muster.

"All depends, Chris. All depends on one question."

"You know I'd never lie to you."

His mouth curled into the sinister grin a serial killer would give after he'd killed his parents just before ordering a hot fudge sundae. "Are you my nigga?"

Better make it convincing.

"Jake, buddy, you've got nothing to worry about. I'm definitely your nigga!"

The moment they left I sank to my knees. I wanted to run into the kitchen, grab a knife, and slit my own throat. If I were out of the picture, maybe they'd be safe. Then again, that could put them in even greater danger. Jake was a wild card; there was no telling. He'd already gone so far as to hire a hit man. That said it all.

When I was in jail, Jake tried to get Missy to give him our new car as a down payment for my bail, but she talked him out of it. He had done some shitty things over the years, true, but this crossed a new line—a line he should never have crossed.

Bawling and shaking with rage, I knew what I had to do. If I had to kill myself to save them, fine. I could always do that later. But right now the person I needed to destroy was Jeffrey Todd Andes. One way or another I was going to take that motherfucker *down*.

But how?

13

Extreme Ways

THE RULES HAD CHANGED.

My friends were now my enemies. Which meant ironically that my enemies could now be my friends. But all that mattered was the safety of my family. What worried me most was Jake pulling his itchy trigger finger before I could circle the wagons. If he misconstrued the smallest detail, my family and I would be dead long before he discovered his mistake. Then again, maybe he didn't give a shit either way. Dead men tell no tales. One less mouth to worry about. He wasn't the brightest light in the sky—his logic and motives a mixed bag of moronic and ignorant—which spelled certain doom for my family. I turned to the only person I could think of.

"Jeff did *what?*" Gary Hill said.

I repeated the meeting verbatim, choking back tears when I explained the hit man's threats against my family.

"That dumb motherfucker."

"What do I do, Gary?"

"Listen to me, Chris. This case is gonna go federal. Do whatever you gotta do to protect yourself."

A silence followed. That was all I needed to hear.

"Thanks, Gary."

"Good luck, Chris."

It was official: I was in no man's land, caught in the middle of a pissing match between an ambitious idiot and Uncle Sam.

There's an old joke among criminals and defense attorneys that federal trials are really just one long guilty plea. The government won't bother going to trial unless they've got you dead to rights. When they do, they rarely lose. Almost all their cases are based on evidence substantiated by informant testimony. But prior to arrest, they've usually investigated you for years to be certain they have enough evidence to convict. For all I knew, Jake was under investigation before I started running for him. Someone could have ratted us out while I was working with him. Everything I had ever done with him could come back to haunt me now, two years later, and he could shoot my family and me for shits and giggles.

I spent the night pondering the situation, wondering what could have precipitated it. It takes an awful lot to pop up on the feds' radar. Was that why I was never questioned while in jail? One guy in the aquarium was a planted cop, I was sure, but my sweetheart deal made me dismiss the idea as paranoia. Had I been naive?

Jake once told me about a busted dealer connection in Kansas City. The guy owed him fifty large, and Jake said the guy had talked to the authorities about him, but which ones? One night in college Jake and I thought we were being followed, but we decided it was just a stripper's jealous boyfriend. Was he being investigated then? Adan's brother had also just been released from the penitentiary. Had he cut a deal for an early furlough? Jake's other friend, some suit-and-tie guy, got popped at the checkpoint. Maybe he was to blame.

My mind reeled. All I knew for sure: rock, me, hard place. At some point during the night I passed out at the kitchen table, atop the pages of notes I was furiously scribbling. My ringing phone woke me.

"Let's go get lunch," Jake said.

"Okay, let me get ready."

"Hurry up. I'm outside."

My throat closed, but there was no time for fear. I stuffed the notes between the mattresses in the guest room, then threw on some fresh clothes. Jake was waiting in a brand-new Eddie Bauer Expedition with twenty-inch rims. I tried my best to act normal, but if you had hooked an EKG to my chest, the machine would have exploded.

"We're gonna go pick up this stripper I've been fuckin'," he explained. "A redheaded nympho I gotta keep happy." He threw the SUV in gear. "God, I love women."

Keep your mind on pussy and off me, I thought, but really, I wanted to kill him on the spot. Tear out his larynx. Jab my finger through his eye into his brain. He was a state champion high school wrestler, though, so if my surprise attack failed . . . then again, if I succeeded, I'd be charged with murder and go to prison. Best to play it cooler than the dark side of the moon.

Jake for his part seemed colder. We picked up his pole dancer and went to a popular buffet restaurant. Everything he did annoyed me: the way he held his fork, sat in his chair, talked with food in his mouth, all of it. But he was so nonchalant that it made me doubt the events of the day prior. Did I blow it out of proportion? Was I being paranoid?

When his gal-pal went to the can, he used our alone time to pounce.

"Why'd you lie to me?" he said, Baco Bits and shreds of spinach leaves falling from his half-open mouth.

"About what?"

"Everything."

"You're going insane."

"You were just trying to scare me about those feds at your house," he insisted, tossing the business cards on the table. "Did they really ask about me?"

"Yes! Why would I lie?"

He leaned back, folded his arms. "I don't know."

"Oh, my god, Jake, this is crazy."

"You lied to me about speeding. Don't think I forgot about that. If you hadn't been speeding, you wouldn't have lost that load."

Un-fucking-believable. I couldn't believe we were talking about this again. I instantly regretted caving. Fucking asshole. I hoped that he'd choke on a cherry tomato. I'd sit there and watch him die.

"And I hated yesterday," he added. "I look at your kids as if they're *my* kids. I've been around since they were born. It would really hurt me if something happened to them."

"So you were serious yesterday about something happening to my family?"

"Yeah, I would hate for something to happen to them."

I wanted to use my soup spoon to hack his head off. Instead, I looked him in the eyes and choked out: "Look, I don't think either one of us has anything to worry about. It's all good. I'm your nigger."

"I like black people and black dogs," the stripper said, taking her seat.

"Uh, yeah, me, too," I said.

"Exactly," Jake added. "There's nothing to worry about. If nothing has happened by now, it never will."

Threatening my family made him my mortal enemy. He should have killed me on the spot because from that moment forward, no matter what he did, no act of contrition would ever close the rift he carved between us. And he really shouldn't have given me back those business cards.

My mind was made up.

— —

I wanted to talk to Gary about my decision, but Jake was one of his biggest clients. I didn't want to put him in the position of having a conflict of interest, especially considering he had already suggested that I do whatever it took to protect myself. He would have handled it with the utmost of professionalism, but my gut told me to hire new counsel. A few days earlier, during one of my infrequent Circuit City shifts, I sold a bunch of equipment to a sharp young attorney named Joe Vasquez. He oozed confidence and had the swagger of a winner. Was he still too green behind the gills to handle something this serious? Then again, what choice did I have? Besides, the consultation was free.

Sitting in his waiting room, I reflected that this was either the wisest path I had ever walked or the dumbest. I hoped this guy would help me climb out of the hole I was in and not help bury me in it.

"Joe? Mr. Vasquez?" I said shakily. "What do I call you?"

"Call me Joe. Why are you here?"

I stared at the floor.

"Chris, what's the story?"

I cleared my throat, straightened up, and threw back my chin. "I want to be a government informant."

That wasn't what he expected to hear. "Excuse me?"

"I wanna be a rat."

His brow furrowed, one of those "hold all my calls" looks. He motioned to the chair opposite his desk.

I sat down and laid out the entire story. Then the million-dollar question. His response literally brought tears to my eyes. He said I was making the right—the *only*—decision. I had found my man. A weight lifted from me.

We agreed on a price and a strategy. While I was walking to my car, the reality of what I was about to do hit me full force and made me feel like shit again. But Jake had threatened to kill my family. It's amazing how quickly guilt can vanish.

Joe called the agents who had given me their cards and made an appointment with them to see what the terms of my involvement would be, along with their expectations. As you can imagine the feds were eager to speak with me, and we agreed to meet two days later. That gave me a little time to get my affairs in order. The TRO had just expired—and not a day too soon.

Missy had moved to a new house in West El Paso. TRO notwithstanding, it still surprised me that she hadn't consulted me. But we were a family again. The reunion with my kids was awkward but heartrending. We hugged, kissed, played, and hugged and kissed some more. When the kids went and played, Missy and I hunkered down for the most serious talk of our lives.

"I'm gonna be an informant for the feds against Jake."

Her eyes bulged. "*What?* Am I missing something? You're not even talking to him anymore."

"A lot has changed in the last 120 days." I took a deep breath. "He hired a hit man to kill us."

She gave me a look that said: *No fucking way.*

I nodded. "Me, you, the kids."

Her tears of sadness quickly turned to rage. Soon, she was yelling. I expected another argument between us, but as I explained my plans and told her everything she needed to know, she calmed down.

"Can't we just ignore this whole thing, forget it ever happened? It'll go away, I know it will."

"No, it won't. I've got no choice. *We've* got no choice."

Missy is a lot of things, but stupid isn't one of them. A day later she fully understood and agreed wholeheartedly with my decision. No matter what friction existed between us, she knew that my love for her and the kids was boundless and that I would do anything to keep them safe. But that didn't stop her from being junkyard dog mean during our discussions. And then she dropped a bomb on me.

"What about us?" she asked.

"You and the kids are my first priority. I'll find a way to keep you safe."

"Yet you still want a divorce."

"I'm happier now," I said honestly. "Aren't you?"

"I won't help you with the domestic violence case unless you get back with me." She paused to let the power of her words sink in. "We have three kids, and I'm pregnant. No way can I do this alone. You're moving in immediately."

She knew she had the leverage she needed. Some nooses you simply can't escape. To her credit, that ultimatum put my priorities in order. The next day I went to buy a life insurance policy.

"Have you ever been charged with a felony or deferred adjudication?" the Allstate rep asked.

Ugh. Again with that question.

"What the hell does that have to do with life insurance? I'm young and healthy and want to give my family some security and peace of mind."

"That's very noble of you, Mr. Heifner, but we do a thorough background check. If you have an untoward past, they often deny coverage because your risk of early death rises. I need to be aware of any indiscretions before we proceed."

Utterly humiliated, I answered all of his questions truthfully and even took their tobacco test.

They denied me the policy.

There are few viable industries in El Paso. The narco biz is chief among them. Several people whom I still trusted might be able to offer counsel on my situation. They didn't get all the details about my situation and plans, just enough to solicit their advice.

"What do you mean he hired a hit man?" one friend said, aghast.

"Yeah, he brought the guy to my house. Some thug from a motorcycle gang." I told him the colors the guy wore.

"Those guys are bad news."

"So it's a valid threat?"

"*Si, mi amigo.* You're fucked."

"Then what do I do? Do I help the DEA put him away?"

"Why don't you just move out of El Paso?"

"Trust me, if I had more than a miniature bankroll, my family and I would already be living on an island somewhere."

"I don't like cops," my friend said. "Don't trust 'em, either. Too many are on the take these days. But I bet your friend is gonna screw up and make this case the fed's priority. I don't know, Chris. I can't tell you what to do."

"I'm never talking with you about this again. If I do go to work for the *tres letres*"—three letters: DEA—"I won't want your number on my call logs. You understand that, right?"

"Yes, I do."

We hugged, knowing this was good-bye. He hated rats, which is why he didn't tell me to do it. He would have had someone eliminate his problems, but I didn't have the resources to move, much less pay for a hit. A rat is the last thing I ever thought I'd become, but threats against my family change everything. Hell, even a joke to that effect deserved a beat-down. To me it was an offense worthy of a cell. If I had to be the one to put him there, so be it.

It was late in the afternoon when Jake called.

"Hey, Jake," I said, friendly as a lapdog.

"Hey. Just makin' sure you're behavin'. Come have a beer with me."

This was a deviation from his normal routine, but everything between us was a test now.

"Sure, where you at?"

"Applebee's on Airways." He was jittery. I could hear it in his voice.

"Be there in a few."

Not Jake's usual hangout, but a public place, so I'd be safe.

"Look, man, I love ya," he said when I arrived, "but I've been under a lot of stress lately."

"You don't have kids or a job," I joked. "You stressed out from trying to decide which strip club to go to?"

He didn't think it was funny. Nor did I actually, but if I didn't make an attempt at humor, I was afraid I might jab a fork in his eye.

He launched into a diatribe about what it was like to take care of everyone, especially John, his brother, and, of course, me. He complained how no one took care of him and about all the pressure he felt simply trying to live how he wanted to live. He rambled on about what he wanted, bullshit vanity stuff like cosmetic surgery for the bags under his eyes, Bosley hair restoration, and laser skin resurfacing. He even had the nerve to complain about getting his five thousand dollar veneers redone.

I let him talk, waiting for him to apologize and take back the threats he made against my family. More than an apology, I expected him to try to overcompensate by offering me cash or sending us on some great vacation. But that never happened. It was all about him.

"So, are we cool?" he finally asked.

"Sure, brother," I shrugged. "I told you that yesterday."

"Alrighty then." He glanced at his gold Movado. "I gotta get home to the missus."

Jake signaled for the check. The bartender brought *separate* checks. Forget the apology or the apology gift, that fucker couldn't even buy me a few beers and an appetizer. He knew I didn't have a dime on me.

"Hey, man, could you get this?" I said. "I don't have any cash on me, and Missy has my ATM card."

He looked at me like I'd raped his dead grandmother with a backhoe. "Didn't you just hear me? I can't take care of anyone anymore."

He walked out, leaving me with a twenty-six-dollar bill that I couldn't pay. I sat there for a minute, completely shocked, then realized that not only did he not pick up my tab, he also stuck me with a few of his beers.

Sonofabitch!

Lifting my empty bottle, I motioned to the bartender. "Could I have another? I'm gonna stay a little longer. But I gotta move my car to the back of the restaurant. My wife's getting off work, and I don't want her to see it out front when she drives by."

"No problem," the bartender said, tapping his wedding band. "I know how that goes. It'll be waiting for you when you get back."

"Great, thanks."

I got in my car and drove off. Fuck him. Fuck Jake. Fuck my life.

❧

D-day arrived. We had an appointment at the Federal Justice Center on South Mesa Hills. I made Joe drive. At this point I couldn't be too cautious. I parked my car a few miles away, took a cab to a spot near his office, and walked the rest of the way.

In Joe's Cadillac Escalade I made him take the most circuitous route imaginable: turning left up one street, right down another, stopping, doing U-turns, speeding up, slowing down. I watched the rear window like a hawk on a rabbit. This wasn't high stakes; it was the *highest* of stakes. To his credit Joe played it cool—a little too cool, which annoyed me—but I'm sure I annoyed him, too. He was probably ready to fit me for a straight jacket by the time we arrived.

The guest parking lot was oh-so-intelligently placed directly in front of the Justice Center. If someone was staking the place out, looking for, oh, I don't know, informants like me, no friggin' way could you enter the building unnoticed. Great.

After the first gate you had to walk fifty yards to reach the entrance. Even a high school photographer or a shitty sniper could snap you in that distance. Once Joe parked the car, I wanted to bolt. But not Joe. He lingered outside his luxury SUV, primping his hair in the side mirror. I ducked behind it, acting like I was tying my shoes, not standing up until he was finally ready to go.

He walked briskly, thank God, and I didn't breathe until we were inside, staring at the security guard and the metal detector.

"We have a 2:00 p.m. at the DEA office," Joe said to the burly guard.

"Sign in, and step through the metal detector."

In the elevator came that same pang in my gut from when I was being taken into the Potter County Jail for the first time. In the waiting area a receptionist sat behind bulletproof glass, the decor out of some cheesy country club—green carpet spotted with a hideous cherry pattern and enough potpourri to mask the stench of a rotting corpse. With George Bush photos on the wall and assorted fishing and hunting magazines on the coffee table, it was only slightly more elegant and no more comfortable than that Potter pisshole. I could barely breathe, so Joe did the honors.

"Excuse me," he said to the clerk under glass. "We have an appointment, Chris Heifner with counsel."

Jesus, who'd want to work in a place like this? It reeked of sadness. All it was missing was that sign from the *Inferno*: "Abandon all hope, ye who enter here." Why does anyone want to work in a prison? I guess I'd feel different if I were the one with the badge and the gun. I just wanted to tell them my story, put my family and me in the Witness Protection Program, and hope the new life they gave us somewhere else was better than the one I was suffering in Hell Paso.

Within moments the two agents who had come to my house, along with three other agents, walked into the waiting area and led us into an adjacent conference room. Every door had electronic key locks, but this room was the only place other than the waiting room where visitors could come and go freely. That didn't make it feel any more welcoming.

Everyone took a seat. Joe started to make his way in but noticed I wasn't moving.

"Chris?"

The wheels of my mind were spinning as if buried in sand.

"Chrisssssss?"

The moment I walked into that conference room, life as I knew it, life as my family knew it, and life as Jake and his crew knew it changed forever. I tried to make my legs move, but they wouldn't budge. *Where's the nearest defibrillator in case I flatline?* I thought.

The agents noticed my hesitation and began to talk among themselves. Then I thought of my wife, my children, and that motherfucker who had hired a vile piece of shit to commit unspeakable atrocities against them. Rage flowed to the surface, my face flushed, my balls swelled and dropped, and I knew exactly what I had to do.

"Chris, are you okay?"

I looked Joe dead in the eyes. "Yes. I am. I'm fuckin' great."

14

Beautiful Disaster

There were no pictures on the walls, nothing else in the room. No distractions. Both the room and table were designed to be non-threatening. The table was round, so everyone was equal. It was meant to be bland, and it succeeded.

Two more agents came into the room carrying thick manila folders stuffed with papers, some undoubtedly pertaining to me. They introduced themselves and shook our hands. If I wanted to stay alive and keep my family safe, I had to start thinking differently—about everything. I'd have to be cognizant of my surroundings at all times, down to the smallest details. For instance, all the DEA agents wore jeans, short-sleeve button-down dress shirts, and what appeared to be steel-toed tennis shoes.

I gave the agents a tough-guy stare and waited for someone to speak. They all returned the look.

The agent from the Texas attorney general's office finally broke the silence. "So, why are you here, Chris?"

"Are you kidding me? You were the ones at my house a couple days ago."

"And . . . what do you want to do?"

"I might be interested in helping you guys out."

"What made you change your mind?" asked the agent who had been with him.

"Jeff threatened to kill my kids and introduced me to the hit man he hired. I know that by working with you guys I'll gain some assurances. Right?"

The Texas AG dodged my question. "Why did Jeff threaten you and your family?"

"Because after you guys left, I went and told him about your visit."

Every agent in the room blew his stack. "*Why did you do that? We asked you not to tell him!*"

Defending my rationale was pointless. Besides, once a bear has been poked, the damage is done. I explained long-form how Jake reacted, and I offered some insight into his logic—or lack thereof. I had hoped for a little F. Lee Bailey or Johnny Cochran from Joe, but he just kicked back and enjoyed the show. Maybe he figured I was doing okay on my own.

"Before I go any further, I want to define our relationship."

"What do you mean?" asked DEA Agent D.

"I mean, am I gonna be prosecuted for anything I reveal?"

"We can't promise anything, but the short answer is no. It's not immunity because the US attorney can prosecute if he chooses. But as long as you don't double-cross us or keep trafficking drugs and you fulfill your obligations as a confidential informant, he won't."

"Sort of like a get-out-of-jail 'not quite free' scenario," I said.

Agent D laughed. "Pretty much."

Joe nodded. Good enough for him, good enough for me. Conditional immunity was a hell of a lot better than a RICO charge.

"What about protecting my family?"

"We do a threat assessment that considers several factors," Agent D said. "But I've only known a handful of cases that required desperate measures along the lines of the Witness Protection Program. There are some things we can do, however, but we'll cross that bridge when we come to it. Just don't go to Mexico. For any reason. We can't protect you there."

Crossing that bridge when we came to it didn't sound like much protection at all. But the meager platitudes he was offering were better than my current situation. I'd be working with a net, only it had gaping holes in it. I just had to be damn careful where I fell.

"Third and final question: What are my obligations as an informant?"

Agent D shrugged. "You do whatever you can within the boundaries of the law to give us the information we need to stop illegal activities and catch the bad guys."

"I have a bullshit family violence charge pending against me. Can you guys put in a good word with the DA for me? I can't help you if my probation is revoked."

All the agents looked around the room at one another like I was a used car salesman. But fuck them, my ass was on the line, and this whole process seemed way too simple. I talk, and that conversation potentially takes my head off the chopping block for a RICO charge and the domestic violence charge and provides my family with some safety from a hired gun. It sounded good in theory, but the reality sent an icy shiver up my spine. Ultimately, I didn't have much choice. If nothing else, that I *felt* safer, especially for my loved ones, was worth it. Also, their asses were on the line, too. It wouldn't look so good in the news if my family or I got murdered and it was later revealed that agents handling the case didn't take the threat seriously.

I took Joe into the waiting room to get his opinion. "So? You know the situation. Am I missing something?"

"No, Chris. It sounds good to me."

"You sure?"

"Yes, but it's your call."

I needed an objective hard-ass, not a yes man with flip approval. But it was now or never. I swallowed my fear and walked back into the room.

"Okay, let's do this."

"Fill out this form, and sign it," Agent D said, pushing a sheet of paper across the table.

It was a simple one-pager, full of pertinent personal info—social security number, phone numbers, the names of my kids, home address, and the one that made me sweat: next of kin—along with the simple rules I needed to follow. There was also a loosely worded disclaimer that the DEA wouldn't be responsible for my death or dismemberment. Wonderful. Joe looked it over and gave the thumbs-up.

Just as I was about to sign, Agent D, who would be my handler, said, "We can do the background interview today. Then we'll get your fingerprints and photograph you for our records."

I froze. "Hold on a sec. Where do you keep this info?"

"Under lock and key. The only people with access to it are my partner, my boss, and I."

This was a big fucking deal that scared me to death. I was crossing a line that guaranteed pain, suffering, and death if I were ever outed. A simple swipe of a pen, and I would be playing for the other team.

"Are you in or not?" Agent D asked.

This was insane but unavoidable.

"Fuck it. Let's do it." I signed the form and pushed it back across the table. Life, as I knew it, was officially over.

"Can we take a break for a minute?" I asked. "I need a Diet Coke, and I gotta take a leak."

"No problem," said the Texas AG agent.

They escorted me to the restroom in a secure area.

"I'll wait for you out here," the escorting agent said at the door to the men's room.

I locked myself in a stall. My head in my hands, I tried not to hyperventilate. I was playing with people's lives, mine included. I would have called Missy, but my cell was in Joe's car. So I sat there, alone, pissing like a woman. When my ass got sore, it was time to face the music.

While I was washing my hands at the sink, two other DEA agents walked in talking about basketball. They barely acknowledged my presence, making me feel like a second-class citizen. But without people like me people like them couldn't do their jobs. When I finally reemerged, the escorting agent was nowhere to be found. Unsupervised, I wandered the bowels of DEA headquarters. Not knowing whether this was a test, I decided not to push it and found my way back to the conference room. A sweating Diet Coke was waiting on the table for me.

"Let's get started, shall we?" Agent D said. "Tell us what you did for Jeff Andes."

"I'm not gonna be prosecuted, right?"

"Right."

I was now a passenger on the scariest roller coaster ever devised. I could hear the clicking as the car climbed the initial ascent.

The meeting lasted about two hours. It was surreal to admit my crimes to a room full of feds, but I removed myself emotionally from the situation, as I did as a trafficker. I stayed cool and played the part.

"What did you do with the money?"

"Well, I bought—"

I quickly clammed up and marched Joe into the hallway.

"Joe, I bought my car and a bunch of other stuff with that money," I whispered. "I don't want them seizing it."

"I don't think they want to do that, but just to be safe, let me check."

Joe popped his head in the conference room and explained my concern.

"We don't want your car," the Texas AG agent replied loud enough for me to hear. "We just want to know everything you did with Jeff."

We went back into the room, and the Texas AG finished his spiel.

"You can testify in court about that stuff, if needed, but it makes things hard for him to deny when we confront him with our evidence. Remember, we're not after you. If we were, we would have reported your probation violations."

I was starting to see a method to their madness, even though they weren't telling me anything. It was a one-way street. But if they were faking their sincerity, they were better actors than me.

Only a few of them spoke, but everyone took copious notes, and if I wanted another soda or a tissue to wipe the sweat from my face, they were happy to oblige. They seemed genuinely concerned with my plight. I was actually impressed.

"So why are you helping us again?" Agent D asked.

"To protect my family. I made a mistake and did some things I'm not proud of. Now I'm paying for it, and I need help. I'm hoping I can right a few wrongs along the way."

"Do you owe Jeff money? Or is there anything else we should know?"

I shook my head. "He threatened my wife and kids. Now he's my mortal enemy, and I want him to burn."

"We obviously have a lot more to talk about," Agent D said. "Can you come back tomorrow? You can bring your attorney if you like."

Joe blanched at the prospect of sitting through more boring debriefings, but I wanted him to shift his focus to my domestic violence charge. I could handle the DEA meetings, and if I ran into any snags, he was only a phone call away.

"I can come alone," I said.

"Sweet," Agent D said. "Is eleven good?"

"No problem."

"We'll do your fingerprints and mug shot tomorrow."

"Great."

That I had officially crossed the line sickened me. But what choice did I have? On the drive back to Joe's office, I barely said a word, just slunk down in the back seat replaying the conversation in my head.

"So how do you think it went?" I asked him.

"It went *very* well, Chris," he said. "You're a skilled negotiator and very eloquent. You should have been an attorney."

"Tell me about it," I said, mentally drop-kicking myself.

After my long walk and return taxi to my car, I finally looked at my cell phone. Dozens of missed calls, most from Jake. He might have had me followed and was calling to find out what the hell was going on. But my first call was to Missy to make sure she and the kids were okay.

"We're fine. How are you? How'd it go?"

"It went. I gotta go back tomorrow. Tell you the rest tonight."

"Okay. I love you," she said, clearly scared.

"I love you, too," I said, just as scared as she was, if not more.

I screwed on my courage and called Jake.

"Nutty! Where the hell ya been?"

"I've had a shitty day. I was with my attorney discussing my domestic violence charge. Then I had to go see my PO. Then I went and met with

Missy to work things out since we're getting back together. That bitch is holding me hostage with the domestic violence charge."

I played it up, criticizing her, knowing I could get a reaction out of him to gain some sympathy.

"Mmmmm-hmmmmm," Jake said. "I was just checking up on you."

"Thanks."

"Wanna go eat?"

"No, I don't have any money. Besides, I have an errand to run, and I wanna take a nap. I'm beat."

He left me high and dry the last time, and I was tired of talking to him. He tried to call back, but I didn't answer. Fuck him and his sudden interest in my everyday life. He should have expressed concern about my well-being before he brought a hit man to my fucking house.

At Scenic Drive, a beautiful vantage offering spectacular views of downtown El Paso and Juarez, I parked my car near the road leading to the television towers, and although it's marked TRESPASSING, I walked up to find a quiet place to think.

A cauldron, my brain roiled with emotions and stupefying what-ifs. There could be no plan for this problem because I wasn't in control. There was no guidebook to study, no one who had done this before whom I could tap. Most informants had been arrested and sang like canaries for lighter sentences. Walking in off the street like I had done was way outside the norm. I was in uncharted waters and, for someone who thrives on stability and certainty, way outside my comfort zone. I called the only person I knew who would give me good old-fashioned advice: my dad.

Not my biological father, my stepfather: the man who had adopted and raised me. He married my mom when I was five and divorced her when I was eighteen, but he was still my dad, and I spoke to him often. A good ol' country boy at heart, he was retired military and one of the smartest people I've ever known. Book smart and street smart, the man had knowledge. Besides, he was always happy, which I definitely wasn't. I took a seat on a big rock overlooking the city and dialed his number. He didn't know about my arrests or problems, but he'd give me honest advice.

"What's up, Dad?"

"Just got back from fishing," he said.

"Catch anything?"

"Nothing worth talking about. But I had to beat a moccasin off the boat with my favorite flipping rod. Figured there was only room for one of us, and he disagreed. I managed to convince him."

I laughed for the first time in days. It felt so good.

"What's going on out there?" he asked.

"I have problems you couldn't even imagine. I just need a lucky br—"

"Stop. I only have a moment, so I'll say this fast. Listen to me. Don't become a victim of your own bullshit, Chris. The only thing you can control in life is yourself. Do that, and leave everything else for the birds. You got that?"

"Yeah."

"Good. I love you. Gotta go."

Five seconds of advice, and everything was clear as moonshine. I couldn't control Jake or the DEA agents or Missy or anyone or anything else in my life. I needed to focus my energies on what I needed to do and let fate handle the rest. For the next couple of hours, I sat on that rock, flicking ants off my leg, staring up at a cloudless sky, enjoying the sheer nothingness of the day.

I could do this. I could win this. I would win this. Rather than dwell on my problems, I counted the blessings in my life. I needed to forgive—and forget—the past.

That night I circled the wagons and made a list of people whom I would quit talking to. Courtesy of my new job, the list was long. I intended to become a temporary recluse until the danger passed. I didn't know how long it would take, but I knew it was better for everyone involved. It was much easier and safer simply to disappear. I contemplated changing my phone number but that would spook Jake. I hoped everyone else would get the hint and give me space.

I was still in the dark about how the confidential informant (CI) process worked. I imagined I'd assemble a mosaic of Jake and his organization and the DEA would use that to close the case, just like they do in the movies. I'd provide the inside details, and then a SWAT team would raid Jake's house a few hours later. If I could keep my head low—and attached—until the end of the trial and sentencing, then everything would be okay.

I showed up early the next day and parked at a local restaurant, the Great American, just up the street. After a quick bite I walked over to the Federal Justice Center, which I nicknamed the Halls of Justice. As promised, I brought documentation and corroborating evidence, which I had kept under lock and key for years. The evidence was nothing more than cell phone records and receipts, but when put into proper context, it was damning.

They took me downstairs to a minijail where I was photographed and fingerprinted. Then back upstairs to the conference room.

This time there were only three agents: Texas AG, Agent D, and some other guy. A fourth agent, a Cuban with a funny accent introduced as the head of the local DEA branch, soon joined us.

"I just wanted to introduce myself and let you know I'm the boss here," Chief O said. "If you ever need to speak to me, don't be afraid to ask."

"Okay," I said, impressed. The guy was hard-core. He came from Miami during the big cocaine days and had seen frontline action for a while.

I gave an exhaustive account of every load I ran for Jake: the loads, the destinations, the contacts, everything. I also gave them a full background on Jake and everyone in his crew. Whatever tidbit I knew, no matter how small and inconsequential I thought it was, they got. I left out anything embarrassing to me or crimes I committed on my own volition. This was about taking down Jake, not digging a deeper hole for me.

Before long my suspicions were confirmed. Turns out the DEA knew considerably more about Jake and his operation than they let on. Every time I thought I was revealing something new—a previously unmentioned person, for example—they pulled out a mug shot and a file and said, "Oh, you mean this guy."

"Do you have my mug shot in there?" I asked.

"Of course," Agent D said. "Which one do you wanna see?"

I realized just how close I had come to getting wrapped up in a federal charge. They already knew everything—well, almost everything. But more than enough to lock me away for a very long time. Looks like some luck had finally come my way.

"So when are you gonna send in the SWAT team?" I asked after the grueling three-hour session had ended.

Agent D's face went sour. "The what?"

"I gave you everything you need to get this son of a bitch. Go get him."

"That's not how it works."

"What do you mean? My job is over. I told you everything."

Texas AG's chuckle was so frightening I had to check my BVDs. "Chris, your job is just beginning." He started packing up his files. "Now we need to catch him in the act."

"Catch him in the act? I don't work with Jake anymore."

"Well, if you can't give us something new, most of this info is useless."

My spine turned to jelly. "I don't understand."

"We need fresh information," Agent D explained.

This wasn't what I signed up for. I wasn't a provocateur or a spy. I was just a pipeline of knowledge—brains, not brawn. What they were suggesting could get me chainsawed into pieces. For a moment I seriously considered taking my chances with the hit man.

Agent D pulled out a tape recorder and a stack of tapes, each labeled Drug Enforcement Administration. He showed me how to use it, pointing out various features and demonstrating the earpiece while I talked. He queued up a practice tape and played with it a few times to prove it worked. I didn't say a word. I couldn't.

"I can tell you're hesitant," said Texas AG. "But everything will be okay. Just don't do a drug deal on your own. Keep us informed, and don't do anything unless you ask us first."

"This means I have to get hand-job close to Jake again."

Agent D laughed. "Can you?"

"Yeah, but it'll take a few months. And that means I'll have to hang around him a lot more than I am now."

Agent D nodded. "Then we're good?"

I shrugged. "I guess so."

I was petrified. Bullets would have bounced off my face. I thought being a CI was just telling a story. Now I was an undercover agent. James Bond got a bevy of superhot girls, wild weapons, and exotic cars. All I got was a shitty tape recorder.

"Let's call Jeff right now and record it," the other agent suggested.

My eyes bulged. "*What?*"

"See if you can get him to say something incriminating."

The agent snatched the recorder and recorded an introduction: *The date and time is such and such, and agents blank and blank and blank are present. We are about to call Jeffrey Todd Andes at this number.* He stopped recording and looked at me. "Ready?"

No. While I knew I could record a conversation with Jake, I didn't want to do it with an audience. Still, I dialed the number, and the agent started the recorder. Jake answered, and just as I was about to say hello, the recorder started *playing* Agent D's voice from when he tested it. The ass-clown agent hit "Play," not "Record." I quickly hung up and gave the agent my fiercest fuck-you stare.

"*Seriously?*"

"Let's try this again," he replied.

Either he was dumber than shit or testing me, so I snatched the recorder, pressed "Record" and dialed Jake again.

"*Nutty!* What the hell are you doing?"

"Fucking phone, I dropped it by the radio," I said, giving the dumb agent another ice-down.

"That was the noise I heard?"

"Yeah. What'd you think it was?"

"I don't know," Jake said, disbelieving.

We chatted for a few minutes, but he didn't like talking to me on the phone. He preferred face-to-face discussions, and for good reason. First rule of drug trafficking: Never talk shop on the phone.

"That was good work," the agent said after I hung up.

"No thanks to you."

Agent D changed the subject. "Can we meet for lunch tomorrow to come up with a game plan?"

"Sure, but not here."

"Okay, here's my number." Agent D scribbled on a scrap of paper. "Call me, and we'll figure it out."

"Will do."

I couldn't get out of there fast enough. Walking off with my new DEA-issue tape recorder and stack of tapes, I had the sinking feeling that I had seriously screwed the pooch.

15

Let's Go Crazy

"What do you mean, they need fresh info? You gave them his organization on a silver platter! Let *them* investigate him."

The moment I returned, Missy bombarded me with questions.

"Apparently, that's not how it works."

"So how does it work?"

I collapsed onto the sofa. "I don't know, exactly."

She looked in my satchel, saw the tape recorder and the tapes, and glared at me. I hadn't even moved back in yet, and already I was in hot water.

Jake was calling me nonstop, suddenly concerned with my every movement. Maybe someone in the DEA was on the take. But I blamed my absence on Missy busting my balls. It was becoming increasingly hard to cover my tracks.

At my grandmother's house the DEA had called four times according to the caller ID log, which read "Drug Enforcement Administration." The last thing I needed was for Jake to pop in unannounced and check the phone log. I had to erase the digital memory of every phone in the house.

The following day I called in sick to Circuit City and met the DEA/ Texas AG dynamic duo at Village Inn, where we discussed ways to get back in Jake's good graces. But first I had to nip a few things in the bud.

"Quit calling my house. You trying to get me killed?"

Agent D gave me a perplexed look.

"DEA comes up on the caller ID." I shook my cell. "This is the only number you should use. And·block your number, too. I'm serious."

"Okay, okay," he said.

"The idea of this makes my stomach turn, but I just need to hang around him. Eventually, he'll trust me again."

"Oh, he'll trust you, especially after you told him about our visit."

"He's a dumbass. Charming, but a dumbass."

"Okay, then, here's the rules," Agent D explained. "You call me every time *before* you meet with him and every time *after* you leave. No exceptions."

"No problem. I'll check in frequently."

"Don't do *anything* on your own.· This isn't a rodeo, so don't be a cowboy. You aren't allowed to participate in anything illegal unless you have my permission and are doing it under DEA supervision. Okay?"

I nodded.

"And you don't need to record every phone conversation. I have to transcribe them, and I don't want to spend hours transcribing audio about whether or not you prefer big boobs to small ones."

"Big ones, definitely." I mimed a rack that bordered on ridiculous and squeezed them for added emphasis.

Blank stares.

"Just take notes about the conversations and put them with the tapes. Date, time, et cetera."

"Got it."

"When do you have time to drive around and show us everyone's house?"

"Might as well do it now."

I walked outside expecting to find a dark four-door sedan with tinted windows. Instead, there was a vomit green two-door Pontiac Grand Am with perfectly *clear* windows.

"Please tell me this isn't your car."

"It's the DEA's." Agent D motioned to the shotgun seat. "Chris, you ride up front, and he'll sit in back."

"How the hell am I supposed to hide?"

"Just duck down."

Fucking ludicrous. And then they frisked me before letting me in the car. Like I was going to carjack a couple of federal agents.

Inside the vehicle was a variety of weapons, cameras, binoculars, and paperwork. Definitely an unmarked cop car, but there I sat in plain view through that big, untinted window.

We drove all over Northeast El Paso, talking about the drug biz the entire way. They saw where Jake, Byron, and Richard lived and the various places we did business. We called the area Narco East, and Texas AG took notes as I pointed out every place I remembered.

Jake's house was on the list—and of course he called me just as we passed. He was standing outside! *Are you fucking kidding me?* Did he plant a tracker on me? I answered the phone and fumbled with the recorder while the agents silenced their phones and radios.

"Wassup, Nutty? Whatcha doin'?"

I almost said I was at work. "Shopping for shoes."

"I called Circuit City. They said you called in sick today."

"What are you, my mother?"

"Nah, man, just wanna make sure you're flying right."

"I'm an arrow. Let's go have a beer. Lemme get out of this store, and I'll see ya in forty-five. Cool?"

"Let's do it!"

Clearly, he couldn't find anyone else to play with.

The feds hustled me back to my car on the west side of town. I should have made them drop me off half a mile from where I parked and hoofed it the rest of the way, but I was still learning.

"You've been very helpful," Agent D said at my car, "but we need to figure out how to catch Jeff in the act."

"Look, it pains me to be around him, but I'll do it. Just give me a few weeks to warm him over."

"Haven't you already been hanging around him recently?" said the Texas AG from the backseat.

"There's a big difference between hanging around a guy and getting all up in his business. Just let me do my thing. And I need you to put in a good word with my PO if she calls you. Okay?"

"Okay," said Agent D.

───

Suffering from a nasty hangover after a long night of drinking with Jake, I made my way to Circuit City. Business was slow, so I formulated a plan. I needed to manage both my DEA contacts and Jake carefully, somehow steering them into a head-on collision. Easier said than done.

Needing some systematic rules, I generated a list:

- Create daily list of priorities, what to do to keep family and self alive
- Weekly status check, determining where I stood with Jake and the DEA
- Train brain to memorize everything
- Research every informant and spy case I can find
- Be disciplined

Not exactly masterstrokes, I realize, but they helped me focus on the task at hand and not lose perspective.

As I wrote my list, I tried to notice everything about my Circuit City surroundings. It took a lot of energy and was easier in short spurts than long hauls. Then came my first test, courtesy of my two least favorite coworkers, whom I nicknamed Gums and Chongo.

Gums was an ugly, short Mexican with a stupid smile perpetually plastered on his fat face. He made fun of everyone and everything but had never seen or done anything cool in his life. Chongo was the size of a boulder and just as dumb, the kind of *guido* meathead who routinely expressed himself through violence. My first day on the job, he asked me what I thought of the girl behind the counter. I picked up on his ruse and said she was cute. As expected, he told me she was his girlfriend and that I should stay away or else.

Because they were low-class losers, spending any time in their vicinity was maddening. They had run off two other employees from our department already, and while I normally had the strength to deal with dipshits like them, the DEA situation pushed me beyond my tolerance threshold.

The two knuckleheads started in with their usual banter and insults. I ignored them at first, working on my list. Then Chongo snatched it from my grasp.

"What's this?" he blurted, and he and Gums began to read it, not understanding the context.

"Another one of your fantasies, like Merrill Lynch and your fraternity?" Gums snarked.

I grabbed the list back, stuffed it in my pocket, and started walking away when they made some nasty comments about my children. I stopped dead in my tracks and about-faced, ready to take them both. But the list flashed through my mind. The last thing I needed now was to get arrested for aggravated assault in the middle of Circus City.

"You want some of me?" Chongo puffed, hoping for an altercation.

"You're not worth it. I quit."

Zapping them with a death ray wasn't permissible, so quitting was my only option. *Enjoy your lives in retail, losers.*

By the time I reached my car, my mind had fully clicked into damage control mode. I dialed my PO in Amarillo, the only one with any real authority over my case.

"Hi, Joyce."

"Hello, Chris, how are you?"

"Well, uh . . . there have been some big changes, and I really need your help."

The call lasted two hours. I laid it all on her.

"Wow." Long pause. "Wow."

"Both my attorney and DEA Agent D will be calling you to corroborate my story. I would really appreciate some leeway."

"After I speak with them, I'm inclined to remove you from local supervision. As long as you pay your monthly fees and report by phone, I can supervise you from up here."

"I appreciate that. I don't know who I can trust down here. And while I like my local PO, there's no telling who he knows."

"Everyone speaks highly of you, Chris. Just get your domestic violence case dismissed, and I'll see about having your probation ended early."

"Thank you. You don't know how much I appreciate this."

"And take care of your tickets. They could cause you major problems."

"My tickets?"

"Just take care of them."

My domestic violence hearing was set for August 2002. If what she said was true, I'd only be on probation for eighteen months. The minimum time was two years, and I could have done the full six, so this was a boon. But the tickets?

The last ticket came after being fired from Merrill Lynch. To blow off some steam, I raced a Mustang down the Border Highway in my Intrepid. We both saw the cop; the 'Stang bolted, but I actually pulled over and waited. When the cop asked me why I didn't try to run, I told him I'd already made enough bad decisions, like getting married, and begged for mercy. He laughed but still wrote me up.

My ticket attorney, Richard Robbins, did his thing, and $60 later it was over—or so I thought. Unfortunately, his notoriously rude secretary neglected to tell me that I needed to enroll in a defensive driving course . . . which resulted in a warrant for my arrest. I rushed to the courthouse, paid the $270, then went to Robbins's office and thanked them loudly for nearly screwing up my entire life. Why the hell hadn't Agent D told me about this? Surely, they knew about it.

Missy and I were preparing for the birth of our fourth child while I attempted to work myself back into Jake's good graces by accompanying him to the strip club every day. It was the nightmare of being a trafficker all over again, except this time I wasn't making any money. In fact, between attorney fees, court costs, and fixing Missy's financial mess, I was broke. Again.

"Can I borrow twenty bucks?" I asked Jake at Tequila Sunrise. Nothing cements a friendship like asking for a loan in a strip club.

"Get a fucking job, Nutty!"

As he launched into a tirade about taking care of people, I turned to Byron. "Man, I really need to borrow twenty bucks from someone."

"Wish I could help you," he said, tucking a fifty-dollar bill into a busty stripper's G-string.

Bastards. They had just dropped a few hundred on lap dances and drinks, but they couldn't peel off a measly twenty? So much for that extra fifteen hundred I gave Byron on the Memphis trip, along with a hundred here and a hundred there when he was broke and wanted to keep partying. Now that I needed a little green, I was persona non grata. The guilt I felt about throwing Byron under the same bus as Jake instantly vanished.

Interestingly, Jake's habits had changed. He still did his daily strip-club routine, but he wasn't going home as early. In fact, he'd often go home just to eat, then head out to another club, usually JB's, a hole-in-the-wall titty bar that offered free popcorn with your meager two-dollar cover. Though, to JB's credit, they did have the most beautiful strippers in El Paso, and maybe anywhere.

But now those amazing sights made me feel guilty whenever I went into a club. I was about to be a father of four. I wanted nothing to do with these places, but now I had no choice.

Jake's business had grown considerably. Byron was now his right-hand man and invested partner. They were using a more sophisticated system of stash houses and warehouses to store the dope. In the warehouses they palletized the drugs and put them on eighteen-wheelers to be trucked to warehouses they owned in other cities. Upon arrival the dope was broken down into smaller shipments and distributed to several new connections in each area. Loads were going to Boston, Memphis, Indianapolis, and Chicago. It was highly mechanized and methodical, but Jake was in way over his head.

Part of me desperately hoped he'd screw up and get arrested on his own. My ratting would lock him up forever then. But it never happened.

He had become a major player. He was running a big money game, and the DEA wanted to nail his entire supply chain and distribution network. It was going to be a long haul.

That's when I noticed two guys at another table who looked familiar. They were the two agents from the bathroom at DEA HQ. Either they were spying on me for backup or spying on Jake for intel. I nearly pissed my pants—but this is what it would be like until my job was finished—or I was.

My days consisted of getting drunk with people I didn't want to be around in places I didn't want to be, then going home to sleep off the buzz and, when I awoke, trying to spend some quality time with my kids. One day turned into a week, a week turned into a month. Then came the morning of Jake's frantic phone call.

"Get to my house. I need your help."

I rushed over, thinking he was being attacked or busted, calling Agent D en route. "I'm headed to Jeff's. He needs help, says it's an emergency. Be nearby, just in case."

"Will do."

When I arrived Jake was struggling to pull a brand-new ATV out of the back of his truck.

"This is your emergency?"

"Yeah, help me. I don't want to scratch it."

"Jesus Christ."

"C'mon, we got another to pick up at Las Cruces Motorsports."

"You bought two?" I could barely afford to eat, and he was out buying multi-thousand-dollar power toys.

"Yup. I don't wanna ride alone. I'm thinking about getting another street bike, too, so I can have someone to ride with." He sensed my desperation for money and salted the wound. "Should have stayed under my wing, Nutty. You could be buying one of your own, and your kids would be *safer* riding these."

Cocksucker. I wanted to grab the shovel in the corner of his garage and beat his head into the shape of a canoe, but with my luck the DEA had him under photosurveillance. Still, this Dr. Jekyll/Mr. Hyde routine had become standard operating procedure. I never knew which Jake to expect. Every weekend he and his crew went to Red Sands, a popular desert recreation area, to ride ATVs. He invited me on half the trips, but sometimes, just to be mean, he'd invite me, then take off without me and tell me about the fun I missed after he returned. He was punishing me for leaving his crew. I couldn't wait to see the look on his face when the DEA nailed his ass.

"I think I wanna buy two more quads for you guys," he said one day on the way back from a ride.

"In that case can I borrow the black one that's been wrecked a lot?" I asked. "I wanna take the family on a picnic."

"Hell, no! They're only for when you ride with *me*."

July was sliding away, and the DEA was itching to get something solid on him. I was almost back in the fold, but he still wasn't talking to me like in the past. We had reached a stalemate. That's when DEA HQ summoned me. When I arrived Chief O was waiting in the conference room with Agent D, along with another agent I had never met, an older Puerto Rican.

"So, where are we?" Chief O asked.

"Chris is getting us some good info but nothing specific," Agent D replied.

"Well, we gotta do something! Jeff's using trucks. Let's introduce him to Agent P," he motioned to the Puerto Rican, "and say he's a truck driver."

Chief O seemed about as strategic as Jake.

"That might work," I said. "But you'll have to hang around Jake for a while until he trusts you."

"Screw that!" said Chief O. "We introduce him, and they do the deal right then and there."

This was the premier drug-fighting organization in the world?

Agent D and I both rolled our eyes. Every possible variation of this plan was idiotic and destined for failure. Jake might have been a dumbass, but he was a smart dumbass. He would have it sniffed out in a cocaine heartbeat. Chief O left for another meeting, and I sat there flabbergasted.

"Did Jake tell you about his recent arrest?" Agent D asked.

I was shocked. "No!"

"He got popped in Georgia with over a hundred grand on him."

"I remember him being arrested once before in Chicago with a lot of money and fighting it."

"Yeah, well, he's a moron. He was smoking pot and driving without his seat belt. They searched his car and found the cash."

"No wonder he's been acting strange."

"You have to help us get something concrete on him," said the Texas AG.

"Just give it a little more time. I'll play the poverty card and ask him to help me make some money. Is that entrapment?"

Agent D shook his head. "Nope."

"My domestic violence hearing is in a few weeks. After that I'll pin him down. I just can't concentrate right now."

When my court date arrived, Missy didn't come because she was eight months pregnant and wanted to sleep late. When Joe saw me, he looked horrified.

"Where's your wife?"

"Sleeping."

"She should have come! They probably won't dismiss if she's not here."

Panic washed over me. I called her at least a dozen times, but no answer. We had no choice but to go into the courtroom without her.

Joe swaggered up to the assistant district attorney, and they chatted while I verged on a panic attack. Normally, I couldn't get Missy *off* the phone. The one time I needed her *on* it, she was MIA.

Joe and the ADA tried calling her repeatedly, in case she was intentionally ignoring me, both to no avail. Eventually, Joe walked back over, looking defeated.

"They didn't dismiss."

"What's that mean?"

"We rescheduled for next week."

As I sped back to the house, my mind conjured horrible thoughts. What if she was in trouble? What if the hit man had come to the house?

She was sitting on the couch watching television.

"*What. The fuck. Are you. Doing?*"

"I watered the lawn, and now I'm watching a show. What?"

"Why didn't you answer your phone?"

"I turned it to silent. I didn't want to be bothered."

"Jesus, Missy!" I threw up my hands. "You knew I was going to court. They didn't dismiss the case because *you* didn't answer."

"You didn't tell me to answer it."

"I don't tell you to breathe, either. Jesus."

16

Fuck tha Police

"Turn the radio down!" Missy screamed.

"Everyone thinks I'm a thug. Might as well act like one!" I said, pulling out of the courthouse parking garage, windows down, sunroof open, NWA's "Fuck tha Police" blasting.

It was a day to celebrate. Joe worked his magic, and with Missy—smiling whenever the ADA looked our way—they conditionally dismissed my domestic violence case. All charges against me would be dropped provided I completed an anger management course.

"I hate you," Missy said.

"I hate me, too," I said, my head bobbing to the beat.

There wasn't another honeymoon, though. I slept on the couch, and we barely spoke. Unfortunately, my shitty luck was rubbing off on her now, too. Loretto Academy fired her from her show choir director position because she didn't have a degree. My grandmother knew the school's president, Sister Buffy Boesen. Knowing Grandma, I figured she probably bitched about my tribulations to her gal-pal, who then associated my problems with my wife. Just speculation, but now Missy was working a call center and I was unemployed. Again.

The birth of our fourth child at the end of August was both our only joy and a welcome break from the insanity of working with the DEA. Jake and Sandra wanted to congratulate us in person, but he probably just wanted to find out where we lived now. I kept him at bay by saying that

Missy hated him for getting me into the drug business and that she'd kick his ass if she ever saw him.

She went back to work shortly after giving birth—which made me Mr. Mom. My son was two and a half, and my other daughter was eighteen months. Factor in the newborn, and I was neck deep in formula, diapers, baby powder, and shit. Even though I was practically mainlining caffeine, I fell asleep at the first quiet moment. As my kids drank their bottles, ate their animal crackers, and watched TV, I wondered: Would they still love me if they knew how much of a colossal failure I was?

My biggest worry was some random bad guy coming to the house. I had three kids, but only two arms. So I went into Rambo mode, working out like a madman and stashing weapons—machetes and lead pipes—strategically around the house, out of view and grasp of the kids. They made me feel safer, but ultimately, it was pointless. If someone wanted to hurt my family or me, we were easy pickin's.

Like me, Missy only wanted to sleep. We took turns watching the kids while the other napped. At some point I tried to study for the GMAT, setting my sights on grad school. I needed something positive on which to hang some shred of hope. Jake knew I was utterly defeated, and he took every opportunity to rub it in my face.

"Guess what I did?" he said.

"Cured cancer."

"Screw that. I bought some rental houses."

"How the hell'd you do that?"

"Simple. I gave the money to my dad, and he bought 'em."

"Must be nice."

"Don't worry, Nutty. You'll be back on your feet in no time."

"I guess."

"Sandra wants to sell her Integra, and I'm gonna get her a new car."

I was recording the conversation, trying—hoping—to prove that Jake was doing something big. He had just bought new furniture and expensive jewelry for Sandra. He didn't spend money unless he had money, so blowing almost a hundred grand on toys should pique the DEA's interest.

"How the hell are you spending so much money without violating the Large Currency Transactions Reporting Act?"

"I'll tell ya later," he said smugly.

Agent D and company were writhing that they didn't have anything concrete. Personally, I don't think they dedicated enough resources to the case. With just a couple of weeks of twenty-four-hour surveillance, they could have caught Jake in the act. But a lot of these guys were eight-to-fivers; when the bell rang they couldn't wait to get home. Why didn't they have a second or third shift to run at full operational capacity, 24/7? Also, they handled multiple cases at once, which complicated matters. To me this was everything. To them it was just another case.

"Chris, the tapes are great," Agent D said. "But I need you to talk with him about the laundering."

"In person."

"Will you wear a wire?"

"Uhh . . . okay."

We met the next day in Narco East to wire me before I met with Jake. No biggie, I thought, just two friends talking.

Agent D had me follow him in my car and wanted to stop in the parking lot of a park, but the park was near the school Byron's kids attended. The other place they suggested was a street near Byron's mom's house. El Paso was certainly big enough to find a spot that wasn't near any of the players. We settled on a lot behind Wal-Mart. Three cars showed up with two agents in each. None of these guys did anything without his partner.

Agent D pulled out a bag. Their gadgetry was less sophisticated than my kids' Speak & Spell—and nearly as large.

"What the fuck is this?"

"It's all we've got," he said.

"You're shitting me, right?"

I was wearing khaki shorts and a polo. To hide that monstrosity I needed long pants and an overcoat. Thank freakin' God I had the presence of mind to bring a pair of pants with me. While agents began searching my car, making sure I didn't have weapons or drugs, Agent D and the Texas AG wired me up.

One part of the wire—like a large pager—stayed in my pocket while its antenna attached to my ankle. The whole shebang was about as obscure as a handheld GPS tracker. The other device was a miniature tape recorder, the same kind you can find at Radio Shack. The microphone went on my waist and connected to a recorder taped to the other ankle. If Jake didn't see all this shit on me, he deserved to be busted.

"Go straight to Jeff's," said Agent D. "Don't play the radio in your car, and don't stand near a TV or radio while you're in his house because it records ambient noise. You have thirty minutes or we're coming in, guns blazing."

"Okay . . ." I said. The thought of backup actually put me at ease. It was the sheer lunacy of the operation and their low-tech tools that worried me. No wonder the government is losing the War on Drugs.

Jake loved to brag and talk shit at the clubs, but there was no way to record anything clearly with all the blaring music. Besides, most of the girls are touchy-feely when they give you dances. They'd find the wire immediately.

Agent D was nervous for me but not enough to keep from decking me out in World War I–era circuitry. On the phone with him, I could hear radio chatter as the other agents got into position. But I still had no plan.

Fuck it, I thought. I got out of my car and went into Jake's house without knocking.

"Nutty! What are you doing here?"

"I was in the neighborhood."

I sat at the kitchen bar, as far away from the television as possible, and tried not to do anything like cross my legs. The TV was extra loud.

"Could you turn that thing down?" I said, indicating the TV and squinting. "I've got a massive hangover."

Jake walked up behind me and—

CLICK! CLICK! CLICK! CLICKCLICK! CLICK!

I knew it was a stun gun and braced for impact. Instead, Jake turned the TV up even louder. I gave him my patented douche-bag stare-down.

"All right, all right, I'm just fucking with you." He lowered the volume and showed me the stun gun. "Like my toy?"

"It's scary."

"It's meant to be." He put it on the table. "What's up?"

"I came over to figure out how you're laundering your millions of dollars from drug money proceeds. Could you please speak into my shirt collar?"

He gave me the weirdest look, then walked over and grabbed my chest. My eyes flashed daggers again. He let go of my shirt but redirected his stare to my groin.

"What? You want to grab my dick now, too, homo?"

Jake laughed and backed off. My heart resumed beating.

"Shiiiit, I ain't launderin' nothin'. But I do need to get rid of Sandra's Acura and get her a new ride."

"About time! That car is what? A '92 Integra? You've had how many new cars in recent years?"

"Hell, I spent five Gs on the rims for my Eddie Bauer Expedition," he said with a shit-eating grin.

"How much you selling the car for?"

"Four grand. I need two cars, actually. One for her and one with a big trunk like your Intrepid."

The trunk in my Intrepid was huge. I could have packed a herd of cattle in that thing and the range they grazed on. It was so cursed now, I was dying to get rid of it. I had paid cash for it, but when the shit hit the fan, I took out a thirteen-thousand-dollar loan against it to put some green in my pocket. I still owed six thousand on it, and now it didn't run so well.

"You always liked that car, didn't you?"

"I love it," he replied.

"So buy it from me. It's worth twelve or thirteen easy. Give me Sandra's car and six Gs, and you'll come out ahead."

Jake beamed. "That's a great idea."

"See, laundering money is easy," I said with a chuckle.

I messed with his head a little longer, but he didn't talk. The plan was for me to go home and get the car, then he'd give me the money to pay off the title. At that point the DEA's needs were secondary to my own. I walked out of his house feeling like a king. I was trading an unreliable, cursed piece of shit with a monthly payment for a reliable, paid-off cherry—and I did it by letting Jake think he was fucking me over.

Even better, I wore a wire and lived to tell about it. Agent D and Company probably weren't expecting me to get any info; I think they were testing me to make sure I was capable of being a CI. As they tore their lo-tech crap off me at Wal-Mart, I asked Agent D if it was against the rules to engage in an economic exchange with Jake.

"He didn't say it was drug proceeds, so go ahead."

Fewer than thirty minutes later, I left Jake's house with six thousand dollars in a Wal-Mart bag and got in my new red car. Once I got him the Intrepid's title from the bank, he would give me the title to the Integra. I flipped the script on Jake and was on cloud nine. If he got buyer's remorse and threatened me again, I hoped that would force the DEA to bust him.

Jeff ultimately bought Sandra an Audi and bitched about the Intrepid. But my Jedi mind trick deflected his complaints while I continued to play the poor card and begged for opportunities to do some work.

"Can you get me anything?" I asked. "A money run?"

"I can get you a load," he said.

"Uh, I don't know about that."

If I was too eager, he'd get curious about my change of heart. But my stellar acting job was winning him over. He started talking to me again, even over the phone—which he never did before. But that still didn't close the deal for the DEA. They needed hard evidence.

As the warm weather was ending, a few hours of picnicking and enjoying the sun with my family helped me forget about the problems we faced. My son saw a basketball court for the first time and walked his little butt all the way across the park to check it out. It was hilarious watching them all cry over getting sand in their shoes and their astonishment as we fed the pigeons. For a few moments I felt like a regular dad.

But the stress revived the cycle of sickness. The GMAT exam took place in a couple of days, and right on cue I could feel myself coming down with a fever.

"What's the deal with grad school?" Missy asked.

"I'll earn my MBA and find a great job afterwards. I'll just have to doctor up my résumé a little. I can't exactly include 'confidential informant for the DEA.'"

"How are we going to pay for this?"

"Financial aid. We'll probably get an extra six or seven thou every semester. Combined with your income, we'll be fine."

"But that's a loan, right?"

"Yeah, but we can worry about that in the future."

She shook her head. "I don't know."

"Join the club."

We needed diapers, and I needed Theraflu, so we stopped at a Walmart we seldom visited. Standing in the over-the-counter medicine aisle, I looked up and saw one of the agents from my debriefings with his family. We made eye contact, said nothing, and moved along.

Being nonchalant about my clandestine activities was much easier than I expected, and the stress over my "job" paled in comparison to the stress I had about money. Running a household of six was an expensive operation. Maybe I made myself sick for nothing. Maybe it was all in my head.

Detouring through electronics to the diaper section, I ran into the agent and his family again. Again, I ignored them and turned down another aisle . . . where I came face to face with my worst nightmare: Hank the hitman. He was looking at cameras with a woman and a child. I immediately turned around, but he caught me out of the corner of his eye.

"Hey, how's the family?"

I acted like I didn't hear him and walked away. My heart was stampeding in my chest like a herd of buffaloes. I beelined to Missy and told her that I'd thrown up and damaged some products. We rushed home, but I didn't say a word about what really happened. Way too close—to both sides.

It had been months since this all started, and I had allowed myself to get comfortable. My brain had to get back into game mode or else I'd be attending the funerals of my wife and children and then meeting them in heaven after being tortured to death.

Agent D called me to DEA HQ, and I took the precautions of old. No more laziness. I figured it was a debriefing about the operation where I wore the wire. Or they were calling me in to chew me out for selling my car. Either way, paranoia had returned.

"We called you in to pay you," Agent D explained.

My mood brightened. "Really? Why?"

"'Cause we liked what you did the other day."

The rules dictated that more than one person had to be present as a witness. Chief O came in, and on a litany of forms I signed here and initialed there ad nauseam. Then he peeled off a thousand dollars in crisp bills. The money couldn't have come at a better time. It may have been just a drop in the bucket to people like Jake—a ho-hum trip to the strip club, nothing more—but it was life support for me.

When my fever hit, it didn't matter that I was on the right side of the law this time. I had been healthy for two years, but the problems and stress attacked my immune system like ICBMs against strategic targets. Worse, the fever hit the day before the GMAT.

Waking to take the exam, I was sweating more than a fat man in a fur coat running in the Sahara, yet I felt like I was freezing to death. I could have rescheduled, but that would have screwed up everything, and there was no refund. I had enough medication in me to open my own pharmacy. The test was supposed to take at least three hours, and I had no idea how I was going to suffer through it. I needed a 540 or better to get into grad school, but even though that's an average score and easily attainable, I found myself skimming through questions rather than answering them. It was a train wreck.

In a drug-induced haze when I finished, I had the choice of accepting the score or dumping the entire exam. I couldn't afford to take it again or wait a month, so the choice was simple. Wiping a sheet of sweat off my brow, I hit "accept." Eyes clamped shut, I prayed to God for a 540. On the screen appeared the most beautiful number in the world: 570. I wasn't sure whether the euphoria came from the success of my achievement or the latest round of meds, but at that moment I didn't care.

Unfortunately, my victory didn't last long. The next day Jake called in a raging panic, wanting me to come to his house again. I put Agent D and the Texas AG on notice, and they promised they'd be in the area.

Walking up to Jake's house, I didn't know what to expect—another ATV, an ass chewing, a shotgun in the face, or anything in between. The front door was open, so I stuck my head in.

"Hello? Anybody home?"

"Over here!" Jake yelled. He was sitting on the kitchen floor, blood gushing from his nose. "Take me to the hospital!"

17

Time Marches On

JAKE HAD UNDERGONE PLASTIC SURGERY TO FIX HIS CORRODED SEPTUM—too much coke—along with some other vanity procedures (veneers, hair restoration, and so on). But with those procedures came complications. A full-on nasal gush was one of them.

Jake at the ER with Sandra gave me the perfect opportunity to break into their house and find some evidence. But my thorough search yielded only a thousand dollars and a file of pictures. In other words: nothing. A hundred grand would have been a different story, and the photos only showed Adan and Jose standing beside planes they'd purchased, tail numbers visible. They didn't prove any wrongdoing. Getting the dish on Jake was like pushing a dump truck up a hill.

By the time October arrived, I was now adept at wearing two hats simultaneously: DEA informant and family man. During family time Missy and I hosted cookouts, kids' parties, and tailgate parties. Balloons, music, and a hot grill were the norm. On DEA time I played the role of Jake's attentive friend. I diligently recorded and documented everything I had done for the feds, giving them a trove of information, everything but the kitchen sink—or a major deal. But if they would just get off their asses and put Jake under proper surveillance, they could have busted him on their own ricky-tick.

My two lives compartmentalized, one would have never known the other existed. Jake and his crew didn't get anywhere near my family. Whenever any of them asked to hang out, I casually changed the subject.

Improvising, if only out of paranoia, had become one of my greatest strengths. I also kept Missy in the dark about my DEA activities. The less she knew, the better.

While I still didn't have much to be proud of, I was exceedingly pleased at becoming what I deemed to be a world-class undercover operative. But that didn't change that I desperately needed a break. My life had become routine: drink with Jake or ride with him in the desert, then drink. Or cookout at Jake's house, where we all drank, then sleep off the buzz at my grandmother's house before going home. The DEA should have put my liver on the payroll, too. The upside of this schedule was that it allowed me to keep my worlds separate, and Grandma's acted as a safe house: Anyone following me from Jake's wouldn't get to my wife and kids.

But many weird coincidences happened during this phase of my life, and I ran into persons of interest in the oddest places. For example, I took a quick weekend trip to visit an old friend—also named Chris—in Boulder, Colorado. On several occasions we ran into the same two guys at area businesses. They looked like DEA, so I figured they were shadowing me. I also assumed my phone was tapped and acted accordingly. To my disbelief, Jake had gotten reckless and was no longer taking the precautions he once had.

On another occasion I ran into a friend's brother who just happened to be an FBI agent working at El Paso's Halls of Justice.

"What are you doing here?" he asked, surprised to see me at the HQ.

"Oh, uh . . . one of my golf buddies is giving me a tour."

"Who's your buddy? Maybe I know him?"

Instead of answering, I feigned being late to take Missy to a doctor's appointment. By the time I turned the corner, I was drenched with sweat.

Paying microscope-close attention to my surroundings, I was dumbfounded that Jake and his crew never noticed the constant commotion around them. Perhaps my new gig had changed my perspective.

The phone rang early one morning, rousing me from sleep. Seeing it was Jake on the caller ID, I fumbled for the recorder and managed to get it set before the third ring.

"Hey, I know you need some money," he said.

"Yeah, of course."

"I got 770 tiles I need to do a wrapping party for. Wanna go buy supplies for me? I'll give you a couple hundred bucks."

"Abso-fuckin'-lutely. When?"

"I'll pick you up at Grandma's at noon."

"See ya then."

I couldn't get off the phone fast enough to call Agent D. "Mobilize the National fucking Guard. I got a deal!"

"Okay, let me talk to Chief O," Agent D said.

It was only 8:00 a.m., so the DEA had plenty of time to organize a team—or so I thought. Waiting for him to call me back seemed like eons. Finally:

"It's on."

"Anything I need to do?" I asked. "Wear a wire?"

"Nope. Just have him pick you up and do your thing."

Waiting for Jake to arrive made me feel like a kid on Christmas Eve. I even called Missy and, speaking in the lame code we created, told her that my DEA involvement might end soon, perhaps today. She was beyond excited. Maybe we'd finally have a chance at a normal life.

Jake was driving one of Byron's cars, a dark green Ford Focus that I think belonged to his mom. That he was trying to move incognito meant that this was a real deal and not a test. The DEA would have no problem following it. Our destination was a catering supply store in downtown El Paso. It wasn't far from my grandmother's house, traffic was light, and I already told the DEA where it was to eliminate any variables. The scenario was so simple and straightforward that anyone with the mental capacity of a houseplant could follow us every step of the way. Poor guy would never know what hit him.

Then he began blabbing about how much money I could make if I allowed him to use my home as a stash house.

"I told you, I don't want my wife and kids around that stuff."

"Byron and Richard do it," he said. "It throws the cops off the trail when kids live at the house."

Not a chance.

He dropped me off at the supply store and ran an errand. I grabbed a couple of rolls of industrial grade plastic wrap and, at the checkout counter, understood why he didn't want to go in. The store was a wholesaler and required a lot of info from me—more corroborating evidence in my eyes. I chatted with Agent D on the phone for a while to make sure everything was fine, pretending to be on the phone with a girl in case someone was watching me.

Jake returned moments after I exited the store, and I hopped in the car to catch another earful about the virtues of using my home as a stash house and my family as a smokescreen. As he shot out of the parking lot like a rocket, I said I'd think about it, but my mind was reeling that in just a few hours he'd be busted.

He dropped me off at my house and drove off with the wrapping supplies. Over and done, good riddance. Enjoy your orange jumpsuit and your jail cell. I danced a little jig in my driveway, mocking Jake's happy dance, and dialed Agent D to celebrate.

"All right, have fun. My work is done."

"What do you mean, your work is done? We're still following you."

"Uh, no, you're not. Jake just dropped me off at my house."

"You mean you're *not* on Paisano Street?" There was panic in Agent D's voice. Godzilla in Tokyo panic.

"Fuck no!"

"Fuck. *Fuck!* We followed the wrong fucking car."

I wanted to cry. To scream. To bang my head against the pavement.

When Jake pulled out of the parking lot, at the next traffic light there just happened to be another green Ford Focus there. I hadn't given it any thought. Trying to salvage the op, I dialed Jake immediately.

"Hey, where you at? I think I left my keys in your car. Could you come back and let me check?"

"I don't see 'em."

"They might be under the seat. I need my keys, man."

"I don't see 'em. If I find 'em later, I'll get 'em to you."

Fuck!

Jake wasn't turning around. We were dead in the water. It was a crushing defeat, yet I couldn't help but laugh at the irony. Jake was an asshole's asshole, but he was also the luckiest asshole I'd ever met. You had to admire him just a little.

That was when I realized that I couldn't depend on anything or anyone, not even Agent D or the DEA. For my purposes now, I was in it alone. Which meant reevaluating my loyalties. Until now, I had been willing to do whatever was asked of me. When they said jump, I jumped. No more. It was time to take the bull by the horns.

Normally, I didn't tell Missy much of anything. If I was busy with DEA work, I said I was TCBing—taking care of business—and she knew what that meant. After this latest debacle I couldn't remain silent.

"What are they, the Keystone Cops?" she said.

"Seems that way. I can only imagine the ribbing they'll get in the office."

"Screw that! What about our safety?"

The DEA gave me another small stipend for that fiasco, and life returned to normal, although my belief in their abilities had diminished considerably. I started my anger management course, which met every Saturday for twelve weeks and cost me six hundred dollars. After my first class I met Jake at Tequila Sunrise.

"Hey, Nutty, can I go to the classes with you?"

"Why would you wanna do that?"

"Because I know they make you angry, and I wanna see how you deal with your anger in a classroom setting."

He wasn't kidding. Jake loved trying to get my goat, and he was damn good at it. I pondered the idea of ending him and giving the cops a *real* offense to charge me with. The notion had its merits: I'd get a place to live, three meals a day, and reasonably decent health care. My wife and kids would be out of danger, too. Hell, I'd probably even get a little sex now and then—just not when I wanted it or from whom!

Hate him or love him, it was good business sense for me to hang out with Jake at the strip club. He gave me money for dances, most of which I pocketed. I usually made around a hundred bucks and drank for free.

"I appreciate you helping me out the other day," he said.

"No prob. That's what friends are for."

"Things went smoothly. It shows I can trust you, and I'll have good work for you in the future."

"Awesome," I said, enthused but skeptical.

I was hoping he'd send me on a money run. The DEA told me I could keep 10 percent of whatever I helped them seize, but I had other plans. If I got a money run, I was going to take it all. Granted, I'd have to beat the living shit outta myself and find a way to launder the cash, but even though I didn't have all the details worked out, if the opportunity came, screw these guys. I was going to take full advantage. What's more, if I robbed the money from myself, I could ultimately sue the DEA for botching the operation. Jake would probably threaten me over the lost cash, instantly giving the DEA enough reason both to prosecute him and shepherd my family and me out of harm's way. Reckless as hell, but sometimes you have to roll the dice.

At the next anger management group session, we had to stand and give some details about ourselves. I shared a little about my past regrets and briefly touched upon my drug trafficking days. Walking out of class, one of the students, a clean-cut, well-spoken Hispanic guy, cornered me.

"Dude, do you still have connections?" he asked.

"Why do you ask?"

"Because I might have some work."

"Are you from El Paso?"

"Yeah, why?"

My bullshit-ometer went off the charts. "Who are you with? DEA? FBI? EPPD? Sheriff?" I laughed. "Doesn't matter. Your undercover persona sucks."

His jaw clattered around his ankles. The guy was probably an undercover newbie trying to make a name for himself. Nobody walks up to a complete stranger and asks him to do a drug deal, especially in Hell Paso. There's so much narco business in this town with people you know from high school and way back that a local would *never* need to prospect—and at an anger management meeting, of all places.

Cop or not, I didn't like this development. If it was a legitimate offer and I turned him over to the DEA, I'd have a new list of enemies to avoid. Whether I was being tested, profiled, or seriously approached, the risks didn't justify the rewards. So I didn't bother telling Agent D.

That night Missy and I watched *American History X* after the kids went to sleep. Half Jewish and half-Mexican, I would never be accepted by the Aryan Brotherhood, which meant if I went to prison and needed a white support system I'd be shit outta luck. But watching someone else's screwed-up life, even a Tinseltown fake-believe one, made me feel better about mine. Also, aspects of Ed Norton's character struck a chord with me, especially the beginning scene.

"Missy, see him standing in the road, arms out, forming a cross? He's surrounded and unarmed, yet when he surrenders to the cops, he's still the most powerful person in the scene. In a pure point of weakness, he's still able to find a way to *be* strong, not just *appear* strong."

"You're giving me a headache."

"I need to find a way to channel my inner strength like that."

She rolled her eyes. "Please."

"In life I'm the guy surrounded by unstoppable opposing forces. I need to be the strong, shirtless guy with the fuck-you look standing in the road." I jumped up, ripped off my shirt, and stretched my arms out.

"That's it. I'm going to bed."

The next day at Jake's house I discovered that, strangely, he'd rented the same movie.

"That's a messed-up flick," I said.

"Yeah. Could you imagine doing real time in jail?"

If he only knew how close he was.

Just as I started to discuss the dichotomy of social values versus individual values, Jake cut me off.

"Shut up, Nutty. You think too much."

"You sound like my wife."

"Then she's the smart one."

I laughed. "Maybe I'll shave my head and become an instant badass like Ed Norton."

"Great fucking idea!" Jake roared. "I'll pay you five hundred bucks to do it!"

I really liked my hair. But for five hundred I was willing to get my head mowed by a tractor. Truth is, I'd always wanted to try the cue-ball look. When I was in the joint, a tough-as-nails inmate went from shoulder-length locks to a chrome dome because he was getting transferred to a state pen and didn't want anyone using his long hair against him in a fight.

Jake brought out a set of clippers, and we laughed hysterically as he gave me a Mohawk, followed by a full buzz. It was going to piss Missy off, but she didn't have five hundred extra dollars. Jake took me to Mulligan's, a local bar in Narco East, to show off his handiwork. He loved having control over me, but I loved that I was learning to let go. At the bar we ran into Byron, his wife, and his two cousins, Chris and Dave.

When we went to JB's later that night, the strippers couldn't keep their hands off my head. I liked the compliment and the attention. I liked how it felt to be reckless, even if it was just a new hairstyle. I had been OCD my entire life, trying to control everything with an iron fist. My obsessions had taken me nowhere. Suddenly, the simple act of shaving my head brought the innermost pain of my life to the surface. My emotions took over. I was ready to let go completely.

Byron, Jake, and I got ass-over-teakettle drunk. I couldn't see straight, let alone walk. I saw three of everything, and I flirted with every stripper in sight, determined to bang one. Groping their tits, putting my hands in their G-strings, I was bad—and I liked it! I asked every patron in the bar if they had condoms before remembering that I *hated* condoms. My next memory was riding in Jake's Expedition.

"I'm gonna get a stripper pregnant," I declared. "On purpose!"

"Don't you have enough kids?" Jake said, laughing his ass off.

"Screw that. I want a dozen baby mamas."

"I've never seen you like this."

"Meet the new Chris."

Jake dropped me off at my grandmother's house and pointed me at the front door. I couldn't figure out how to get into the house, though, so I slept in her car. Despite having the hangover from Hades the next morning, I felt great. I fully expected Missy to come unglued over my not coming home.

"Oh, my god! What happened to your hair?"

"The movie."

She began bawling. "I don't even know you anymore."

Neither did I.

———

Everything was getting away from me, and I didn't give a damn. The first week of December the home phone rang at 3:00 a.m. Missy answered, woke me up, and pushed the phone in my hand.

"What's wrong?"

"Dad died," my sister, Lisa, choked out between sobs.

"What?"

"He had a massive heart attack."

A shocked and shattered "I love you" was all I could muster. I was numb. I handed the phone back to Missy and rolled over. I wanted to cry. I wanted to scream. I had been so busy fighting my own battles for the last two years that I hadn't taken my kids to Fort Myers to meet him. He was one of the few people whom I respected with every fiber of my being, and now he was gone. The only legacy that remained was that my kids carried his name.

Missy hugged me. She wanted to talk, but I couldn't. When the weight of sleep hit me, it felt as if I had been given anesthesia. Next thing I knew I was dreaming and talking to him.

"Listen to me, son," he said.

"I love you, Dad."

"Listen to me. Missy ain't never gonna change. And you need to behave. Don't let go."

"I miss you."

"I know, Chris. Just be good, okay?"

18

Take This Job and Shove It

WE BARELY HAD ENOUGH MONEY SAVED TO BUY THE KIDS CHRISTMAS presents. We'd be eating sand with gravy for New Year's, but Christmas was going to be good. If I went to the funeral, the flight alone was seven hundred dollars, an impossible expense considering our finances, so I asked my grandmother, who was well off.

"Sorry, Chris, I can't afford it," she said, lying to my face.

"But it's my dad!"

"I never liked Ben. He spanked you."

"Grandma, show some respect."

"I always hated him."

She wouldn't budge. I hated her with a passion.

Missy told me to use our savings, but Dad wouldn't have wanted that. He was a no-nonsense, gruff old country boy—a real R. Lee Ermey type (Gunnery Sergeant Hartman in Stanley Kubrick's *Full Metal Jacket*). He would have pitched a fit if I deprived my kids of Christmas to attend his funeral. I could hear his voice in the back of my head. *Dammit, son, I'm dead. There ain't nothin' you can do for me. Don't be selfish and waste your time comin' to see me. Give them kids a proper Christmas.* As much as it hurt, I listened to the voice in my head and gave my kids the Christmas they deserved, the Christmas my dad would have wanted them to have.

Then Jake offered me an early Christmas present during a 7:00 a.m. phone call.

"What are you doin' today?"

"Nothing. Christmas is in three days, and I need to save money."

"I'll pay you five hundred bucks to take care of something for me, but it'll take all day."

He had made a new friend in the narco biz, a guy who had done some serious time but was out on parole and had started a successful document shredding business. Jake talked about how he was going to use the guy's connections and transport for him to Chicago and Boston, among other places, but there was a catch: He'd be screwing Byron out of a lot of money. Apparently, he and Byron had become partners, but this new player wanted to cut Byron out of the picture on certain stuff.

"Do you think that's right?" I asked.

"Fuck it," Jake said. "Guys like Byron grow on trees."

"So what do you want me to do?" I said, still half-asleep.

"Fly to Houston. Daniel will pick you up at the airport. He used my maroon F-150 and new trailer to tow a salvaged Escalade he brought to his house in Houston. I need you to bring my truck and trailer back."

"Five hundred won't even cover the plane ticket and gas."

"I'll buy your ticket online right now and give you $250 for gas. Are you down?"

"Let me ask Missy, and I'll call you back."

"Hurry up."

I didn't need to ask Missy; I needed to ask Agent D. He told me, if I saw anything unusual in the car, to report back to him immediately and we'd go from there. He probably still felt guilty about the wrapping party fiasco. Normally, he went by the book, and I'm sure this was against protocol, but he didn't argue or request authorization. Flying to Houston two hours later, I didn't give a damn either way.

The trip was uneventful. Daniel picked me up, and just as Jake had described him, the guy was a nervous Nellie chain-smoker. A total amateur, too, testing me with what he thought were tough questions. Jake had obviously talked to him about me, but I made short work of his lame interrogation. I even flipped the script and had him stuttering from my counterquestions.

Since I was in the area, I had lunch with my biological father. It shocked him to learn that this was a DEA-sanctioned trip, but his opinions had ceased to matter to me. Not once did he or my half brother come to El Paso to visit and meet my kids. When I met them for the first time in 1997, I made it a point to reach out to them, but they never reciprocated. *Who could blame them?* I thought. Apparently, not even Jesus loves a loser. But now their feelings were farts in a hurricane.

When I worked at Circuit City, I hooked Jake up with XM satellite radio. Now I enjoyed it traveling through the nether regions of Texas where normal radio reception is nonexistent. Towing the trailer was a challenge, but the F-150—complete with leather, seat warmers, cruise control, and sunroof—was a luxury car wrapped in a pickup truck's skin. I went through both the truck and trailer with a fine-tooth comb but found nothing.

The weather report for my return trip forecasted flurries from San Antonio to El Paso, a six-hundred-mile stretch. During the last two hundred, Mother Nature dumped nearly five inches of snow and made the driving treacherous, but the 4x4 handled like a dream, so I slowed down, enjoyed the view, and took the extra time to think. Meeting Daniel was a coup from a DEA standpoint, but it made me worry, because new and powerful players were coming into Jake's life at an alarming rate. Daniel had connections in Monterrey, Mexico, which meant he was in deep—and so was Jake by default. I was playing in the lion's cage wearing a meat suit.

Grad school started in January. Certain that my pops would have wanted me to do it this way, the right way, I determined to turn my ship around. The first few days of classes made me feel that I was in over my head, though. The professors lectured at breakneck speed, and all the other students speedily took notes like they knew exactly what the professors were discussing.

The initial days were especially awkward. They all introduced themselves and talked about hometowns, undergrad degrees, majors, and jobs. I tried to dance around the perfunctory bio, to no avail.

"Hello, my name is Chris Heifner. I was born here but grew up in Alabama. I have a BBA in finance, and I am an MBA student."

But the professor wanted more. "Where do you work?"

"Umm . . . work?"

"Yeah, you know . . . your *job?*"

"Oh. I, uh . . . day-trade."

Listening to people describe their pleasant lives, in contrast to how fucked up mine was, made me want to crawl into a hole and die. At the end of class, the reminder of all my failures was waiting for me. In a way he was actually a welcome sight.

"What's up, Nutty? I wanted to see what grad school looked like."

"It looks the same way it did when we earned our bachelors. We met in that classroom right there," I said, pointing.

"I think I might want to earn a grad degree."

"If you want me to write your papers for you this time, I'm charging double."

"Deal."

We had a beer at Hemingway's.

"Make some money," he said. "I need a stash house."

"Lemme see what I can do. But I might need you to front the deposit."

He nodded. "I can do that."

I met with Agent D and laid out the plan. After I found a place, I needed him and Jake to put up the deposit and rent money. Jake told me what he wanted, and Agent D, the Texas AG agent, and I drove around looking for houses that fit the bill.

Jake thought he was helping us both out. Missy and I had our problems, but I exaggerated. I made her out to be an ogre to keep him from coming over. He probably knew where we lived at that point, but I didn't want him anywhere near my children. He thought he could use the situation to encourage me to move out on my own, where he'd get carte blanche to use my garage. Win-win.

In central El Paso a lot of houses had detached garages. If I found one that met his criteria, Jake wanted to use it as his personal storage unit.

"I'll have the only keys to the garage. It will be *my* space," he insisted. "And to keep people from calling the stash house hotline, have your kids play outside."

"That's brilliant," I said, trying hard not to roll my eyes.

We chose a house on Cincinnati Street, a nice three-bedroom built in the '50s with a garage at the end of the driveway, essentially in the backyard. At $775 a month, though, it was out of reach for my broke ass. To move in I'd need first and last months' rent, along with another month's rent for security deposit. That was over $2,000. Jake offered to put up $750, so the DEA had to cover the rest. I wore a wire when I picked up the money from Jake, but this time there was much less gadgetry.

"Wow! We're moving up in the world," I said, indicating the better equipment.

"Seems that way," Agent D said with a chuckle.

It was business as usual to go to Jake's and get the money. It was almost too easy. By now I was cold, calculating, and fearless—and it was starting to be fun. It reminded me of my motorcycle riding days. But when a rider quits fearing his bike, that's usually when the purring kitty turns into a roaring lion and bites him. Lease signed, Jake offered me one of his transport vans to move my things, an old AT&T work van made to look like a tradesman's. It never occurred to me that I would actually have to move into the place.

"Hey, are y'all gonna help me move in?" I asked Agent D.

"No. Don't get too comfortable. You won't be living there."

"I have to make it *look* like I'm living there."

A long pause. "Oh, yeah. Good point."

"God, I hate you guys. . . ."

"No, you don't," he said. "Once you're settled, I'm gonna send a guy over to do some wiring. You won't be able to go near the house for a few hours tomorrow."

"What if Jake comes by?"

"We'll cross that bridge if we come to it."

From my grandmother's house I took one of her guest beds, a TV, some chairs, and a bunch of bathroom stuff. Agent D and the Texas AG scrutinized the van for documentation purposes. Then I loaded it up with clothes, toiletries, plastic dishes, and enough other personal stuff to make a convincing bachelor pad. I even took some of my kids' toys and food from her fridge to complete the look.

The few nights I spent at the new place really creeped me out, and I missed my kids. A few outdoor motion lights doubled as cameras but otherwise no evidence of wires and cameras. I didn't spend many daytime hours at the house because it didn't have cable. All I did was study and sleep there.

It took a lot of convincing of both Jake and the DEA to front the money, and they only gave me enough to cover rent and utilities for one month. Agent D and I stressed over the situation; both our necks were on the line. After a few weeks I began to worry that nothing would happen. Was Jake's amazing luck going to save him yet again?

After a couple of weeks, Jake chided me for not making the house look more hospitable, so he and Byron showed up to do some yard work. Which meant something was about to go down, and Jake was feeling me out. But he had to do it quick.

One night he came over unannounced with a twelve-pack of cold beer. "Whatcha doin'? There's no TV."

"Studying."

"I was studying, too," he said.

"Lemme guess, *Playboy* or *High Times*?"

Handing me a beer, he sat in one of my plastic chairs and rambled on like a Dr. Phil session. He told me about losing the money in Georgia and how much Byron was annoying him lately. Apparently, all Byron wanted to do was party—coke and strippers 24/7. Jake had wanted to use Byron's home as a stash house but feared that the constant partying would draw too much attention. He talked about how irritating Richard had become and how Jake continuously pissed him off by not paying him on time or at all, even though it was only fifteen hundred a pop or so. His brother, Eric, owed him money, which he hated, and John had lost two loads.

The same kind of Texas state trooper task force that nailed me snagged John with one of the loads, a few hundred pounds. He had been dating a stripper from the Lamplighter, and because Jake didn't bail her out, he worried now that she would rat him out.

"Why are you playing with Richard's money like that?" I said. "You know he's poor. Just pay him, and be done with him. And why didn't you bail her out? You bailed John out. That's just bad business."

"I needed to teach them both a lesson."

"You're not in the business of teaching lessons. Don't do things that will hurt business. Out of curiosity, did you accuse John of speeding on that trip?"

Between his head games and that "my way or the highway" mentality, Jake was his own worst enemy.

Then he explained how John lost the second load. Seems he got drunk and passed out on the side of the road somewhere in Oklahoma. The cops pulled up, and it was game over when they searched the trunk. John had been in jail, but I didn't know why.

"Remember when you were working at the bank and John and I swung through Birmingham on the way to Indianapolis?"

"Yeah."

"We lost a load that trip. John took the fall so I could stay outta jail. Now he's facing that charge, along with two other loads. He'll be away for a while."

John was Jake's best friend, best man at his wedding. They had a lot of history. This was heavy stuff.

"It's all that stupid bastard's fault. If he wasn't a drunk? No problems."

Nothing was ever selfish, narcissistic Jake's fault. John, Byron, Eric, and I all had gone to bat for him, but he didn't give a damn about any of us. When he left I sat there in that quiet little house with no TV, no noise, thinking about the situation. At times Jake was the most charming person I had ever met. Others, he was the Antichrist. It boggled my mind that he didn't realize the effects of his behavior on those around him.

Jake called me on his way home. "You drive me crazy sometimes, but I'm thankful I can depend on you. Your house is gonna save my ass."

You'd think that was a tremendous compliment, but all it really meant was that I was less of a pain in the ass than Richard or Byron. If I crossed him, even a little, he wouldn't hesitate to threaten my kids—again. But this time I didn't ride the emotional swing. I just did my job and had a long debriefing with Agent D at the Halls of Justice the following day.

"He said all that?" Agent D said, amazed. "Did he say when he wanted to use the stash house?"

"No. But knowing him, it's soon. Be ready."

"Okay, but this is on you."

I knew it was on me. I tried to take notes in my macroecon class, but my mind kept drifting to the pretty redhead sitting beside me. What would she think about my situation? The instructor scratched on the chalkboard, and my mind wandered around the room. Some of my classmates wore shirts bearing the logos of the jobs they had just come from; some picked at what appeared to be their dinners; none looked particularly happy. Why did I want to live their lives so badly? Many told me they were bored out of their minds and completely unfulfilled. But at least they could pay their bills.

As I was getting out of class at 10:00 p.m., my phone rang. "Meet me at JB's," Jake said. "I wanna talk business."

I called Agent D and told him to be ready, but Jake was as random as a slot machine. In JB's all my senses sparked. I could smell every scent, hear every sound, see everything in sight. My entire life hinged on Jake's words. It was time to fight.

I grabbed a beer and made my way over to a table near the wall where Jake was sitting. His facial muscles were twitching as he tapped his feet. He was wearing jeans and an old T-shirt. For a guy who normally dressed preppy, this meant he left home in a rush. Something was up.

I selected the chair nearest the wall to give me a view of the entire room in order to spot anything out of the ordinary, like someone watching us and not the strippers. Still on my guard, I sat far enough away from Jake so he couldn't stab me with a weapon under the table. Not that I was expecting to be attacked, but I wasn't taking any chances. Not with that loose cannon.

"Are you ready?" he asked.

"Sure. For what?"

"Are you my nigger?"

"I think I've already proven that with my loyalty."

Jake rubbed his hands together like a miser, and a cheesy smile crept onto his face. "I got a load coming in tomorrow."

"How big?"

"Didn't I tell you?"

"No."

"Maybe 'cause I didn't want you to know."

I rolled my eyes.

"It's big, but not so big that it won't fit in your garage."

"How much you gonna pay me?"

"Standard amount. Twelve hundred."

Feigning enthusiasm, I nodded excitedly. "Okay, then, let's do this!"

"*Let's do this!*" he parroted.

We had a few drinks and continued the innocuous small talk before leaving at 11:30. Jake and Byron would come to my house at 6:00 a.m. the next day.

I called Agent D, waking him up.

"Code red! Code red!" I blurted.

"What's that mean?"

"Jake is dropping off a load at the stash house at 6:00 a.m.."

"You sure? This is for real?"

"Yes!"

"Okay, 'cause I'm gonna have to call Chief O and get the crew rolling. Everyone is going to hate you tomorrow."

"Good. That's why y'all get paid the big bucks."

"They're gonna hate me, too."

"What do I do?"

"Just meet Jake and do the business you gotta do. We'll be there, taking care of business, too, but you won't see us."

"Am I gonna wear a wire?"

"No. Just call me in the morning when you're on your way over."

19

If It Ain't Ruff

"Are y'all awake?"

They'd flubbed ops before, so as I rushed to get to the stash house by 6:00 a.m. after spending the night with Missy and the kids, I called Agent D.

"Yes, we're in position. Just relax, and do your thing. Call me when you can, and keep me updated."

"Y'all aren't gonna lose me today, are you?"

"We got the entire office on this."

His answer didn't reassure me, but at this point I had no choice.

I had spent enough time in the neighborhood to get a feel for what was normal, but nothing seemed out of whack on Cincinnati Street. No unusual sights or sounds. I pulled up to the house just as Jake and Byron raced up in their car.

"Where ya been?" Jake asked.

"I picked up a girl at JB's last night and stayed at her place," I said, thinking fast.

"That's what I'm talkin' 'bout!"

"How long y'all been here?"

"A while. We wanted to see if we noticed anything."

"And?"

"And the only thing we noticed is that this 'hood is graveyard quiet."

Was Agent D pulling my leg about being in position?

"So you're back in the biz, huh?" Byron asked.

"I guess."

I liked Byron. Always did. Stand-up guy. He had no idea that Jake screwed him every chance he got. When I flipped I tried to play devil's advocate for him whenever possible, asking him whether he thought Jake's strategies were foolish or reckless and doomed. I had to be *really* careful, but Byron always dismissed my comments or laughed them off. If he had half a clue, he would have realized that I was trying to warn him.

They went into the house to use the bathroom, but I think they just wanted to look around. I looked around, too, but nothing was out of the ordinary. Back outside in the front yard, they seemed spooked and checked out the surroundings again, but I distracted them by being talkative, especially since I noticed a plane in the air, only about two thousand feet up, doing circles. How could they not see this? Fortunately, Jake's phone rang.

"Hello. Uh-huh. Uh-huh. Got it."

"What's the word?" Byron asked.

"Village Inn."

Same place where I'd met with Agent D. We jumped in Byron's green Ford Focus, Jake in the driver's seat, and I smiled inwardly at the coincidence. Out the rear window was a slew of cars, far more than usual for that area of El Paso at 6:00 a.m. And of course, the bulk of the abnormally heavy traffic consisted of vehicles and faces that didn't fit the profile of typical UTEP students or El Paso morning commuters. The DEA's moving net was more obvious than a blue whale in a bathtub.

There was also that fucking crop duster. A plane like that should have been flying over farmland whacking bugs with pesticide and scaring the shit out of cattle, not barnstorming a college campus. It had zoomed directly overhead a couple of times already, dropping a little lower on each pass. Amazingly, the two yahoos up front, totally oblivious, were yapping away like a pair of chuckleberries.

We looked for the rendezvous vehicle for what felt like an eternity. Insanity is doing the same thing repeatedly but expecting a different result each time. After eight passes along the exact same route, I was ready to fit

Jake for a straitjacket. How had he or Byron not noticed the commotion following us? It was beyond absurd.

The vehicle we were scouting, a nondescript white cargo van, had just come across the border with a monster load of dope in the back. A white four-door Ford Explorer was tailing us way too closely as we searched up and down Mesa Street. The government bastard's surveillance skills made me more nervous than the last lobster in a restaurant fish tank. I made Jake pull over, claiming unbearable stomach pain.

"It's all that goddamn coffee you drink," he said with a laugh. "Fuckin' stuff's worse than prune juice." He pulled into a Whataburger and threw the Focus into park. "Don't spend all day wiping; I wanna get this shit over with."

I bolted from the car like a thoroughbred out of the starting gate, unbuckling my belt en route. Jake and Byron were no doubt laughing about my frantic behavior, taking bets on whether I'd shit myself before I made it to the john. Inside the bathroom I threw the lock, turned on the faucet full-bore, dropped trou, and mounted the porcelain throne. This was my last chance to be alone before finishing this job with Jake. It had taken me two years to regain his trust. I wasn't about to throw all that hard work away by letting the DEA be careless. I quickly keyed the number I'd committed to memory into my cell.

"What's going on?" Agent D asked.

"You tell me," I said, voice hushed but agitated. Even with the water running, the bathroom's acoustics didn't allow for the most private of conversations. If someone stood outside the door, I could have been in a world of hurt. But the DEA's operation was starting to resemble a monkey fucking a football—and I didn't want to be the football.

"Chris, what's wrong?"

"For one, the tails are *way* too fucking obvious. Back them the hell off. And Jesus Christ, who the hell does that pilot think he is, the Red fucking Baron? That plane's about as unobtrusive as a three-foot black rubber cock in a convent."

"That bad, huh?"

"Seriously, reign 'em in, or call the morgue and reserve me a slab."

"I'm on it."

The line went dead. I wiped my ass out of habit, flushed, threw some water on my face and rushed back out to the car.

"Feel better?" Jake asked back in the car, sincere as a used car salesman.

"Yeah, much," I lied. "Thanks."

We hit the road again. Byron made a show of wafting the air with his hand as he took a hearty whiff. He frowned, shook his head. "Damn, I don't smell nothing," he said to Jake. "You win."

"Of course I win," Jake replied. "Nutty's already got a big load to worry about. He didn't need another in his pants."

They giggled like kindergartners at a puppet show. How the hell were these two going to survive in prison? A small part of me momentarily felt bad for their inevitable incarceration and the unending rectum ravaging that would go with it . . . but you know what? Fuck 'em! Literally. That's what they get for threatening my family. I mean, seriously, what the hell did Jake expect me to do when he promised unspeakable atrocities committed against my wife, my kids, and me?

Turning into the Village Inn for the tenth time, we finally spotted a white Chevy Astro van parked in the back of the lot. Byron and Jake were debating over who was going to drive it back to the stash house when I volunteered and jumped out of the car. I had immunity to do whatever I wanted for the next few hours, and I was going to enjoy it.

"Meet ya at the house!" Jake yelled out the window before driving off.

The van had huge clear windows on the side, and looking in, you could see the pot plain as day. There wasn't even a blanket over it. Jesus fucking Christ. The only seats were the driver's and front passenger's. No center console, either. Just bundle after bundle of pot stuffed from the rear door to the seat backs, stacked to just below the windows. There were also bricks of varying sizes wedged between the seats and on the floorboard of the passenger side. The only things missing were pictures of Cheech and Chong painted on its side.

I called Agent D. "I'm in it."

"We see you," he replied.

His radio was buzzing with activity in the background. It sounded like the D-Day invasion.

"What's it look like in there?" he asked.

"A Mary Jane convention. Two thousand pounds easy. But without tinted windows or a blanket covering the dope, how the hell'd it get over the bridge?" No time for chitchat, though. Before he could respond I hung up.

With Johnny Law in my back pocket, speed limits didn't matter. I nearly beat Jake and Byron to the stash house, where I backed the van into the garage. I tried to snap a couple of quick pics with my cell's camera, but Byron and Jake came into the garage too soon.

"*Woo-hoo!*" Jake roared. "Look at that!"

Even I was awestruck at the size of the load.

We locked the van in the garage and went to breakfast back at Village Inn. Jake was glowing; he loved playing the contraband kingpin. Byron and I ate our pancakes and chatted while Jake jabbered on the phone. At the tables and booths next to us, at least half a dozen DEA agents were also having breakfast. I did everything I could not to look at them, and if I could keep Byron occupied, he wouldn't look around, either.

"Baller status," Jake said into his cell. "Just got a big load of tile." He paused. "Yeah, yeah, we're rolling. Just gotta divide the tile and send it out of town." Another pause. "Nah, we should be able to get the tile past the checkpoint."

His attempt at narco code was hilarious.

After breakfast Jake drove to Home Depot, where he and Byron bought black contact paper. I wasn't sure why, but I didn't care. I wanted to go back to bed. I had done enough. Fortunately, the tails backed off while we got supplies. They only wanted the drugs. Driving back to the house, Jake did four laps around the neighborhood before finally parking on the street.

"Byron and I have work to do," he said. "Leave us alone in the garage for a while."

"*No problemo,*" I replied. "I'm gonna take a nap. But piss outside. I don't want you waking me up by coming into the house."

I went inside and jumped into bed. My bedroom window faced the garage door, and with Jake and Byron safely ensconced inside, I called Agent D.

"The frogs are on the lily pad."

"Huh? What the hell are you talking about?"

"It means they're in the garage."

"Oh, okay. What are they doing?"

"I don't know, probably ass-fucking each other."

"Really? I didn't think they had that kind of relationship."

"Jesus, I'm playin' with you."

"Oh, okay." He wasn't amused. "What's the plan?"

"I don't know," I said, annoyed. "I'm taking a nap."

"What?"

"Next step is your job. The cute couple in the garage is busy, so I'm going to sleep. I have class tonight."

I hung up and dozed off. Strange dreams of trying to survive a riot in a foreign prison while naked haunted me. Yeesh.

When I awoke, Jake and Byron were standing at the foot of my bed, serious looks on their faces.

"What did you do?" Byron asked, menacing.

"What?" I said, still half asleep.

"We saw you," Jake said.

"*Huh?*" My mind was racing.

"We saw you," Byron said again, "jerking off."

They laughed their asses off again.

"We're done," Jake said. "We're leaving."

"What's the plan?" I asked. "How long is the tile gonna be here?"

"We're just getting started, my friend. We gotta pick up another load tomorrow."

"No shit!"

"I wouldn't shit you, buddy!" Jake said, grinning.

Jake and Byron had used the paper to black out the van's windows since they were going to use it again tomorrow. Byron hopped in the empty van and took off for Mexico, leaving Jake and me in the front yard. After a brief chat Jake pulled out a wad of cash and handed me twelve hundred dollars. I hoped the DEA caught that. The second Jake left, my phone rang.

"What was in the van?" Agent D asked, "and where was it going?"

"It was empty. Byron's taking it back to Mexico. All the dope is in the garage."

He calmed down. "Oh. Okay."

"But I got bad news for you," I said.

"What?"

"They're bringing over another load tomorrow. Same plan?"

"We gotta do this again?" Agent D said, annoyed.

"Yup!"

The DEA had operatives tailing both Jake and Byron. When they were a safe distance away, Agent D came to the house, and we looked inside the garage. Stacked against the back wall was a tower of pot tall enough to get all of El Paso high at the same time. Agent D snapped a couple of pics. He estimated the load at fifteen hundred pounds; another agent at closer to eighteen hundred. He took more pics and made a slew of calls and radio transmissions. After locking up the garage, Agent D took the money from me and documented it.

"Twelve hundred? That's it?"

"Yeah. He's fucking me, big time," I said.

"He sure is!"

"The going rate for stash houses is a couple dollars a pound, so he should have paid me at least three to five thousand, especially since more pot is coming over the bridge tomorrow."

"The nerve," Agent D said dryly.

In class that night a sense of peace came over me. It was the first time I had felt this sensation in years. Pretty damn pleased with myself, I had a mental boner the entire night. We were sitting around doing group work, and some of the other students were talking about the excitement of their weekend.

"How was your weekend?" someone asked me.

"Insanely unbelievable would be an understatement."

"Deets."

I shook my head. "I don't kiss and tell."

I desperately wanted to brag that I helped organize a DEA task force for the eventual arrest and capture of hardened drug traffickers. I pictured myself accepting the key to the city when—

"I know what you did," said one of the girls.

"You do, huh?"

"I was at the gas station when you walked into JB's the other night. That place is disgusting. People that go there are disgusting."

She got up in a huff and moved to another group. There went my sense of peace and accomplishment. I had forgotten for a few short moments that I was a loser. So I tucked my mental boner between my legs and left.

Back at the stash house, I checked everything out again before crawling into bed. All the hopes and dreams of my youth, all my skills, all my hard work . . . all of it was locked in the garage, and it all amounted to nothing more than a blight on society.

The next morning, start to finish, repeated the previous day. Byron and Jake even wore the same clothes. Agent D and the gang weren't as noticeable, but that stupid plane was still there. The second time, though, the rendezvous went much more smoothly. Pulling up to Village Inn was the same shitty Astro van, its windows now blacked out. I wondered whether Agent D had watched the bridge this time.

Business as usual—except when I opened the door a brick of pot fell out from underneath the seat. The damn van was so loaded the tailpipe was nearly dragging on the asphalt.

"We hit a home run," I said to Agent D en route back to the stash house. "This thing is stuffed floor to ceiling, at least twenty-five hundred to three thousand pounds. I don't know how it's even driving."

At the end of the run, the entire back wall of the garage was stacked floor to ceiling with dope, truly a sight to behold.

Jake took the Focus to exchange it for the Dodge van and left Byron and me at the house. We settled into some plastic chairs in the living room and tried to watch whatever the antenna could pickup. Only soap operas came through. Fitting.

"What do you do here?" Byron asked.

"Study or sleep."

He gave me an odd look.

"I'll buy furniture once I get going. But it's gonna be hard to get rolling on twelve hundred."

I knew Byron was banking a lot of money—well, a lot more than me. I was hoping he'd do something redeeming and offer me some out of his pocket, like I did when Jake was fucking him on the Memphis drive.

"You'll get rolling again."

"On twelve hundred bucks? Don't you think that's cheap for watching a stash?"

"Yeah."

If Byron had done me a solid, I would have figured out a way to get his ass out of the fire. I would have warned him somehow. It was Jake I wanted to take down, not him.

"Don't you think Jake is just asking to get busted?"

Byron shrugged. "Nothin's happened yet."

Christ almighty, what fucking rock had he been living under? Everyone who worked with Jake had bad things happen to them sooner or later. How could he not see that? We talked for an hour, but he wasn't listening. We relived old war stories, and I even reminded him of the load I took through the checkpoint for him and how I had helped him. But he didn't redeem himself in any way. Time to wash my hands of him.

I wanted to call Agent D, so I tried to leave with the excuse that I wanted to go to Walgreens to buy a snack and a magazine, but Byron wasn't about to be left alone in the house. He bounced with me. So I decided to test him.

"Hypothetically, what would you do if Jake did something stupid and got you pinched? Would you rat him out?"

"I'd rather be an animal on the inside than a rat on the outside," he said.

"Even if he threatened your girls?"

"I'd deal with it, but I'd never rat."

I was trying to deal with it, too, in a way that would have made my father proud. Eventually, Jake came back and killed the boredom.

"Adan is coming by to check things out."

"*Adan* Adan?" I asked.

"No, another Adan from Chicago, jackass."

A few hours later Adan, a short, skinny Mexican who didn't look a day over twenty, showed up. I tried to position us all in front of the outdoor light camera because I knew that the DEA had no clue who the guy was. On top of that I didn't appreciate Jake's bringing some guy I didn't know around a house where my kids were theoretically staying.

Jake, Byron, and Adan locked themselves in the garage. When they emerged, Byron and Adan left, and Jake asked me to take him home.

"Hey, man, don't you think twelve hundred is a little cheap for all this weight stored at my house?" I said.

"Man, you're lucky I'm paying you at all. You still owe me for that load you lost 'cause you were speeding."

"What the fuck are you talking about?" I blurted. "We had an agreement. Besides, losing loads happens. You said it yourself. And I wasn't speeding."

"I'm teaching you a lesson," Jake said. "Just like I'm teaching John a lesson by letting him sit in jail and sober up."

"So what's the plan?"

"We're gonna move it out tomorrow."

"Sweet."

"By the way, who's that bitch across the street from your house? She seems nosy."

"I know. But don't worry about her. I'll take care of it."

"Bring your kids over," Jake suggested. "Have them play in the front yard."

"Not while the drugs are there."

He got rabid-dog mad. "*Just do it, goddammit!* I pay you, and *you do what I fuckin' tell you to do!*"

End of conversation. I was still seething long after he'd gotten out of the car. But I had work to do. Agent D looked in the garage again while I relayed Jake's plan.

"Great, here we go again," Agent D said. "What are you doing tonight?"

"I've got class, remember?"

"Oh, yeah. Could you look at one thing for me first?"

Agent D showed me a video of some girl with long hair walking over to the garage and asked if I recognized her.

"Nope. Should I worry about this?"

"Nah. Probably just a nosy neighbor."

"What if she calls the police or the stash house hotline?"

"Don't worry. We've got that covered. Again, great job, Chris. See ya tomorrow."

Sitting in class that night, I noticed the same girl from a class the night before. I smiled, but she rolled her eyes and looked away.

"I have a job available to any MS Econ students that are interested," the professor announced. "It's with the Economic Development Center in City Hall. It's a security-sensitive position that looks at everything, including credit. Anyone interested?"

Everyone looked at me. They all knew I was unemployed. Of course I was interested, but I would never pass the background check. I wished I were invisible.

"Mr. Heifner?" the professor said.

"Thank you, but I just took on a new and exciting entrepreneurial project."

Nobody believed me, but everyone went about their business. I wished I could fast-forward through time or travel back and do things over. Anything was better than this.

20

Bring Me to Life

"You won't play by my rules," Jake scolded. "You're lucky I don't demand a refund." He was fuming that I wouldn't allow my kids to play at the stash house. He insisted that the drugs were being moved early because I wouldn't put up a better front. But I didn't care. It forced him to move the drugs; the sooner that happened the sooner he was Agent D's problem and not mine.

Jake and Byron showed up around 9:00 a.m. the next day. Everyone in place again, including that damn plane. I hoped the pilot, flying counterclockwise ad nauseam, was a NASCAR fan. To my amazement they still hadn't noticed the plane. Someone breathing too loudly annoys me. How a Cessna 180 doing parade laps in the airspace just above the house didn't even register on their collective radar confounded me.

Jake and Byron worked in the garage. They put a portion of the pot into the Astro van and the remainder into the bigger Dodge work van. Byron was driving the Astro to Albertsons to rendezvous with a contact who would take it to parts unknown. This was the Adan contact. Then Byron would take the Dodge van to his cousin's house. I wanted to be present at the Albertsons meet, but Agent D ordered me not to, and I didn't argue.

I woke up on the wrong side of the bed, though, in full-blown fuck-you mode. Jake and Byron were in the garage dividing the load, so I called Agent D.

"Hey, fuckface," I said.

"Okayyyyyy," Agent D replied testily.

"You're gonna arrest these guys tonight, right?"

"Probably."

"Well, after the Albertsons meet, I'm gonna make a citizen's arrest."

"Uhh . . . that's not part of the plan."

"When I start doing jumping jacks, rush in. That's the signal."

"Uhhhhhh . . ."

I laughed. "*Relax.* I'm just fucking with you."

Silence on his end, which made me laugh even harder. For the most part I liked Agent D—as much as any former narco could like a DEA agent—but when all this was over, I was never gonna see him again, so what did it matter? I hung up, went to the garage, and started pounding on the door.

"Hey, Jake, if you don't pay me more, I'm gonna call the stash house unit myself."

He opened the door and popped his head out. "What the fuck is *wrong* with you?"

"Nothing. Why?"

"You better be kidding!"

"Of course. I love you," I gave him a big bro hug.

Byron left a few minutes later and quickly returned from the UTEP Albertsons meet, where he handed the van off to some girl named Betty.

"Was she hot?" I asked.

"Not really, but she had nice legs."

"Would you hit it?"

"Maybe, but I like 'em hotter."

"Your ex, Sandra, was hot. Jake and I talked about her. I'd hit it."

Byron looked like he wanted to gut me with an ice cream scooper. I smiled. I didn't give a damn what anyone thought. Today I was a wrecking ball, and everyone else was a straw house. Fuck *everyone.*

Byron hopped in the Dodge and took off. Jake followed in the Focus. *Suyonuru, motherfuckers!* My across-the-street neighbor was out watering and watching again; I glared at her, and she glared back.

"How long can you water those fucking plants?"

She dropped the hose and ran into the house. I scratched my balls for a moment. She was watching me through the window—I could feel her eyes on me—so I flexed and pointed at the sky, striking that old Rowdy Roddy Piper pose and screamed, "*Woooooooooo!*" I was feeling my oats.

Although I recognized her from the surveillance video and should have appreciated that she was a concerned citizen, with my wrong-side-of-the-bed 'tude that day she was just another nosy bitch. No one in the world was going to make me feel like shit right now. No one.

For the next hour on pins and needles, I knew the fireworks were gonna fly, but I had no clue what was going to happen. I told Missy to take the kids to her mom's for the day. Then I sat in the plastic chair in my living room and waited, staring at my phone, watching its signal strength bounce from three bars to four and back again.

Ten minutes passed.

Thirty.

An hour.

Then my phone rang. It was Jake. I had the tape recorder ready. This was going to be classic.

"What are you doing?" he asked, out of breath.

"Just sitting here studying. Wanna go get lunch?"

"No."

I was waiting for the other shoe to drop—one of those heavy hip waders, considering the amount of shit he was in.

"What's wrong?" I asked.

"I'm in Mexico."

"What? Why?" A long silence. "Hello?"

"Byron got pulled over on the freeway," Jake said. "I was following him and a state trooper came outta nowhere."

"I bet he was speeding. Cops won't pull you over unless you're speeding. Why was he speeding? Didn't he realize he had a load? He shouldn't have been speeding."

"He wasn't doing anything," Jake insisted.

"Yeah, right. He had to be speeding." Slamming the ball back in his face felt damn good. "Did he get arrested?"

"Yeah, the trooper and some unmarked unit pulled up. They looked in the van and hauled his ass away."

"How'd you see all this?"

"I parked nearby."

"How'd you get to Mexico?"

"I just freaked. I'm over here with Adan. I'm gonna spend the night. Haven't thought past that."

"Holy shit! Hold on."

"What what what?"

"I'm leaving this house!" I said, trying to sound frantic. "I'm not gonna hang around here. Should I come to Mexico?"

"Yeah, yeah. Come down if you want." I wasn't gonna set foot in Mexico, but I did have to act like I was in the same boat. "Where ya gonna go? Whatcha gonna do?"

"I don't know yet. I just wanna get outta this house. Fuck. I hope Byron is okay."

"I dunno, man, I dunno. Someone had to rat us out."

"Who?"

"Probably that nosy bitch across the street," Jake said. "I bet she called the popo. She gave me a nasty look when we drove off. I'm gonna knock her fucking teeth in."

I loved it. He gave me the perfect excuse to break the lease. I'd tell him that I couldn't afford to keep the house if I wasn't getting supplemental income and I definitely didn't want to stay with nosy neighbors across the street.

By rights Jake should have been arrested with Byron. Since he wasn't, I had to placate him until he was because he could always call Hank and seal my family's deal. "Listen, follow my logic," I explained. "*You* weren't arrested on the spot. If she had turned us in, the cops would be over here already and have pulled you over, too. Maybe it *was* just a traffic stop."

"I dunno."

"I wouldn't hide in Mexico too long," I warned. "That could be suspicious."

"I gotta go. Let me figure this out."

"Be safe, man. Keep me updated, and I'll do the same."

"Okay."

Agent D fumed that Jake went to Mexico, but he had his hands full with Byron and the other load.

"We'll probably pick up Jeff when he gets back. Talk him into coming back soon. And be available later."

I napped at Grandma's, then went to class. Hank could still show up on my doorstep at any moment, though. At least I'd see it coming and had a fighting chance. I had a pocketknife in my right pocket and another in my sock. Plus, I had machetes and other weapons around both my grandma's and Missy's house. If they walked up and shot me, I was screwed. But they would probably try to kidnap me and take me to Mexico to interrogate me first. The key would be fighting like hell to prevent the kidnapping.

It was officially the longest day of my life. When Agent D called around 8:00 p.m., an eternity had passed.

"Chief O wants to see you. Can you come to the East Side?"

"Sure. Where?"

"Target on George Dieter."

Agent D's car sat beside a black Mercedes-Benz S500. Chief O was driving with another agent up front; Agent D and I hopped in the back. Chief O whipped around the back and pulled up alongside a trailer in the corner of the lot.

"Great work today," he said.

"Thanks. Is this car my reward?"

Everyone laughed, but I wanted the Benz and the decadence it exuded more than the kudos they were bestowing on me.

They didn't go into details, but Byron had been arrested with over two thousand pounds of dope in the Dodge van. They popped the white Astro at a stash house on the East Side, nabbing cash, another ton of pot, and a couple more people. Agent D and company were giddy. They had learned something important, but whatever it was they weren't telling me.

"We might not arrest Jeff when he comes up for air," Chief O explained. "We can get him any time we want now. So we might just give him some more rope."

Not what I wanted to hear.

"Of course, we'll call you into the office and take care of you," he continued, "but I wanted to give you a bonus."

Chief O pulled out an envelope and handed me two thousand dollars—which I needed a lot more than praise. We did the paperwork, and when they dropped me back off at my car, they told me to distance myself from Jake and take a break. No arguments from me.

Over the next couple of weeks, they gave me two more payments for my troubles, seventy-five hundred and five thousand. Much needed and greatly appreciated, but if they weren't going to arrest him so that they could monitor his supply chain, then I wanted to move, and I needed more money to do that.

"How's it going, Chris?" my Amarillo PO, Joyce, asked.

All I had to do was fill out a sheet and send it in with my monthly checks now, but that didn't change the fact that every time I hung out with Jake I was violating my probation.

"Great," I said. "I helped the DEA do a five-thousand-pound drug bust," I said, exaggerating the weight.

"Did they arrest everyone?"

"No, they're letting some continue to operate. You know how federal investigations go. I wanna move and get my family away from all of this, though. My job is done."

She got the hint. "I see you still owe over a thousand dollars on your fine. Pay that off, and I'll get your case dismissed and probation/deferred adjudication removed immediately."

"You're the best."

"Just behave."

Jake settled down, returned to the United States, and ran around like a squirrel in the middle of a traffic circle for the next two weeks. He bailed Byron, who had only been charged at the state level, out of jail. But federal charges were imminent, which gave a much better picture of how the feds ran the show.

Jake and Byron asked me to meet them at Mulligan's again—another test for sure. But my job was done. Agent D had told me to stay away, but agreeing to the meeting kept up appearances.

"Byron, you okay?" I asked, acting genuinely concerned.

"I am now."

"Fuck, dude, that sucks."

"Anyone call you or talk to you?" Jake asked me.

"Nope. I moved out of the house already, too."

"Why?"

"'Cause you freaked me out, and I didn't think we would use it anymore. Besides, I couldn't afford to keep it without extra income."

The day after the busts, the DEA collected their equipment. I shut off the utilities and turned in the keys. The leasing company yelled about it, but Agent D made a phone call, and that was that.

"Just trying to make sure you're flying right," Jake said.

"Duhhhhh."

"We still can't figure out what happened," Byron said.

"You shouldn't have been speeding."

"I *wasn't!*"

They got the exact same look that Jake gave me when I assured him that I wasn't speeding. Maybe my bust three years earlier was just like this one, but I didn't care anymore. My ass was out of the fire, and there was only one more fish to fry.

Jake stared at me, then: "I believe you, Nutty. I believe you."

"You damn well better."

We had had a few beers when a motorcycle pulled up and in walked Hank. My blood ran cold, and my throat started to close. He shook our hands and had a beer with us. He didn't glare at me or even cast any untoward looks, but he was absorbing my mannerisms and everything I was doing. My mind raced. Was he trying not to alarm me because he was going to kidnap me? Should I sound the alarm and tell Agent D I was in trouble? How was I going to get to my car?

I ordered another beer and some food. Then I told Jake that I was going to my car to get my asthma medication. As soon as I got outside, I bolted. Jake called a little while later and wanted to know what happened. I said it was an emergency with the kids. Even though I was scared witless, I took down the plate number on Hank's bike. Just in case.

"Agent D!" I shrieked into the phone. "I did what you told me *not* to do: I went to the meet. Hank was there."

"Did he threaten you?"

"No, but he still scares the shit out of me."

We discussed the conversation, and he took down the plate number as well. The next day he summoned me to the Halls of Justice. He was visibly worried for me. Chief O was there, too.

"I'm giving you another five thousand," the chief said. "Put it away for an emergency."

"Yeah, save it," Agent D added.

What the fuck did that mean? They weren't telling me something, but I didn't have time to overanalyze it. I had a plan. Flawed as it was, it was time to get getting before I got *got*. The plan was family and school and nothing else. Ignore the fear, and stick to the plan.

A few weeks later one of my old fraternity brothers came into town to see his parents. With the looks of Bradley Cooper and the boyish charm to go with them, Jeff had a new job as a pharmaceutical sales rep, making six figures pimping medical supplies. I hadn't done the college party scene or been to fancy nightclubs in years, but Jeff dragged me out with the promise of a good time.

"What have you been up to?" he asked.

"You wouldn't believe me if I told you."

"Uncle Jeff is all ears. Spit it out."

"Lemme get a few more beers in me first."

Jeff opened my eyes to being around normal people, doing normal things, talking about normal stuff. I had forgotten what it felt like—and I fucking loved it. *I have to do more of this,* I thought. That's when the plan got its code name: *Operation Normal.* My goal was to be normal or die trying.

"That's an amazing story," Jeff said. "You should write a book."

"Fuck, no. This isn't a story I want anyone to know. It's one long, bad memory."

"Whatever it is, it's a warning. I would've never pictured this happening to a guy like you. You were our fraternity president, who wanted to work on Wall Street and start a family. Hell, you don't even *do* drugs. It's crazy."

"Could you take a break from cheering me up?"

"Sure. Order another Amstel. Uncle Jeff is taking care of you tonight."

21

Dammit, Man

SHE DIDN'T UNDERSTAND, AND NO AMOUNT OF EXPLANATION GOT THROUGH to her. Every time I walked out to my car, I feared for my life. But I understood her frustration. Missy married me because she thought I was a winner. Turns out I was anything but. The last three years had ground us down brutally, but I was turning it around. I just needed a little help, even if only emotionally. Marriage is a team effort, but we were playing against each other. The last thing I needed was a new enemy.

But divorce was out of the question. My kids were just babies. If I left they wouldn't remember living with their dad. Besides, married life made me happy. The certainty and steadiness of waking up to someone, waking up to my kids, spending time together on weekends made me happy. I couldn't imagine living any other way. So I surrendered.

I surrendered to everyone in my life with whom I had had any sort of strife: my biological father, my in-laws, my grandmother. No matter what had happened, I shrugged it off and tried to compromise. If nothing else the nice guy routine would give me better karma, right? Problem is, people are wild dogs. When they smell weakness, they go in for the kill.

The spring semester was coming to an end, and my macroeconomics grade was worrying me. The material was comprehensible but complex. As a grad student I needed to maintain a 3.0 to keep my financial aid, the crux of my strategy. But macroecon was kicking my ass. The many hours I spent helping the DEA dragged me behind on course work, and I couldn't catch up. Missing the midterm meant my final counted double. My term paper had earned a B, but I wasn't sure how heavily that weighed.

"Professor Sprinkle, do you curve?" I asked hopefully.

"You missed the midterm," he said. "Foolish decision."

"What if I said I had a bunch of personal problems that I don't want to discuss?"

"I only look at the work you've given to me, but you should be fine."

I didn't know what to do next. One voice told me to speak up while another told me to stay mum. I couldn't make a decision, and the voices howled in my head when I bombed the final and got a D in the class.

"I thought you said I'd be all right," I said to the professor.

"I was generous, trust me."

Barely eking out Bs in my other classes put me once again behind the eight ball. Both my summer class grades needed to be As to keep my financial aid for the fall. Talk about stress. My plan hinged on staying in grad school for more than a couple of semesters, and I needed that degree.

Using some creative financing—I wasn't studying econ for nothing—I bought Missy a new van, a new trailer, and a new Kawasaki KFX 400 quad. It was nice to finally have a vehicle big enough to hold the entire family all at once, and it was great for the entire family to go off-roading out in the desert. The van was an olive branch. Yes, it had a useful purpose, but I hoped she would see that I was trying to make life better. For *us*.

Jake and I kept our distance. I checked in occasionally, but he was spinning in damage-control mode. He owed a lot of money for the loads that he lost, which of course turned him into even more of a paranoid freak. The same went for Agent D. I checked in sporadically, but he had other operations now.

In one of my summer classes, a guy named David convinced me to give his church a try. He and I looked like brothers, but the similarity ended there. He had been homeschooled and hadn't been around many people, especially women, until college. He had married a beautiful girl, and I'd bet all the miso soup in Japan that they lost their virginity to one another on their wedding night. He was pure as Telluride snow.

That purity frustrated me to no end. Though on the same side of the political aisle, we debated any number of subjects because his value system was black or white. Gray didn't exist.

"All drug dealers should be put to death, just like in Asia," he said.

"What if they're just trying to feed their families?"

"They're still spreading poison."

"There's no room for discretion in this value system of yours?"

"Nope. The law is the law."

"You're an idiot, David. Man makes the law, which means the law is flawed."

"No, criminals are flawed."

He made my blood boil. He hadn't experienced the vagaries of life enough to know any better, and it made my intestines constrict. Every story I told him, every scenario I painted, he took an opposing stance. But to an extent he was right, and his naiveté, as well as his vim and vigor in defending his beliefs, made him a great guy. Comparing myself to Jake made me look like a saint, but comparing myself to David made me look like Jeffrey Dahmer. Unfortunately, there aren't therapy group sessions for failures working as confidential informants.

Well on my way to making the grade in my summer classes, I applied for one of the TA positions in the Economics and Finance Department. No dice. They told me it was because of the D I received in macro, but they didn't like me. I wasn't one of their peers, and it showed.

It's insane to say that I missed Jake and Byron, I know, but I had been living that life for so long that I had *become* that life. Turns out that the old saying, "When you dance with the devil, you don't change him; the devil changes you" is true.

After our first Tuesday night class of the fall semester, a bunch of us went to the Cincinnati Bar to grab a beer and get to know each other. Most of the conversation centered on careers, so I sat there like an outsider and tried to laugh at the appropriate times. Then their stories grew boring—fast. How many stories can one group tell about 401(k)s and finagling vacation days into cash? After a few beers my liquid courage took over.

"Tonight's ladies' night at Jaguars," I said. "Who's down?"

Half the group balked that I would suggest something so crude. The eyes of the other half gleamed.

Four of us—three guys, one girl—made our way to the club. Walking into the club made me feel comfortable again. This was my element, where I belonged. A cocktail waitress who formerly worked at the Lamplighter gave me an enormous bear hug, to the total surprise of the rest of the students.

"Hi, honey, where ya been?"

"Hiding."

"Oh, my god, sit over here in my section."

She gave us a great table by the bar, prompting the girl from my class to ask if I had been there before. I smiled sheepishly. Then stripper after stripper came up and hugged me as if I were her long-lost lover. The girls all sat in my lap, and we gossiped and talked and caught up on old times. My classmates couldn't believe the attention I was receiving, mouths all agape.

"How do you know all these people?" one of the guys asked.

"They're in my church group," I deadpanned.

Spreading the love, some of the strippers gave my friends free lap dances. I refrained, happy just to enjoy the music, people, and action that I missed. In my heart of hearts, I knew this was ultimately a destructive path. It had been a nostalgia trip more than anything.

Church, Sunday school, grad classes, and family activities returned a relative degree of normalcy to my life. Jake's business, meanwhile, was back on track and growing like an Arizona wildfire. It always seemed like the DEA was going to arrest him at any moment, but it never happened. Still, I kept Agent D updated on any information Jake shared with me:

- He could get free tags and registration for his cars, useful for mule vehicles.
- His drugs now came over the Rio Grande in a low-tech bucket-and-pulley system.
- He was moving huge amounts via eighteen-wheelers to at least a dozen cities.

Some of it made sense, some didn't. But it wasn't my job to figure out. I was just the messenger.

On my usual weekly check-in, I dialed Agent D's phone number, which I had committed to memory and called a thousand times.

"Hello?"

It wasn't his voice.

"Hello?"

Who was answering his phone?

"Helloooooooooooooo?"

I hung up, double-checked the number, and dialed again.

"*Hellooooooooo?*"

What the fuck? Panicking, I hung up again. A minute later my phone rang.

"Hello?"

"Who's this?"

"Who the fuck is this?"

"You called me."

"I was looking for Agent D."

"Why do you want Agent D?"

"Could you identify yourself, please?"

"Purple."

"Are you fuckin' serious?"

"Yes."

I thought for a few seconds. "Do you work with Agent D?"

"Yes. I have his phone now."

"Tell me where he works, and I'll trust you."

"For the government," the voice said.

"Too vague."

The voice sighed. "DEA."

"Why didn't you say so? I work with him."

"You a CI?"

"I still don't know who you are. What's your boss's first name?"

"O."

"Chief O," I corrected.

"What's your name?"

"How 'bout you do your homework, and I come in, and we meet face to face?"

"Fine. Tomorrow okay?"

"Yes."

Back to the Halls of Justice with a knot in my stomach. How I didn't get an ulcer during all of this remains a mystery. Purple—tall, lean, muscular, late-40s, Mexican—was sporting a Stetson and large, calloused hands that looked like they'd roped more than a few head of cattle.

"What happened to Agent D?"

"Transferred to Oklahoma City," Purple explained.

"If you talk to him, tell him thanks for saying goodbye and to eat shit."

"I will," Purple said, laughing.

The quick chat turned into a long debriefing. Purple knew nothing about my case but assured me that it would proceed as planned: Jake and Byron would pay the price.

I wanted to throw up.

My family and I had put ourselves in mortal danger, and now the case was sinking into a bureaucratic quagmire. If the defense ever read the discovery, my name as primary witness might very well come out. The room spun.

"Are you sure you're gonna close this?" I asked. "My family . . . my kids were threatened by a hit man. They won't be safe until those guys are behind bars, and they're making more money now than ever."

"Don't worry, I'm on this," Purple said, clapping me on the shoulder. "Now, what's the name of the guy you're informing on again?"

22

Reeling in the Years

ONE STEP FORWARD, A HUNDRED BACK, AND DÉJÀ VU ALL OVER AGAIN going over the particulars of the case with Purple, who assured me everything was fine and that the case was proceeding as planned. But he didn't give me a firm time line, and unlike Agent D Purple was just a local cop on loan to the DEA. Locals are all sizzle and no steak. This sucked ass big time.

Despite what he said, the case was obviously losing steam. Purple didn't care. I didn't know what to do next. Jake remaining free and rolling in dough after everything I had suffered through made it more than personal. So in an effort to shut him down, I spent even more time with him.

One perfect September day he and his crew took his quads out for a ride. I grabbed my ATV and surprised him.

"Nutty, where ya been?" Jake said, shocked to see me.

"On probation. It just ended, so I'm free and clear to hang out again. That house incident scared the shit outta me."

"Me, too," Byron said. "I lived through it."

The whole clan was there: Jake, Richard, Byron, Byron's cousins Chris and Dave, and a slew of people I didn't know. Trying to remember all their names and license plates was dizzying. But I figured they were truck drivers or warehouse workers. It was obvious that I lay outside their circle of trust.

"Jeez, guys, I'm not feeling the love today."

"There's a lot of unanswered questions about that day," Jake said.

"Yeah, no shit. But you might want to take a look at yourself."

He gave me the hairy eyeball. "How's that?"

"You haven't changed your phone number in seven or eight years, and you do business on that phone. How smart is that?"

As Jake considered that notion, I flipped the script. Phone numbers, patterns of behavior, talking on the phone . . . all signs of amateurs. They had been operating this way for years.

"Seriously, guys, you haven't taken any evasive actions in forever. Both of you have been arrested on numerous occasions, and you haven't done a damn thing to make it hard for the popo to watch you. And you want to lecture me and be suspicious? Fuck you both. If I wanted to put you guys inside, you'd already be there."

I wished it were that simple, but it was clear what the DEA was doing. They were giving the guys more than enough rope to hang themselves. And there it was. I had to find new ways to put myself in Jake's life again, but this time there wasn't any backup to save me, only a contact to forward my info to. Purple was great on the phone, but he didn't have a proactive bone in his body when it came to my case. The only way my family would be safe was if Jake sat behind bars without access to his riches. Sure, I could have let it all play out, but once I made the commitment to cross that line, I knew that holding course to the bitter end was my only salvation. So while sitting there on my quad, I hatched a plan to steer Jake into the maw of the law. I would act as his *consigliere,* and all my advice would outwardly help but ultimately damn him.

I had just started feeling normal again, and here I was fucking around in the desert with a bunch of "bad guys." Always a funny term, that, but that's what most law enforcement agencies used to describe their targets. *What are the bad guys doing? Where are the bad guys now? What info do we have on the bad guys?* The bad guys were out in the desert, riding a bunch of quads with strippers, talking about all the money they're making, and the bad guys were becoming a royal pain in my ass.

The first mistake that ruined the normalcy I had created was telling Missy. We had just found some stability, and I blew it.

"I can't go through this again," she said.

"*You? I'm* the one who went through it. You wouldn't have known anything if I hadn't told you, and I only hid it to spare you."

"So why are you telling me now?"

I wanted to scream.

"Fine," she said. "I just don't want to know about it anymore."

I was sleeping on the couch again. Thank God I'd purchased an expensive and comfortable one during my trafficking days.

The new stress made me gain weight. The only way I could find enough energy to get through the day was through large amounts of caffeine and sugar: donuts and Diet Coke—a contradiction if ever there was one. I stopped working out altogether. My hair, which grew back after Jake shaved it, was starting to fall out, both from stress and from male-pattern baldness. The charm that had served me well in so many dicey situations had evaporated. I couldn't even get ugly girls to flirt with me. But I held strong.

Every couple of weeks Jake and I met in the afternoon at the strip club, where I gave him business advice; nothing too devious or obscure, just enough salient info to get his attention. Then I called him later and did a follow-up conversation. He was consistently buzzed around 9:00 p.m. and usually when driving home, so I kept the recorder in the car and talked during the ride. He never thought I could record a conversation while driving, but I forwarded the incriminating tapes to Purple.

"Fucking Larry," Jake said one night.

"Memphis Larry?"

"Yeah."

"What'd he do now?"

"He owes me $455,000. I'm ready to take some drastic measures."

"Like what?"

"I don't know. I got people."

"What people?"

"You've met some of 'em."

An icicle shot up my spine. "Yes, I have."

"Have any suggestions? You always give me great advice. Do you wanna take care of it? How 'bout a hundred?"

"A hundred what?"

"A hundred grand," Jake said casually.

After the call I immediately scheduled an appointment with Purple to drop off the tapes. "This is some good shit," I explained. "Jake is planning a murder and even offered me a hundred grand to do it."

"Okay, I'm on it," Purple said.

Agent D would have put his foot stomach-deep up Jake's ass, but Agent D was elsewhere, so it was pointless even to think of calling him in his new field office. Purple had me recertify; I signed the CI paperwork again and redid my fingerprints and photos. A new boss, Big S, was running the office, and he was completely underwhelming. After hearing my summary of the case and urging him to act, he repeated the same line Purple had given me: We're on it.

Great. Thanks.

The only place left to turn? A beer bottle. I had finally gotten the hang of grad school. My grades had improved. I even got to the point that I didn't need to buy the books anymore. I took notes and googled key terms or concepts. Book-specific passages I copied from a friend. But as soon as class let out, I beelined to the bar Uncle Jeff had taken me to months earlier, Geogeske, which felt normal. Beers and an appetizer became as a essential as a morning cup of joe.

One of my classmates, Yadira, a short, attractive Mexican girl with blonde highlights, who had accompanied my group to the strip club, was also stressed and unhappy, so she frequently joined me. We commiserated and talked about the future. Drinking buddies who talked about life without really talking, we were both in a holding pattern. As Missy and I grew further apart, only three friends gave me the support I needed: puritan David, my buddy Chris from Colorado, and her.

Chris—a six-foot-four dark-haired Adonis with chiseled features and washboard abs—knew every gory detail of my life. He and I had the exact same logic about the ways of the world, and I could bounce ideas off him without worrying about entangling him in any problems because he lived so far away. Chris also had the luck of the Irish, one of the few people who truly had some of Midas's DNA.

"What's your plan after you get your MBA?" he asked.

"I'm gonna ride your coattails."

"How the hell are you gonna do that?"

"When you're a CEO, you'll finally be in the position to hire and justify employing a loser like me."

He cracked up.

I wasn't laughing, though. "Honestly, I don't have another plan."

Those three friends anchored me. My home life wasn't normal; school wasn't normal; my DEA relationship wasn't normal; and my relationship with Jake and his crew wasn't normal. And then my home life took a turn for the worse. By Christmas my marriage had seriously hit the skids.

"Missy, listen, is it possible that you'll skip doing any of the Christmas programs this year? I know you enjoy them, but you're teaching at a private school, and they're going to have you do a program. Then your mom's church will want you to do a program. And our church will want you to sing. That's an awful lot of time. I would rather focus on us as a family. You're an amazing singer, and it would be worth our time if you sold Christmas CDs after the concerts, but you don't have one."

"Fine," she said to my utter surprise. "I won't do more than one, and I'll get a CD made. They're easy."

She lied. She did all three programs without a CD. Our marriage had dissolved to shit on a stick—minus the stick.

I should have tried to help more with domestic things, but she wasn't being a team player. Then again, I didn't give her the kind of life she deserved. I hoped better times would come. I desperately wanted my sweet, loving wife back. I couldn't imagine myself with anyone else—but it might have been too late.

The pipeline of info from Jake to Purple was continuous and juicy going into the spring. Jake had likely expanded into coke and meth, both a huge priority for Big Brother. Then Byron asked if I'd be interested in running a few loads from Memphis to South Carolina because I knew the South so well.

"Drive a pickup truck with some of those acetylene canisters in the back of it," he explained.

"Lemme guess what's hidden inside: tile?"

"Bingo."

"How'd the stuff get to Memphis?"

"We got trucks now. We're a big deal."

Jake took every opportunity to bring me back into the fold, where he could control me.

"How's grad school?" he asked.

"Great. I just hope I get a good job afterward."

"I got one for you. Go to truck-driving school. Or earn your pilot's license."

"Why?"

"You can either fly loads to the canyon in Mexico or truck it across the country."

"You kiddin' me? Who's gonna pay for this?"

"I will."

"But I want a real, normal job and a real, normal life."

Jake laughed, but he wasn't kidding. He even had his new partner, Daniel, take a shot at me.

"Hey, I got some computers I need to go to Mexico."

It sounded like a money run, which meant the DEA would pay me a percentage.

"I'm down. Is it just computers?"

"Yeah, of course," Daniel said. He was smoking a bowl over the phone. *Yeah, of course.*

Purple had a much different interpretation of the events than I did.

"I think they're trying to get you hammered."

"Hammered?"

"Killed."

"So send me on the Memphis trip with a female agent. She can play my girlfriend and kick ass if something goes wrong."

"No, too many variables. Don't do any of this."

"When are you gonna arrest their asses? You have an airtight case from the stash house."

"Relax, I'm on it."

What a joke. I turned Jake and Daniel down and blamed it on school.

My hands were tied, and Purple wouldn't let me do any more deals or work for Jake. How much secondhand hearsay could Purple really process and add to the case? He probably just took what I gave him, filed it, and focused on his other cases. I felt like a bitch.

Outside Jake's on a weekly visit, I spied a brand-new gold Ford F-150 pickup outside, riding on twenty-two-inch custom rims. Inside the house Byron was glowing like a broken nuclear reactor.

"See my new ride?" he said. "I'm rolling. I just bought a '69 Impala that I'm gonna restore, too. Life is fuckin' great."

I grinned, thinking about how badly mine sucked.

When I ran into Jake, he tsk-tsk'd me. "You should have stayed under my wing, son."

"I thought I still was."

"Nope. That's why you met Hank."

"Well, your brother, Eric, stole fifteen grand from your Charles Schwab account. Did you send Hank to meet him?"

"I thought about it."

It drove me insane. I was trying to fly right and struggling mightily. They, however, were living high on the hog and talking openly about having people killed—friends and family no less—to protect their ill-gotten gains. So I did what any other rational person would do when faced with insanity: I went crazy.

For most of my life I had been a goofball, a master purveyor of pranks and sarcasm. I refrained from those antics while working with the DEA. Granted, I had my moments, like inserting the phrase "chicken-pot-chicken pot-chicken-pot-pie" into each recorded conversation for a month. I laughed hysterically at the thought of the agents transcribing that and trying to figure out what the fuck I meant.

But this was going to be different. First order of business: shaving my head again. It made me look and feel crazier, not to mention that it empowered me with an extra helping of inner strength.

Next, I plotted how to make Purple's life and Jake's life miserable. Purple was easy: I made appointments with him and didn't show up. Then I called him and hung up a dozen times, making him think something was wrong. I was done being his bitch—so I cried wolf.

Screwing with Jake was even more fun. I knew his Social Security number and birth date, so I applied for credit cards in his name and had them sent to his house. I filled out magazine subscriptions for him, using names like Jeff Goingtojail Andes or Jeff Isgonnagetcaught Andes. You can imagine the anxiety they caused.

Jake suspected me right away, but he had made so many enemies over the years that he could only be slightly suspicious. I vowed to continue the pranks until the game blew up in my face.

When the Economics and Finance Department turned me down for what would be my final shot at a TA position, I snapped, bitter and ready for a fight. I just didn't know whom to pick it with. At lunchtime I got shit-hammered and drunk-dialed anyone and everyone who had ever pissed me off. Sitting in my car, sipping from a bottle of tequila with a straw, I unleashed verbal hell.

"You are just a bumbling idiot," I stammered to Purple. "I can't believe you've done nothing with this case. I hand you an airtight case on a silver platter, and all you do is wipe your ass with it. Go fuck yourself."

Jake was next. "You make the dumbest decisions, and everything works out for you because you were born under a lucky star. You fucking idiot."

To my biological father: "Thanks for nothing, you piece of shit. I wish I'd never met you."

Not even Missy escaped my wrath. "You are a fool. A *selfish* fool! It takes two people to build something worthwhile, you fair-weathered pain in the ass."

That was just the beginning. If you had angered me at some point and I could remember your phone number, or if you were in my cell's directory, you got roasted. It wasn't one of my finer moments, but I had spent so many years working my ass off, massaging and finessing so many situations, only to get the worst results imaginable that I just snapped.

Beat me. Kick me. Hit me with a stick. I didn't give a damn anymore.

23

My Home's in Alabama

A maid knocking on the door woke me. How I got to this cheesy motel before passing out, I hadn't a clue—but my alcohol-fueled escapade had stirred the pot something awful.

On my cell phone was a slew of missed calls and voice mails. Everyone was off-with-my-head pissed. The levee finally had broken. As the hurricane raged around me, I sat back, calm and collected. *Bring it,* I thought. *I can handle anything.*

Over the next few days various people pieced together for me the full extent of the mess I made. Missy called the Halls of Justice looking for Purple and gave him the mother of all ass-chewings. She may even have spoken to Big S. Jake called Missy, and she chewed him out, too. My grandmother called all my aunts and uncles as well as my mom because of an uproarious speech I made about our family only caring about money. The stories of the destruction I had wrought were endless—and priceless.

All my life I'd wanted a chance to be heard, and they had definitely heard me. But now everyone was avoiding me—*everyone.* Not a single person called me. Part of me wished I had recorded my rants, but ultimately, I was glad I hadn't. If I couldn't remember them, they hadn't happened. You can't unring a bell, as the saying goes, so I went back to work. After a month had passed, the situation stabilized. Surprisingly, Jake was the first to call.

"What's up, Charlie?"

"Nothing," I said.

"Are you through being a big baby?"

"I guess."

"Then come have a beer with me so I can make sure you haven't become government witness number one."

Idiot.

Purple and I started talking again right around that same time, too.

"I thought you wanted to fight me," he said.

"Nah. You have a badge and gun and are probably authorized to shoot me. I'd rather send a thousand magazine subscriptions to your house. Have you ever read *McCall's*? Some useful tips in there."

The year I had spent working with Purple became the biggest waste of my life. He only succeeded in making the file fatter. I was done with the DEA bullshit.

At summer's end my credit and financing skills enabled me to sell my Kawasaki ATV and buy three new Yamaha quads: a Raptor 660, a YFZ450, and a smaller one for the kids. Better yet, a small technical school called Business Skills Institute gave me a job. They offered soft-skills classes, technical classes, and a few nursing classes. None of the degrees was accredited—and they were expensive as hell but the gig paid fourteen dollars per hour, which was a helluva lot better than a kick in the junk. A twenty-five-year-old with zero management skills ran the place, but that wasn't my problem.

"Have you ever wondered what that office complex is downstairs?" the director asked. Above a pear-shaped body, his big head sported small glasses. He worked hard, but he didn't lead—but that certainly didn't stop him from having a high opinion of himself.

"I know the Border Patrol has half the building, and I saw a sign for the Census Bureau in the other part."

"Well, don't say anything, but there's some sort of drug task force down there."

"Really?"

"Yeah, but don't tell anyone."

"Just out of curiosity, how many other students have you told?"

"All of 'em," he said flatly.

"How many is that?"

"Hundreds, I guess."

Some secret. Why not put a neon sign out front? Agents came and went in highline cars—Porsches, Benzes, BMWs—with Mexican plates and didn't appear to be concerned about the students above blowing their cover.

This job made me discover my love for teaching and speaking to large groups. It also didn't hurt that I was good at it and felt a genuine connection with my students. A few paychecks in, my swagger returned. Not only was this hugely satisfying, it paid the bills. Every six weeks, though, all the instructors sweated waterfalls waiting to see if enrollment was high enough to warrant a full course load. BSI was a business first and a school second.

Classes and riding the quads got me through the summer, and it looked like I'd be graduating with my MBA in less than a year. Then I could springboard this job into another and never look back. As far as I was concerned, the DEA guys were on their own. But I still needed to turn in some tapes, so I called Purple.

"Hey, Purple. Long time, no speak."

"Who's this?" A voice I didn't recognize.

"Uh, who is *this*?"

"Agent J."

"Are you shitting me? Where's Purple?"

"His assignment ended."

"Fuck me with a French horn! What'd he do, come out of the closet and change his name to Rainbow?"

Agent J laughed riotously, but I was in no mood for fun and games.

"So are you DEA or just another wannabe city cop on assignment?"

"I'm DEA."

I introduced myself and told him I needed to drop off some tapes. I planned on quitting in person, so we made an appointment to meet. For once this clusterfuck didn't stress me because I finally accepted that my luck sucked monkey nuts.

Walking into the Halls of Justice for what I figured was the last time, I wanted to take a dump on the reception room's coffee table. Jake had told me stories about how he had taken a couple of shits on his commander's desk in the army and how everyone in the platoon got in trouble because there was a shitting bandit on the loose. Which gave birth to a running joke between us about leaving a mess of paperwork on someone's desk. A pair of agents came out to meet me.

"I'm Agent J, and this is my partner, Agent B."

"Call me Shaft," I said. "No offense, but Agent J and Agent B are the lamest code names I've ever heard. You guys look more like Shaggy and Scooby."

They laughed. At least these clowns had a sense of humor. We went into the conference room, and Agent J produced an insanely thick file, giving me a "What now?" look.

"Have you read it?" I asked.

"Kinda."

"I'm sure you've got a ton of good cases, but that's some solid shit."

The agents shared a look. Agent J leaned forward, all business. "Actually, I don't have any good cases. Tell me why it's solid."

He was genuinely interested. They heard my whole rant about Jake, how big he'd gotten, how many connections he'd amassed, how many cities he'd entered, how Agent D had been transferred, how Purple had dropped the ball. What should have been a fifteen-minute meet-and-greet turned into a three-hour diatribe, which ended with, ". . . and if you ever run in to Purple, give him a swift kick in his vagina for me."

"Lemme check some things out," Agent J said. "But I want the case."

"You're not just jerking my chain, are you?"

"I may be a lot of things, but a chain jerker ain't one of 'em," he said. "Let's take this prick off the streets."

This wasn't music to my ears—it was a fucking symphony!

"Your yearly certification is almost up, so let's fingerprint and photograph you again, okay? You up for this?"

One look at the box score told the tale: I already had two strikes. This was my final swing. But it looked like I was finally going to get a pitch I could hit. *Please, God, just this once, throw it down the middle.*

———

At the end of that BSI teaching period, the director summoned me to his office.

"What's up, Edgar?" I said.

"I'm not renewing you to teach anymore."

"Why not?"

"It's a decision I made."

Apparently, he had gone to a job fair prospecting for new students but instead found of cadre of prospective new teachers. I should have expected this. He'd recently fired a close friend for sleeping with a student—an offense that trounced the fraternization guidelines—and with the majority of the student body being young women, more than a few of whom openly flirted with me, he wasn't taking any chances. Hiring a woman who would work for less money killed two birds. But that didn't mean I had to like it.

"You could have at least given me some advance notice so I could have put away some cash."

"Sorry, not my problem."

"You're not sorry. You completely screwed me over."

"I have to do what's best for the school."

I wanted to spit in his face. "It's chickenshit. I dropped one of my fall classes to teach for you . . . because *you* asked me to!"

"Please, don't tell anyone."

I told every single one of my students, sending a shock wave through the school. Several of the students threatened to drop out in protest. Instead of letting me finish the last six weeks, he fired me on the spot and booted me from the premises. But I didn't go quietly. My lunatic persona had me screaming and hollering in the hallway.

"Could you please just leave quietly?" he pleaded.

"Why don't you have a cup of shut-the-fuck-up?"

"I never expected you to act like this."

"Nor I *you*, motherfucker!" I yelled, my finger an inch away from his face. The outpouring of love from students via e-mail was overwhelming. They commended me for putting up a fight. The girls applauded that I didn't succumb to their advances. They said I was the first instructor at that school to prove himself worthy of respect. Their compliments made me swell with pride. It was the first time anyone had ever put me on a pedestal. I showed the e-mails to Missy and told my biological father about them, but all that mattered to them was that I had been fired. Again.

The best way to look at yourself is through the eyes of others. If you're lucky, you'll like what you see. For the first time in forever, I loved what I saw.

But life can be funny: Just as one door closed, another opened. Agent J called, requesting a meeting. Instead of rendezvousing at the HOJ, we met in the parking lot of the Sunland Park Mall—and this time it was only him, which undoubtedly broke about fifty rules of DEA protocol.

"Can you get back in with Jake?" he asked as we sat in the cab of his truck.

"I'd have to have a damn good reason. Why?"

"He needs to go down, but we need fresh info. I can't get the guys at work to see how big he's gotten. As of right now, the case is dead."

"That was my worst fear." I breathed an exasperated sigh. "Am I or my family safer pursuing this or quitting altogether?"

"I don't know," he said.

We talked for an hour, reviewing important details of the case, including whom Agent J should investigate and how. He was breaking the rules by meeting me solo, not to mention showing me parts of the file. As much as it pains me to admit it, I had a real man-crush on the guy. He was the guy I wanted to be when I grew up. Beyond just his physical traits—handsome, buff, former football hero—he exuded strength and courage. That he was sticking his neck out for me—an expendable confidential informant he barely knew—said a lot about him. He impressed me tremendously . . . but that didn't mean I didn't have misgivings.

"I'm still not sure that I'm doing the right thing."

"What do you mean?"

"Missy, my family . . . they all think I'm a loser for messing with this. I just got fired the other day, too. Nothing works out for me."

Agent J put his hand on my shoulder. "I read the file. You're a stand-up guy, Chris. Fucking brave as hell, too. You did what's right, and that ain't easy."

Not a single compliment in years, and then in a matter of days: dozens.

For what it was worth, I asked Missy for her input. You don't need Nostradamus to predict her response.

"*Again?* Are you fucking *kidding* me? This has been going on for *two years! Two years, Chris!* Don't talk to me."

We had a roof over our heads, the bills were paid, and just enough gravy to have some fun as a family, but it wasn't a normal life, and that's what she wanted: the white picket fence and all that went with it. We didn't own, we rented. The kids were on Medicaid. We used food stamps. Our combined income weighed in below twenty thousand a year. My financial aid kept us afloat with just enough to keep us from total poverty, but nothing in that equation made me a winner.

At some point you have to take responsibility for your own actions, though, and it was time to answer the questions of life and carry this load across the goal line.

In that spirit I met with Robert, a local psychic who I hoped would provide me with answers to the questions I didn't even know to ask. When he greeted me at the door of his house, he looked as if he'd seen a ghost.

An intense odor of incense suffused his home, and weird mystical paraphernalia hung from the ceiling and walls. In the center of the reading room sat a small, round table atop which lay a deck of tarot cards and an ornate wooden box. We sat, and a long silence ensued, during which he stared *through* me. The memory still gives me gooseflesh. When he broke the silence, his voice rang hollow and cold.

"You're gonna get shot. You need to get out of El Paso."

All I could muster was: "Okay."

"You'll live, but you'll have a nasty scar on your face."

"Uhh . . ."

"I see nothing but jail and death surrounding you and your friends. . . . But you can change the future. . . . Nothing is written in stone. . . . I would leave."

Who wouldn't be disturbed? But what worried me was the safety of my kids. Using pictures of my family, he gave his readings, indicating that my kids would all be safe. He said Missy had been unfaithful, though, and even gave me the name of the guy, which unfortunately rang a bell. I asked him to put a spell on the guy, something to make his dick fall off, but he said that "cock curses" weren't his area.

"But you can change the future," he reminded me. "It's like riding on a freeway. Take the nearest exit, and find a new route. You'll be successful in a city or state that begins with an A."

"I wanna move back to Alabama. My heart is in Dixie."

"Then do it," he said. "There's nothing good for you here. I see you in Arizona, Albuquerque, or Austin."

"Not Alabama?"

"Did I say Alabama?"

"No."

At the end of the reading, he returned his focus to the shooting and said it would happen near a building with books in it.

And since I always parked near the library at UTEP, I assumed that's where it would occur.

The psychic powwow left me with more questions than answers. Yet I was surprisingly calm. Some people believe in omens and are terrified by them. I wasn't scared at all, just annoyed. Annoyed with the path I had chosen and that I wasn't smart enough to get off that path when I saw the direction it was taking me.

But that was about to change.

24

Killing in the Name

2005 BEGAN WITH A WHIMPER.

In the home stretch for my master's, on course to receive it in July, I was certain my DEA involvement was coming to an end as well. It had to. I couldn't continue living like this—and I didn't care about the personal ramifications anymore, either. If this was a suicide mission, so be it. Everyone would be better off. Screw Russian roulette and that one round in the cylinder bullshit. Let's load it up all the way, and see what happens.

Jake and Byron had bought a bar they were renovating. En route to the desert with my quad, I decided to pop in unannounced but called Agent J before that, just in case.

"I'm going to the Players Lounge to see what's up."

"I'm already in the neighborhood, but don't do anything stupid."

"Define 'stupid.'"

Most of Jake's crew would be there. Robert the psychic had told me that I'd be shot if I showed my face, but probably, there were not too many books in a bar being reno'd. There was no telling how he'd react. It was one thing to chat on the phone occasionally, but it was another to try to hang out like best pals in the company of his underlings. I walked in feeling like I had a two-foot prick in my pants.

"Wassup, Nutty?"

"Nothing. Just wanted to see your new scheme."

"Whatcha think?"

All far classier than the two schmucks who now owned it. He'd spent forty thousand on new air conditioners, sixty thousand on the sound system, and who knows how much on ubiquitous plasma screens, a wraparound polished wood bar with separate taps, and a multi-hundred-gallon saltwater aquarium behind the bar. He also added a new point-of-sale system and refurbished the back patio stage overlooking a pond and grassy area where patrons could smoke in style. The pièce de résistance? A private office on the other side of the fish tank, hidden behind one-way glass.

"I bet girls are gonna wanna come back here!" he gushed.

"Cool, but aren't you gonna be a dad?"

"Fuckin' A right I am, but that doesn't mean I can't have a little fun."

I tried to rekindle some of the old magic from our friendship, but he didn't trust me anymore—although it seemed he no longer trusted anyone.

"How's your job going?" he asked.

"You mean BSI?"

"Yeah, isn't that the last place you told me you were at?"

"They fired me."

"Once a loser, always a loser."

"Thanks."

"Just kiddin', Nutty."

He went out of his way to make me feel unwelcome, but I strutted around like I owned the joint. I even walked into his office, sat in his chair, and threw my feet up on his desk.

"What the hell are you doing?"

"Seeing what it feels like."

"Seeing what *what* feels like?"

"Being the man. I'll have my own place by year's end."

"Oh, yeah? And just how are you gonna pull that off?"

I double-pumped my eyebrows. "I've got my own plan. Let's just say some mutual friends in Juarez are helping me out. I've got my own people now, too."

Jake looked like he was trying to shit a cinder block. He knew that if I wasn't bullshitting him I was probably working with Adan and Jose. They had a cut-your-head-off policy regarding not talking about the business they did with other people. It's how they lived so long in a country and industry where anything was fair game.

Curious, Jake took a gander at my rig out front—my wife's Dodge minivan hitched to a fourteen-foot custom trailer loaded with all three quads. He jerked a thumb at my ride and the toys it was hauling. "How the hell'd *you* afford *that?*"

"Told you, I got a scheme. You're not the only gringo who's got this game figured out."

If he bought the bluff, there were a zillion ways I could play it. If he didn't, I'd look like a fool and would be putting my family in danger. Again. The hair stood up on the back of my neck.

He went outside for a closer look at my YFZ, which I pulled off the trailer for him.

"Holy shit, this thing is quick! If you punch it, it shoots out like a bullet."

"You haven't even revved it out yet. With the new computer, redline is thirteen thousand rpms."

The quad impressed him, which annoyed him. Feigning work to do, he went back inside.

"So you got a plan, huh?" he pried after I rejoined him inside.

"Maybe."

He was bursting to know more, but he knew he wasn't going to get any additional info. He tapped his watch. "Alrighty then, I got things to do. But don't be a stranger. Come back tomorrow, and let's chat some more."

Then he gave me the oddest look. Either he believed I was going into business on my own or he was sure I was lying and had just decided to have me killed. Either way, time to make like lightning and bolt. As I headed out to the desert, I called Agent J and told him what I'd done.

"Clever. Did he buy it?"

"I don't know. He's incredibly perceptive for a dumbass."

"I know what you mean."

"I'll go back tomorrow. If he's gonna do anything to me, he'll probably do it then, so be nearby."

"Okay. We'll coordinate in the morning."

Before heading over to the Players Lounge the next day, I stopped for a mint chocolate chip milk shake, my version of a last meal. If I was walking into a firing squad, my taste buds deserved one last thrill.

"Hey, where y'all at?" I asked Agent J between slurps.

"We're parked up the road and across the street. You sure there's no way I could walk in there and not be noticed?"

"No way. Place ain't open yet. But you should see it. It's really nice. I can't believe they're spending seven hundred grand!"

"That's a lot of money."

"How'd you guys miss Jake blowing up like this?"

"I don't know."

"I'll try texting you every fifteen minutes, but if I'm not out in an hour, send in the cavalry."

"Count on it."

Most of the DEA guys drove GMC pickups, a few of which were sitting in the parking lot. What *wasn't* comforting were the motorcycles and other cars, including a fucking Cadillac, that I didn't recognize. I knew what Jake and Byron drove, and there should have been work trucks. The diner scene from the last episode of *The Sopranos* came to mind.

A million questions raced through my mind. Were the motorcycles from Hank's gang? Was the Caddy for me, so they could stuff my body in the trunk? Were the workers dismissed because they planned on killing me in the bar? Could Agent J get to me in time? Would Missy have enough sense or money to leave El Paso and start over someplace else? Would my kids be okay growing up without me? Was this really the—

I took a deep breath, willed myself out of the car, and went inside. It was cemetery quiet.

"Hello?"

I had already punched Agent J's number into my phone, so all I had to do was hit the call button. Nobody at the bar or in the office. Walking back to the patio made me wonder if I was already dead. Maybe I had been shot when I walked through the door and this was heaven. When I pushed open the door, the sun hit my face. Nope, Hell Paso.

"*Hey!*"

Byron's cousin Dave scared me so bad I nearly shit my pancreas. He, Jake, and the guys were sitting around a table, having a beer.

"Where the fuck is everyone?" I asked.

"They went to lunch," Byron said.

Jake was talking to two slicked-out Criminals-R-Us guys who clearly weren't in the hospitality biz. I tried to introduce myself, but Jake waved me off. One of them was complaining about the brakes on his Toyota—one of the cars in the lot—which put me at ease and gave me an idea. Feigning shortness of breath from the scare Dave gave me, I returned to my car. Using my asthma inhaler as a visual cover, I got the license plate and texted it to Agent J.

Back inside, I headed into the office to install a keylogger and some spyware on Jake's computer surreptitiously, a tactic about which Agent J knew nothing. When the DEA raided the place, if their forensics didn't yield as much damning evidence as they needed, my techno-efforts would save the day. Leaving nothing to chance, I had practiced installing the software at home—but I needed two solid, uninterrupted minutes.

My heart was pounding in my throat as I mentally counted time. Once an idiot always an idiot, Jake kept his password on a scrap of paper taped to the desk. Just as I was about to pull the flash drive from my pocket, the guys from the patio walked back into bar. Thank God for one-way glass. A few seconds later Jake's eyes flashed hatchets when he saw me at his desk.

"What the hell are you doing?"

"My Internet at home went out, and I needed to check my e-mail. Look at what someone sent me." I turned the monitor to show him a porn sequence.

"Lemme see that," Jake said.

Two smokin' hot girls wearing college football jerseys were going to town on one another. Jake's eyes were glued to the screen, but his voice belied suspicion.

"Damn, Nutty, I thought you were snoopin' on my computer."

"Why would I do that?"

"It don't matter anyways. I would've seen what you were doing." Jake pointed to a painting on the wall. "That's a hidden camera. I gotta keep my eyes and ears open at all times."

Too close.

The hour was ending, but as I made for the door, Jake ran me down.

"Hey, I'm headed to the strip club tomorrow afternoon," he said. "Come hang out. I have an errand to run, but we can go afterwards."

"How's he reacting to you?" Agent J asked as I drove back over the mountain from Narco East to the Westside and gave him the plan.

"Strange, but we'll figure this out. Tomorrow I can meet him at the club, so I'm not worried about getting jumped."

"Just be careful."

Jake stood me up and never called or answered my calls. Days two and three came and went. Ditto four, five, and six. I couldn't figure out what went wrong. Where the hell was he? I finally tried calling his house, and to my surprise the sonofabitch answered.

"Where the fuck have you been? I've been blowin' up your cell."

"Don't have it."

"O-kay." A long, cold silence. "So what happened the other day? I thought we were supposed to grab a beer."

"Couldn't."

"Damn, dude, don't be so talkative."

"Busy."

"Want me to come by the bar later?"

"Sure." He hung up.

"Something's up," I said to Agent J. "I called Jake at home, and he wouldn't talk to me."

"Can you wear a wire today?"

"If I have to. Why?"

"I think I know what's going on."

"What?"

"Wear the wire, and I'll tell you later."

"Am I in danger?"

"Probably not."

"That's reassuring."

He laughed. "It'll be okay. See you in a few."

Right on cue in the park overlooking Cohen Stadium on Trans Mountain Drive, four GMC extended cab pickups came winding down the mountain. As they pulled up to my car, the insanity of my life crystallized in my head. How many people could say they'd worn a wire? Or organized a drug bust that devolved into a monumental clusterfuck? Or met a hit man in their own living room? Or held a few hundred thousand dollars' cash? Oh, the stories I could tell at a high school reunion—if I lived long enough to attend one.

Agent J and company got out. We chatted for a minute or so, and the mood was so lighthearted that you'd never guess that someone's life was on the line. There was someone new, though—a beautiful young woman.

I sidled up beside Agent J, indicated her, and whispered, "She should go into the bar with me and act like my girlfriend."

"Yeah, right. Everyone falls in love with her. Just cool down, dude."

"Easy for you to say. Your ass ain't the one in the crosshairs."

"Are you nervous?" another agent asked, overhearing us.

"Fuck, no. I'm *annoyed*. I'd rather be doing anything other than this. This case should've ended ages ago."

Of course I was fucking nervous, but I wanted to look cool for the new agent.

"So what's going on that you're not telling me?" I asked Agent J.

"Relax, not yet."

This time they wired me up with higher-tech gadgetry, just a small beeperlike device. The case budget was increasing. I hoped Jake would have diarrhea of the mouth.

For once a whole fucking army was backing me up as I pulled into the Players Club, and it felt damn good. As long as I avoided music and other external noise sources, I could come through with some first-rate dirt.

Boom! Boom! Boom! Boom!

It took a moment to figure out what the sound was: the concussive effects of heavy bass, Tupac followed by Biggie. Jake was messing around with the sound system, exploring the speakers' limits.

Shit.

Jake told me to help myself to some beer while he screwed around with the system. One turned into five—nursed, not slammed—as I texted Agent J.

Dickhead is playing dj
Ass clown is STILL playing dj
Might as well fill bar w feds. Bag o dicks is oblivious

Midway through my fifth beer, I walked over to the DJ booth and told Jake the music was giving me a headache.

He turned off the music and sneered.

"Damn, dude, what crawled up your ass and died?"

"Nothing. Just in a shitty mood."

"Why are you driving Sandra's car?" I asked.

"I don't wanna talk about it. Just have all the beer you want, and let me be."

Yep, something was definitely up. I tried to convince him to have a beer with me, but he wouldn't budge. Nothing was going to drag him out of his world right now. In all the years I'd known him, he'd never acted like this before. Dave, and a couple of the other guys, clearly knew what Jake's problem was, but they all just shrugged their shoulders. Time to go before I pissed someone off.

Agent J and his Goof Troop met me at El Paso Community College's Narco East campus. We parked in a corner of the backside lot to discuss the scenario.

"He seems upset," Agent J said.

"Gee, you *think?* What the fuck is going on?"

"I can't tell you just yet."

"It's all your fault," I said to the female agent.

She was aghast. "How?"

"You should have gone in there with me," I smiled.

She rolled her eyes at me and got back in the car.

"Agent J, seriously, do I have anything to worry about with whatever you're *not* telling me?"

"I don't think so," he said after a pause.

"If something happens to me, you're gonna tell my kids how you screwed up."

"Just be patient."

How the fuck was I supposed to be patient? My guts were twisting tighter and tighter. Once again, the only person looking out for me was me. Which meant getting info on Jake and quick. But doing the same stupid thing over and over was getting me nowhere. Jake wasn't talking to me anymore, and I wasn't going to spend six months riding his jock to open him up.

Wanting to keep my buzz going, I headed over to Geogeske and had a few more. Had Jake had me followed? Had he tapped or cloned my cell? What if he put Spyware on *my* computer? Maybe he'd hired a private investigator to watch me.

"If someone hired a private investigator to watch you," I asked the waitress, "what would they find?"

Her eyes bulged. "Oh, my god, what kind of question is that?"

"Humor me."

"Wow, I would *hate* that!" she laughed. "I don't do bad things, but there are some things I wouldn't want everyone to know."

"Wait, what did you say?"

"I said th—"

"You're a genius. You found the solution to my problem."

"I am? I did?"

I knew what I had to do.

25

We Don't Need Another Hero

JAKE WAS GOING TO COMMIT SUICIDE.

If I could gather enough dirt on him and plant a few strategic bombs, he'd hang himself with his own rope—which would protect my family from a killer and protect me from further criminal charges. It's what I should have done all along.

Jake's wife, Sandra, had tried to catch him cheating on numerous occasions, but he always stayed one step ahead. She would yank him back on a short leash, if not worse, when presented with solid evidence. Playing some of the strippers whom he routinely dated against one another would seriously harsh his daily entertainment. Revealing how he'd screwed over Byron, Richard, and his brother, Eric, would insert a big fly in his professional ointment. His parents' knowing about their sons' laundering antics would create a mountain of stress for him, too. The possibilities were endless, but they all hinged on getting evidence.

A quick survey of my PI tools revealed a digital camera with a telephoto lens, my trusty DEA-issue tape recorder, baseball hats, sunglasses, several shirts, a couple of Diet Dr Peppers, a bag of Funyuns, and a metaphorical pair of brass balls. I had no clue what to do. But sometimes you just have to go for it. I mean, it couldn't really get any worse, could it?

Knowing Jake's routine meant I also knew Agent J's schedule; he was shadowing Jake nonstop. Knowing where both men would be at all times gave me enough confidence to tail Jake without being discovered.

My first bite at the apple occurred when Jake went riding in the desert with some friends. They were heading to Red Sands—one of my favorite sand-roosting areas—for some kind of manly bonding experience complete with strippers. Catching him in the act would be a slam dunk.

Taking my wife's quad because it had a quieter exhaust, I parked my trailer at the far west end of the dunes, carefully avoiding where I figured they had set up camp. There would be some scrub brush, but it was the middle of February, so most of the creepy-crawlies—snakes, scorpions, spiders, and centipedes—were chillin' for the winter.

Trekking to the nearest mountain on the far east side, I found a vantage point high enough to look down over the dunes. Even if I didn't see them directly, their tracks would give me a fix on where they'd be doing the bulk of their riding.

As luck had it I spotted them quickly and edged my way down through the back trails to a boring and therefore avoided area. Only a hundred yards away from their position, covered with an abundance of scrub brush, lay a spot perfect for clandestine observation.

I parked my quad and crept through the foliage as silently as a panther in slippers. It would have been one thing to bump into Jake and his crew while riding, another entirely if they discovered me lying prone in the bushes holding a camera with a telephoto lens. They'd have buried my body where it lay.

Lying flat on the sand, eye pressed to camera, I focused completely on Jake and his cohorts. What I failed to notice—until it was too late—was that I had lain down on a nest of carpenter ants, nasty black inch-long fuckers that sting like bees on steroids.

The first few stings on my fingers didn't alarm me in my zone of concentration. My hand had probably just brushed against a pricker plant. But by the time it felt like it had caught fire, dozens of the ferocious little bastards had covered it. There were so many, I could barely see my skin.

If I had jumped up or shrieked, Jake and his crew would have spotted me. I bit hard on my lip to stifle my scream and performed some sort of impromptu spastic rolling backflip. This unorthodox movement cleared my hand of ants, but my predicament deepened when my body rolled over the entrance to their nest.

For the next minute or so, which felt like an eternity, I rolled back and forth, silently cursing the little creatures that were gnashing me with razor-sharp mandibles. It looked like I was suffering a spastic seizure. But my defense worked, and the biting stopped.

Now gun-shy of the area, I crawled back to my quad, rolled it down the back side of a dune, fired it up, and rode to the top of a hill, wasting half an hour just getting my bearings. Of course, my original location was the best place to be—I just needed to look before lying down.

By the time I reached my new hidden recon post, my hands and arms had swollen with angry bites. But the discomfort was a small price to pay for the suffering Jake was going to endure when my PI tactics paid off. A bushy yucca plant offered a good bivouac. After a thorough search of the ground, I crawled into a huge opening in the middle of it.

In retrospect I had no idea what I was hoping to photograph, but then again my plan was ill conceived from the start.

Time passed, and my limbs went numb—especially my legs. To alleviate the stiffness I kicked my feet, trying to rekindle circulation. That's when a huge hole just an arm's length away from my face came into focus. How I hadn't noticed it before was a mystery, but there it was. No footprints coming or going from it, only a series of undulating, smoothly packed ripples. Just as it dawned on me what creature had made the hole, its owner confirmed my suspicions.

Fear gripped me like a frozen fist as the four-foot rattlesnake as thick as a PVC pipe slithered from its den. Trying not to make any sudden movements, I slowly began to inch my way back, but the snake kept coming.

"Nice snake, good snake," I whispered, wishing for a silencer-equipped pistol instead of a camera and some Funyuns.

Fully emerged, the snake changed directions and aimed for me from a sharp right-to-left angle. Desperate to put more distance between me and the reptile, I shifted my path—but the snake slithered forward faster than I could crawl backward. I froze. First I was stuck between a hit man and the law. Now I was pinned between a drug trafficker and a venomous reptile.

The snake's tongue's flickering hadn't quickened, though, so it didn't feel threatened. I'm no Ranger Rick, and my knowledge of snakes—especially the kind that can kill a man with one bite like this bastard, fresh from rest and full of venom—comes strictly from nature programs. But it didn't seem agitated. Just when it looked like it would slide harmlessly past me, it changed angle and moved directly alongside my body. Fine, the snake was going to pass. Then it stopped, its head barely a foot past my own.

There are times in life when discretion is the better part of the valor. This wasn't one of those times. My hand lashed out, grabbed the snake's tail, and flung it like a live hand grenade. The reptile pinwheeled ass over teakettle for what felt like the length of a football field before disappearing from sight. Within a breath of emptying my bladder into my pants, I scurried out of the yucca bush, jumped on my quad, and hauled ass. My heartbeat pounded over the throb of my ATV engine.

A few days passed before I worked up the courage even to think about following Jake again. I needed a different tactic. I knew some of the places where he partied in Mexico, and I also remembered where Adan lived. Breaking the cardinal rule given to all DEA informants, I trekked across the border.

A few times Jake had mentioned a strip club connected to a brothel in the Pronaf Circuit, an area of intense commercial activity. Good place to start. I ordered a beer and looked over the girls. Soon, one of them approached me. She spoke Spanish, and though I understood her, I acted like I didn't and smiled.

She switched to English and sat on my lap. "Would you like a dance, Papi?"

"No, thank you."

She looked at me as if I had called her a whore in church. "Do you like boys?"

"No!"

"Then why are you here?"

"I'm looking for a friend of mine."

"What does he look like?"

Idiot that I am, I pulled out my camera and scrolled to a picture of Jake. A huge bouncer—more of a side of beef with eyes—came over, and she told him in Spanish that I was an American cop and he should kick my ass.

Mamba fast, I jumped up, dumping her onto the floor. The bouncer took a swing at me, catching me on the ear. I'm not built like a flower, though, and took the punch without wavering. Before he could throw another, I forearmed him in the chest and made a run for it. A smaller bouncer tried to block my exit, but he obviously never played American football. I lowered my shoulder and trucked him, knocking him flat and nearly through the cheap wooden floor. Breathless moments later I was Taco Bell-ing at full throttle for the border. My ear was throbbing, but my pride hurt more as the umpire of fate called strike two in *Operation Fuck Up the Home Front.*

Sitting on the bridge, I laughed. My foolhardiness reminded me of the time Jake had gone to the Lamplighter and verbally sparred with some dolts in the shitter. He leaned forward and smiled, daring them to do something. One of 'em promptly decked him in the face, knocking out his front teeth. That dental emergency had precipitated his expensive veneers.

Over the next week I tried everything to bump into Jake when he was partying with a girl other than his wife. I could have gone the strip club route, but snapping a picture there would have been nearly impossible. Too bad I hadn't used my cell phone camera all those years when partying with him, snagging a little rainy day insurance. No sense dwelling over past mistakes, though. Then Jake called.

"Hey, whatcha doing?"

"Running an errand," I lied, desperately wanting to say, I'm outside your gym, you fucktard, waiting for you to get your ass off the treadmill and do something stupid so I can take a picture of it, show it to Sandra, and wreck your marriage.

"You should see the girls at the gym."

Like the one on the treadmill beside you?

"I'll bet," I said. "Hey, I gotta take this call."

I clicked over to the incoming call from Agent J.

"Hey, just checking up on you," he said. "Whatcha doing?"

Fucking déjà vu.

"Running an errand."

"Too bad. You should see the girls in this gym."

My heart stopped. "*What* gym?"

"Jeff's gym. I'm here watching him work out."

I threw my car in gear and raced away. Jake was a horn dog and would hit on at least one of the girls there and possibly leave with one—but it wasn't worth letting Agent J see me following him.

A few minutes later Jake called me back. "What side of town are you on? I need a lap dance."

"Great minds think alike."

"Pick me up at my gym in fifteen."

I called Agent J and told him the plan, almost hitting him pulling up to the gym's parking lot.

Inside JB's Jake and I chilled, drinking beer, as my mind wandered. How did he do it? The guy was a fucking genius. Had to be . . . his results were unfathomable. Either that, or he was the luckiest guy in the universe. Or maybe he thought every situation a thousand moves ahead like chess grandmaster Bobby Fisher on steroids. The white flag raised itself in my head. I couldn't defeat him, and I knew it, so it was time to stop trying.

Jake went for his usual round of lap dances in the VIP area while I nursed my beer. A few of the girls tried to chat me up, but I shooed them away. A cold drink was more appealing than a warm body. He returned two songs later wearing an impish grin.

"Dude, I wanna fuck that girl."

"So do it."

At some strip clubs, if you say the right thing, you can bang a stripper while getting a dance. You usually have to pay for the pleasure, but every so often you can get laid for free. Jake had to hit the ATM.

"I'm gonna do it when she gets off the stage," he said, snapping the cluster of crisp bills in his hand.

When the song ended, the stripper came down from the stage, grabbed Jake's hand, and led him to the corner of the VIP area. Here was my chance.

When the first song had almost ended, I grabbed a stripper of my own and led her to the VIP area. The quality wasn't going to be great, but if I could snag a video of Jake getting his noodle wet—in the strip club, no less—I'd be golden.

They were doing their thing to my right, so I had the stripper sit on my right leg, her back to them. Holding the phone in my right hand behind the stripper's back, I flipped it open and punched the buttons from memory, preparing to film.

"Do you want a dance or not?" my stripper asked impatiently.

"Not this song. I'm really picky. Next one."

"You still gotta pay me for this song, though."

"No problem."

Squinting past the girl on my leg, I could see that they were clearly doing the deed, so I pressed the "start" button.

Flash!

Mother of fucking god! I hit the wrong button; the camera took a picture using the flash, which lit up the strip club like lightning, scaring the shit out of everyone. Even worse: The couple I thought was Jake and his date *wasn't*. Just some poor schmuck getting lucky. Judging by the way he shot out of the club—the stripper chasing after him, screaming to be paid—he had spooked big-time.

But I had a bigger problem: Club security and some of the other strippers surrounded me instantly, screaming at the top of their lungs. I explained that I was trying to turn my ringer off but accidentally hit the wrong button. The lame excuse pacified no one.

Jake walked over, laughing his ass off. "What's going on over here, Nutty?"

I explained my version of the story while strippers and bouncers barked at me. Jake handed out twenties like candy, which soon sent everyone about their business with a smile.

"Christ, man, I can't take you anywhere."

"No, you can't. But thanks."

Driving Jake back to his car at the gym, I didn't say a word. There was nothing to say. He rambled on about the size of the tits on the stripper he boinked, but all I could think about was that he was Teflon. Nothing stuck to him.

"I'm going to Mexico tomorrow," he said at his truck. "Afterwards, let's go back to JB's."

"Sure, whatever."

He bounced into his truck. Where was his Expedition? It had been MIA for weeks. Then it hit me. He was going on a money run. If he was using his F-150 for a money run, I knew where he'd hide the money. The truck had a keypad entry system on the door. If he left it unattended for just a minute, I could steal the cash, relocate my family to Alabama, and forget all about all of this shit.

"You're calling me early," Agent J said the next morning.

I had decided to play it straight. "I think Jake and Byron are up to something today."

"Well, it's gonna have to wait. I'm taking a personal day."

"Oh, then never mind."

Maybe it was meant to be. Sitting up the street from Jake's house in my grandmother's blue Honda Civic, I was just getting settled when Jake's garage door opened and out came his F-150. Now, all he had to do was leave the truck alone for a moment. But he never did. Burger King drive-through, gas station, drive-through pharmacy, a small tire store. *Christ, Jake, how many fuckin' errands you gonna run today?*

The sweet taste of success turned to bitter fear as he headed across the bridge to Mexico. Idiot that I am once again, I followed. As I crossed the Bridge of the Americas, my window of opportunity was closing—fast. Once he arrived at his destination, my opportunity died. But I wasn't paying close enough attention, and following him too closely, next thing I knew the *federales* were flagging us both to the inspection area.

Before his truck even came to a stop, he handed a twenty to the men, who immediately waved him through. I had to stop, pop my trunk, and answer questions. The delay put distance between him and me, but the answer to my prayers was also driving away. They finally let me go after he had long vanished from sight.

The plan had been so ridiculously simple—yet I blew it. If he had gone straight to his destination, it was toast; if he ran into me in Mexico, *I* was toast. It was the perfect place to have me snatched, questioned, tortured, whacked, and dumped. Mexico has different rules, especially for anyone in the narco biz. Tail between my legs, I decided it was time to head back to the safety of the good ol' US of A.

Finding my bearings took me in circles before putting me on the street I wanted. Then—*no, it couldn't be.* At the traffic light, emerging from a haze of sorrow and self-pity, I noticed an enormous maroon Ford pickup with Texas plates *directly* in front of me.

It was Jake.

All he had to do was look in his rearview mirror, and I was fucked, so I pulled my front bumper to within inches of his rear bumper—so he couldn't see me over his tailgate—and threw down my visors. All he could see was my roof.

Just as *Good thinking, Chris* ran through my head, brakes squealed, and tires skidded. In slow-motion horror in my rearview mirror, a piece-of-shit car barreled toward me. Terror lined the driver's face as he slammed into my rear bumper, sending my car into Jake's truck. The hit didn't cause any damage—it was more like a love tap—but it was jarring nonetheless.

I couldn't . . . fucking . . . believe it.

While frantically trying to think up a good explanation for why I was literally tailing Jake, the unexpected happened. *Both* vehicles—Jake's truck and the car that hit me—raced off as if they had jet engines under their hoods. In Mexico, if you're ever in a car accident and not killed or otherwise incapacitated, *run*. The *federales* will detain you until you've proven you can pay for the damages—and them for their troubles. Even if you have to abandon your car, do it, and let your insurance deal with it.

No wonder they canceled *Magnum, P.I.* Tom Selleck must have been sick of it, too.

Strike three.

26

My Way

DEATH WAS HANGING ON MY NECK LIKE AN UGLY TIE.

When the DEA investigates people, they do the full sleuth: phone taps, video surveillance, forensic accounting, DMV inquests, computer dumps, interviews, eyewitness Q&As, rap sheets, and so on. They also do more simplistic investigating, like drive-bys of suspects' homes to document visible vehicles. Tailing suspects yields registration tags. On some occasions agents follow a suspect into a bar or restaurant and engage in direct conversation, not to get damning evidence but simply to know *everything* about him: friends, enemies, relatives, lovers; favorite restaurants, bars, and hangouts; daily habits; hell, even the type of contraception they prefer and who they voted for in the last election. For their profiles the smallest nuggets of info carried the same weight and respect as the largest. Yet no matter what resources the DEA and other major agencies have at their disposal, confidential informants are still the best way to mine information.

But you never hear about them. No one hears about an informant's role because the government takes the informant's information and expands upon it, sometimes for years. The strength of their investigative power combined with an informant's testimony results in a wicked one-two punch designed to crush the defendant. In many cases, barring an insanity plea, refuting the testimony of a CI with up close and personal knowledge of the suspect is impossible.

Passing along overheard or observed information to the DEA is one thing, but it's another to acquire it by going into the field alone without backup. With my meager resources it proved next to impossible. If the DEA made a mistake, the case suffered. If I made a mistake, I suffered. Or died. It felt like an invisible Sicilian necktie.

Missy, the kids, and I moved into a new house a few streets away. Just two classes away from earning my MBA, I returned to my normal surveillance sessions with the DEA. See it, hear it, tell it—end of story. Jake had become increasingly busy with the bar, which meant not seeing him as often, but we still talked regularly. As May was warming to an end, Agent J asked me to meet with him. He had new information.

"I'm gonna pick you up at your house."

"Okay . . . any chance we could meet somewhere else?"

"No time. Just be outside."

It was nice finally to sit in a vehicle with blacked-out windows rather than some look-at-me machine like that puke-green Grand Am.

"Where's your partner?" I asked.

"Never mind. I wanna show you some stuff."

For three years DEA information flowed strictly one way—me to them. Something was going on.

"Did you know a narco lived on your street?"

"He doesn't live right beside me, does he?"

Agent J laughed. "No, there were two, but the one across the street from you recently moved."

"No shit! I thought those people were shady."

We drove over to Narco East, and Agent J pointed out various locations, telling me about each. He clearly had received a ton of fresh intel, but where had it come from: good old-fashioned footwork or another informant?

"Have you ever seen this house?" he motioned to a residence in the middle of the block, on the same street as Byron's.

"No."

"Have they ever talked about it?"

"Nope."

"See the camera system on the roof?"

A hard look and there they were: multiple cameras. "Holy shit."

"Check out the gate."

Two more cameras on either side of the gate. Wide-angle lenses could easily cover the entire street.

"Wow."

"They call this place The Spot."

Impressive. The state-of-the-art closed-circuit television system had cameras covering every side of the home from every angle. A huge gate in the back provided access to several large storage sheds. Sitting back there among the sheds were a couple of trailers, various cars—my old Intrepid among them—and Jake's truck.

"How'd you find out about this place?"

Agent J was asking the questions, not answering them. He motioned to a tire store as we drove past.

"Ever seen this place? Have they ever talked about it?"

"No, but they talk about using a warehouse to palletize the drugs. Is this the spot?"

"Did you know a guy named Jimmy?"

"Yeah, he was a supplier for Jake who lost a load and went to jail. I think he was Byron's supplier. Met the guy once or twice. Didn't he just get out of jail?"

"Yeah. He's going back."

"Really? Related to Jeff? Did he give you this info?"

"I can't say, but you're free to infer whatever you want. Ask yourself, though, would *you* be happy if you went to jail twice for a guy and never got anything out of it?"

"Fuck, no."

"Jeff has been pissing off a lot of people lately."

"How?"

"He fucks over everyone he works with."

An old man doing a money run for Jake got busted in Sierra Blanca, losing eighty-six thousand dollars. Instead of bailing him out, Jake let him sit in jail and rot. Jimmy and John had also been busted with loads and were going to do serious time, yet Jake denied them any severance. Jake was purposely holding out on Richard, to whom he owed money. Jake had been shortchanging Byron from the beginning and every chance he got. He also fucked over the previous owner of the Players Lounge in the transaction. And a serious rift had formed between Jake and his brother Eric over—what else—money. Jake had parked funds in a brokerage account using Eric's name, and when a disagreement between them arose, Eric withdrew the money and kept it for himself.

Every story has two sides of course, but all of this was Jake's MO. The stories were undoubtedly gospel. He may have been shrewd and savvy in certain areas, but cheating your associates is beyond idiotic. In addition to making him a high-profile target, it completely erased any loyalty. The last thing you do when running an illegal enterprise is stoke the ire of the very people who have your back. He was about to learn this lesson the hard way.

"So I take it the floodgates are opening?"

"Like a busted dam," Agent J confirmed. "I'm working this case hard."

"Whatever happened to all the other details of the case? Like, how did the loads cross back in 2003 without being noticed by Customs? Or all the info I gave you on how they crossed it and who they crossed it with?"

"I can't talk about that."

A recent news story had reported the arrest of a Customs agent for letting a bunch of loads cross. Had that started with my case? Cops busted a local license plate retailer for providing bogus registrations specifically for mule cars. Did that connect with the info I gave the DEA about Jake being able to register his drug cars for free? Too many coincidences. . . .

"So what *can* you tell me?"

"Jeff's Expedition was stolen last month. He was on a money run and went to pick up a stripper to take to Juarez with him. She had her boyfriend jump him in the parking lot, and they jacked his ride, keeping the money. That's why we made you wear a wire, to see if he'd talk about it."

"What happened to them?"

"El Paso Police Department recovered the Expedition, but I'm assuming the stripper and her boyfriend got the cash. A couple of weeks later, her and her boyfriend were shot up in their new car."

"I saw that on the news. Did they live?"

"Yeah, they're fine. Jake tried to get another guy to do that job."

"Jimmy?"

"I can't be too specific."

We turned the corner and drove past a couple of parked big rigs. Agent J nodded toward them. "Jake bought his own eighteen-wheelers, too. Have you ever seen these trucks or talked about them with him?"

"Uhh . . . no."

Jake had grown so large that he needed camera-monitored stash houses, his own trucks, and warehouses in El Paso and other cities, *and* he was ordering hits. He had figured out a way to launder the profits through a new bar and a slew of rental properties. Insane from a growth perspective, it broke every narco biz rule Jake had ever taught me about staying low key. His sinking ship was going down fast.

"I saved the best news for last," Agent J smiled.

"What?"

"This case is about to be handled by a multistate task force."

"Is that a big deal?"

"The biggest."

As Agent J drove me home, it became clear that my job was done. New informants were playing the game, gathering new intel, and breathing new life into the details of my former miseries. Agent J unwittingly reaffirmed every one of my worst fears, making me realize just how lucky I was to have jumped ship when I did.

"Who are you going to arrest when it all goes down?"

"Everyone," he said flatly.

"What do you mean by that?"

"Anyone and everyone, all known associates. You're lucky you're on this side of the law 'cause we would have arrested you, too. We're gonna take everyone in and see who talks."

If I had never ratted, Jake would have grown his business to the elephantine proportions it had reached now, and the expansive net the feds were trawling would have ensnared me along with all the other narco fish.

"Whatever happened to those guys I gave you the license plate for from the bar?"

"Tags belonged to a car lot. We tried to follow them, but they drove like madmen and we lost 'em."

"Smart criminals."

"Yeah. I don't see many."

"Jake's an idiot."

"You don't know the half of it. He may have diversified to coke and ecstasy. He may even have teenage girls dealing it."

Agent J detailed more particulars about the case. It was mind-boggling. He had screwed over *everyone*. Agent J had confirmed my worst fear, but he had also given me hope and closure. My job was done, but that meant I was about to become as useful as a windshield wiper on a goat's ass. DEA had passed the torch to other CIs. They didn't trust me to know all the new information, so there was no sense in stressing about it. Sure, I wanted to smear Jake and make him fight more than one battle, but he had created most of those problems himself. Time to grab some popcorn and watch the implosion.

Talking to Jake became a problem because I had so much information about him, most of which he didn't know that I knew. I had to tiptoe through minefields, making sure I didn't slip and accidentally reveal anything during our recorded conversations, trying not to lead a conversation in any way, especially because I knew what I was trying to achieve.

He was moving thousands of pounds a month to various cities using a highly sophisticated distribution system. As much as I hate to admit it, he deserved credit. He had come a long way: from country boy to army sergeant to the CEO of a multimillion-dollar drug empire. What a waste. He could have used those skills and talents to do something worthwhile with his life, something positive. But his selfishness was incomprehensible.

DEA was going to crawl up the ass of every person who had ever shaken hands with Jake, following each trail to the bitter end, no matter where it led. Once his associates saw the writing on the wall, they'd sing like Pavarotti at the Met. If the authorities had assembled a multistate task force, there were going to be innumerable loose ends. The investigation alone would last ages, a year or even two.

Thank God I was done.

As I finished my MBA, it was time to move on with my life. The relief I felt was indescribable, but there had been consequences: I had gained weight, lost hair, grayed a bit (prompting me to shave it all off), and my marriage essentially had ended.

Time started to slide by. I had the occasional conversation with Jake or Agent J. I drove by Jake's, or Byron's, or The Spot, or the Players Lounge to see if the DEA had raided—but nothing out of the ordinary. Then one day Agent J called and asked me for a favor.

"What do you need?"

"As agents we constantly have to take lie detector tests."

"Okay."

"It's no big deal, but sometimes they want to interview CIs to make sure everything is on the up and up."

"No problem."

For the fourth time the Halls of Justice recertified me as an informant with the customary photographs and fingerprints. Someone from the Department of God-Knows-What had another Q&A session with me, and Big S, the department boss, sat in. I wanted to laugh my ass off at the tedium of the interview, but because people's lives and careers depended on it, I refrained.

Big S had nothing unkind to say about me, but that didn't fix my life. I still needed a job, so my search began anew. Problem was, companies were looking not only for criminal pasts but also new criteria, such as perfect credit—another strike against me. Juggling my finances had put me $135,000 in debt.

In October I called Agent J to check in. "I've been trying to reach you. Where you been?"

"I'm laid up at the house," he said.

"What happened?"

"Tore my knee up stepping out of a van during a bust."

"That sucks. You didn't accidentally shoot anyone, did you?"

"No. It would've been messy, too. I had a shotgun."

"How long you out for? Does this affect the case?

"Six months maybe, and no, Agent B is on it. Deal with him if you got anything."

Another changing of the guard. It was time to do things my way. The right way.

27

Renegade

The motel resembled an early-1980s Best Western, woefully outdated, abandoned. The room was a junior suite: kitchenette directly ahead, bed against the far wall, a couch and two chairs facing each other in the center. Five black guys—intense-looking dudes with violence in their eyes—were standing around as if waiting for someone.

I sat in one of the chairs, and the smallest but scariest of the guys took a seat opposite me.

"What's the deal?" I said after a long, uncomfortable silence.

"You tell me."

"What do you mean?"

"Byron says to go fuck yourself. You had this coming."

Shit.

I leapt from my chair and lunged at my counterpart, grabbing him around the waist. We wrestled, but the other guys quickly pulled me off him. A pistol hammer cocked distinctively behind me as cold metal pressed against the back of my head. I never heard the shot.

It was pitch black. No sound, just darkness. Slowly, my vision returned, and they were standing over my body. The sound of arguing crept into my ears. Apparently, they were supposed to shoot me before I got out of the chair. They wrapped me in old, stained bedsheets and dumped me behind some decrepit warehouse, arms swaddled to my sides. Then someone started speaking to me.

"So you were a DEA informant, huh?" It was Jake.

"No. Uh . . . I mean . . . I didn't—"

"Just help them find me," he said. "I have a son."

"What?"

Then they shot me in the back of the head again.

———

My body bolted upright in bed, sheened in sweat. I touched the back of my head to see if there was a bump where the pistol's muzzle had been jammed against it in my nightmare. Further sleep was impossible, so I went into the kitchen, where I stood quietly sobbing for almost an hour.

Somehow I showered, dressed, and got to work on time, but the vision lingered. As I sat on the forklift, freezing my ass off, nothing I did could shake that horrific thought.

My new job—management trainee with Ferguson Enterprises— was the only offer I received after getting my MBA. They mainly sold housing and plumbing supplies. It was a good gig that paid the bills. I was miserable. But not why you might think. Their warehouse stored as much dust as it did merchandise, aggravating my asthma to dangerous levels. Training required working every job in the warehouse before moving into management. I had to suffer. They denied my request, practically on my knees, for a week of desk duty to let my condition stabilize. These were old-school, blue-collar guys who wanted me to tough it out. When I asked how long, they all said, "As long as it needs to."

The others from my recruiting class had the luck of the Irish. I was lucky as a lamb in Irish stew. They loved their coworkers; I hated mine. My body hurt more and more, slowing me down. Ferguson heard my concerns, but the only action they took was to nickname me "Flash." But I refused to let them bring me down. I was alive, my kids were healthy, and beer and college football were still legal. So long as those things were in my life, I was fulfilled.

Missy and I had separated again, which meant living with my grandmother—again. Bored, I decided to have a beer with Jake to see what was happening in his life, hoping some of his mojo would rub off before the implosion. When he didn't respond after a few days, I tried calling again. This time the call went straight to voice mail. Odd. Had I been excommunicated? Discovered? I called his house.

"Is Jeff home?"

"No, he's not here." Sandra said.

"Can you please have him call me?"

"Okay."

So where the fuck was he? Agent J was still on leave. His standard response to my questions about Jake was to call Agent B. The prospect of getting to know a new agent again made my head spin, but I didn't have any other options.

"What's up, Agent B? I've been trying to get a hold of Jake but haven't spoken to him in a while."

"When was the last time you spoke to him?"

"Before Christmas."

"Can you come in? I want you to talk to some guys."

"Sure, no prob."

Two DEA agents from the Wichita office met me in the Halls of Justice the next day.

"We're just doing some background info on the case," one of them said. "Can you tell us about it?"

"Where do you want me to start?"

"From the beginning," said the other agent.

"Seriously?" My shoulders slumped. "How much time you got?"

"As long as it takes."

Ugh. We settled in, and I started at the beginning as if I were giving a speech: If I hadn't sold my soul on December 28, 1999, none of this would have happened. They gave me a funny look, so I made a mental note that perhaps audiences didn't like that opening. During the four-hour debriefing, they got the whole enchilada. They didn't ask many questions, grateful that I was saving them the hassle of deciphering the time line. We shook hands at the meeting's end, and that was that. Agent B walked me to the elevator.

"So what's going on?"

"Nothing," he said.

"Where's Jake?"

Agent B looked me dead in the eyes. "Just don't call him or his house for a while. And stay away from the Players Lounge."

"Sure. Anything I should worry about?"

"Nope."

Something was going on—but what? As I left the Halls of Justice, I called Agent J. Something about what had just happened bothered him, but he wouldn't explain. Typical bureaucratic bullshit probably.

Ferguson was killing me—slowly but literally—so I quit to reenroll in grad school to work toward a second master's, an MS in economics, which, because I had taken more hours than required to earn my MBA, I could earn in under a year. My professional and personal lives were in shambles, but I was actually happy. It could have been worse. It can always be worse. Always.

Spring break rolled around, and with a week's worth of free time on my hands, my curiosity flared again.

"Enough of this bullshit, man," I said to Agent J. "What's the deal?"

"Call Agent B. I'm not at the office every day. I don't see the file."

"Will he give me answers?"

"Just call him first."

What was the big fucking deal? What were they not telling me?

"Agent B, what's up? I haven't talked to Jeff in months. Do y'all have him at Guantanamo or something?"

"I can't discuss this."

"Why?"

"I'll tell you soon. Hopefully."

He hung up, and I cursed the air he breathed. This customary "I can neither confirm nor deny" response was driving me crazy. I had heard it a thousand times:

"Agent D, is that y'all's plane in the sky?"

"I can neither confirm nor deny."

"Agent J, is Jimmy now an informant? Do you have other informants?"

"I can neither confirm nor deny."

"Purple, did you blow the other agents in the men's room?"

"I can neither confirm nor deny."

Four goddamn years without a single screwup on my end—they owed me more than "I can neither confirm nor deny." So that's exactly what I told Agent J.

"He told you nothing?"

"Not a goddamn thing."

A long silence.

"Please. I've got to know."

"Go to a pay phone and call me back at this number."

"What?"

"I'm not gonna say it again."

DEA agents don't play telephonic cat and mouse on a whim, especially with informants. I raced to the nearest gas station and called Agent J from the pay phone as instructed.

"Where you at?" he asked.

"Diamond Shamrock, corner of Mesa and Executive."

Silence.

"What's the big deal?"

"Jeff is dead," he said.

"I'm sorry, would you repeat that?" I'd heard him, but I didn't really hear him.

"He's dead, Chris."

The world spun. A cavalcade of emotions surged through me, from elation to anger to sadness. He could no longer hurt my family or me. But someone had killed my friend. And the fucker got off easy. I wanted to sit on the witness stand, point my finger at him, and put *his* ass in jeopardy. Someone had saved me the trouble.

"Are you sure?"

"Actually, no. That's the problem."

"Is that why I was questioned by the Wichita office? I'm a suspect?"

"We looked at everyone."

"I guess you haven't really lived till you've been suspected of murder. Am I still a suspect?"

"No."

"Where's the body?"

"We don't know. We still don't know what happened. He spent Christmas at his folks' in Wichita, then went off to do something, like pick up money. He disappeared on December 28. We found his truck in St. Louis with his wallet and phone in it."

"Did you say December 28?"

"Yes."

An icy shiver ripped through my spine. The first load I ever ran for Jake was on December 28. A chunk of my soul died on that date. Eerily fitting.

"We heard a story that he was kidnapped and taken to Mexico and held for ransom. Five hundred thousand. But no one knows for sure."

"Why didn't Agent B tell me? I could've been in danger. Shit happens to informants all the time."

"You're right. An informant in Atlanta hadn't checked in for a few days, so his handler found him using his cell phone's GPS. When the agents stormed the apartment, they found him tied to a chair with someone standing over him with a chainsaw, *Scarface* style. Another few seconds, and he was meat."

"Jesus."

"Every bad guy I ever busted had a copy of *Scarface* on his shelf."

"Figures."

"If I were Agent B, I would've wired you up and sent you to Jake's house and the bar."

"I would've wanted a SWAT team for backup."

"You would have had it, too."

"What now?"

"Can you get any information?" he asked.

"I can talk to Gary Hill."

"Do you feel safe doing that?"

"Gary intimidates the shit out of me, but I can do it."

"Then do it. Call me from a pay phone at this number after you finish."

This whole situation was seismic. My body was trembling. In the narco world, or any hierarchical criminal enterprise for that matter, when something like this happens, there's no telling what the fallout will be and who will or won't be affected. Fingers get pointed. Doors get broken in. People disappear. Anything is possible, none of it good. All the angles of the last few months replayed in my head at a rapid clip. Did Sandra know?

"Missy, round up the kids, and meet me at Grandma's in two hours."

I hung up before she had a chance to speak and continued analyzing the situation. What did I need to do? What could I do?

If anyone knew what was going on, Gary did. Walking into his office gave me the same scared feeling as when I was arrested and on the days I went to court. It was torturous.

"Hey, Donna, is Gary in?" I was willing myself not to stutter.

"Hi, Chris! Let me check."

Moments later she ushered me back to Gary's office. There was no reason for me to know anything about Jake or his predicament because I didn't speak with Byron and Sandra didn't tell me anything. I was exposing that I had privileged information. I had to be careful. I never told Gary that I was an informant. I didn't think he'd look down on it, but I respected him so much that I didn't want to draw his scorn. He also represented Jake.

"I need to talk to you about something," I began.

"You want to know if Jeff is dead."

"How'd you know that?"

"Because I'm smart. But the answer is, I don't know. We've hired private investigators to look for him but have gotten nothing. There are a few stories about what might have happened, but nothing solid."

"Wow."

"He's pissed off a lot of people lately. He left that guy to rot in jail in Sierra Blanca, and he's not paying people what they should be paid. Then his dumb ass went out and bought that bar."

I nodded.

"All of that is bad fucking business."

"So nothing?"

"There's always the possibility that he felt the heat. You can't do what he's done without drawing the ire of the DEA sooner or later. He could have made a run for it, but I don't think he's that smart."

"Jeff never was the sharpest knife in the drawer," I said.

"No, he fucking wasn't, and with all the dumb shit he's done, I'm surprised this didn't happen sooner."

"Well, I appreciate your time."

"My pleasure, Chris."

I was still shaking as I left Gary's office. He knew that I had flipped. He had to know.

"I spoke with Gary," I said to Agent J from a pay phone.

"What did he say?"

"Same thing you did. Everyone has the same info."

"Damn."

"Gary intimidates the shit outta me. That was rough."

Agent J chuckled. "You know he threatened to kick the prosecutor's ass in the Sierra Blanca case, right?"

"No, but I fuckin' love that guy. That's the kind of attorney who gets his defendants off the hook."

"I guess."

"So now what? Agent B doesn't want to use me, and I don't talk to Byron. Sounds like the end of the road."

"I guess it is."

———

Missy met me at my grandmother's. Motioning for her to get out of the car, I pulled her off to the side.

"What's going on?" she asked.

"Jeff is dead."

"*What?* How did it happen? When was the funeral?"

"They haven't found his body. Apparently, they had a service for him, but nothing official like at a funeral home."

She put a hand to her mouth. "Oh, my god."

"He went missing on December 28. I couldn't make this shit up if I tried."

"I guess we'll never know."

"Either he was kidnapped and held for ransom in Mexico, or he was killed in the Midwest during a deal gone bad. There's a chance he's just disappearing for a few years until the statute of limitations expires, but no one thinks he's that smart, myself included."

"Are we in danger?"

"I don't think so. But be vigilant for the next few weeks."

"Okay." She looked into my eyes and saw that I was struggling with the news. "Are you okay?"

"I want to celebrate and vomit at the same time. I listened to 'Renegade' by Styx at least a dozen times on the way over. The one where the criminal says he's in fear of his life, the gig is up, they finally found him."

"I know the song."

I mimicked Jake's happy dance, the one that made me laugh and want to smack him at the same time. Then I put my hands on Missy's shoulders and looked into her eyes. "I guess he can't hurt us now."

"We hope."

"Bottom line, I won."

Missy shook her head. "We all lost."

Epilogue

On August 31, 2007, after a five-year investigation called Operation Players Lounge, Byron Segura was arrested and named as the head of the Segura-Andes Drug Trafficking Organization. The execution of the warrant yielded 10,000 tablets of ecstasy, 4,800 pounds of marijuana, 332 grams of cocaine, and approximately $1.25 million in cash.

Attorney Gary Hill is still kicking ass, taking names, and getting sweetheart deals for his clients. On July 22, 2009, Hill had his own brush with the law when he was arrested for pulling a pistol following an altercation in the parking lot of his law office. He is innocent until proven guilty in a court of law.

Purple, Agent D, Chief O, and Agent J are still in the trenches fighting the war on drugs. They aren't winning.

Jeff "Jake" Andes (March 31, 1969 – ?December 28, 2005) is still missing and presumed dead. No evidence of his remains has ever been found. The statute of limitations on his crimes expires in 2015.

Missy and I are still legally married but separated, doing our best to raise our four children right in a world of wrongs.

I have become an *anti*motivational speaker, empowering people to live their lives for all they can be, not simply cheerleading them on. Rumors of a bounty on my head are false. Maybe. I have never been convicted of a felony.